Britain and World Power since 1945

Britain's descent from status as a global imperial power began in the Second World War and continued over the subsequent decades, with decolonization, military withdrawal, and integration into the European Union. Yet, Britain's foreign policy decision makers continued to behave as if the nation remained a great power.

In *Britain and World Power since 1945,* David M. McCourt maintains that the lack of a fundamental reorientation of Britain's foreign policy cannot be explained only by material factors such as economic strength, trade flows, and business interests or even by an essential and immutable British international "identity." Rather, he argues, the persistence of Britain's place in world affairs can best be explained by the prominent international role that Britain assumed and into which it was thrust by other nations, notably France and the United States, over these years.

Using a role-based theory of state action in international politics built on symbolic interactionism and the work of American pragmatist philosopher and social theorist George Herbert Mead, McCourt puts forward a novel interpretation of Britain's engagement in four key international episodes: the Suez Crisis of 1956, the Skybolt Crisis of 1962, Britain's second application to the European Economic Community in 1964–67, and Britain's reinvasion of the Falklands in 1982. He concludes with a discussion of international affairs since the end of the Cold War and the implications for the future of British foreign policy.

David M. McCourt is Assistant Professor in Sociology at the University of California–Davis.

Britain and World Power since 1945

CONSTRUCTING A NATION'S ROLE IN INTERNATIONAL POLITICS

David M. McCourt

The University of Michigan Press
Ann Arbor

Published in the United States of America by
The University of Michigan Press
Manufactured in the United States of America
⊚ Printed on acid-free paper

2017   2016   2015   2014   4   3   2   1

A CIP catalog record for this book is available from the British Library.

Library of Congress Cataloging-in-Publication Data

McCourt, David M.
  Britain and world power since 1945 : constructing a nation's role in international
  politics / David M. McCourt.
      pages   cm. — (Configurations : critical studies of world politics)
      Includes bibliographical references and index.
    ISBN 978-0-472-07221-7 (hardback) — ISBN 978-0-472-05221-9 (paperback) —
  ISBN 978-0-472-12037-6 (e-book)
      1. Great Britain—Foreign relations—1945–   2. World politics—1945–1989.   I. Title.
DA589.8.M44   2014
327.41009'045—dc23

                                                              2014005569

For my parents

Contents

Preface and Acknowledgments

IN DECEMBER 1962, former US secretary of state Dean Acheson caused a minor storm in US-UK relations when he told an audience at West Point Military Academy that Britain had "lost an empire and not yet found a role." Britain's attempt to play a world power role, "a role based on the Commonwealth and the 'special relationship' with the United States," he went on, was "about played out." British Prime Minister Harold Macmillan privately hoped his country would be "big enough" to shrug off the comments. In Macmillan's view, the American's tailoring had always been sharper than his judgment, and in any case, the speech had touched on Britain only briefly, and the former secretary was a noted Anglophile. However, Acheson's words caused anger and resentment in the UK, no doubt because many people felt he had put his finger squarely on Britain's international predicament. Macmillan thus thought it prudent to issue a rebuke. He did so by comparing Acheson to Hitler, Napoleon, and others who had underestimated Britain in the past, assuring the country that Britain had and would continue to have an indispensable role on the world stage.[1]

Transatlantic tempers soon cooled, and the incident was chalked up as an unfortunate diplomatic slight and nothing more. But Acheson's words remained, firmly entering the lexicon of British foreign policy and quickly becoming something of a cliché. Indeed, no discussion of Britain's postwar international relations—and certainly not one focused on the concept of "role" itself—could avoid citing what Tony Blair would later call "Acheson's barb." Readers familiar with Britain's postwar international history will hopefully be relieved to have it out of the way early, even if they are entirely unsurprised to see it recounted here. Nonetheless, the assertion that Britain has "at long last found a role" has been heard at regular intervals since 1962, and many observers still consider Britain "in search of a role." Beyond simply

an astute observation about Britain's predicament in the early 1960s, therefore, Acheson's West Point speech raised questions that have remained prescient long after the words were uttered: in short, in an age of US hegemony
and continent-sized powers, of complex interdependence and globalization,
what role can an island at the edge of Europe with a relatively small population possibly hope to play on the great stage of international politics? Acheson's ghost still haunts the corridors of Whitehall.

The power of Acheson's barb, of course, lies in its rhetorical nature, but it is
no less real for that. In this book, I show that Acheson's words resonated with
a central feature of international political life: states are role-playing actors in
international affairs. Their foreign policies are conditioned by the social roles
they come to play in their interactions with one another. I demonstrate the
importance of role-playing in world politics by developing a role-based approach to the explanation of state action. I subsequently put this approach to
work in an examination of Britain's foreign policy since 1945.

The book can be positioned firmly within the constructivist research
agenda in IR, which has placed the social construction of state behavior at its
forefront. Crucially, however, the approach I develop is put forward as a corrective to the accepted wisdom in constructivism, which downplays the
genuinely social bases of action in favor of explanations based on the notion
of state "identity," with all of its presocial connotations. This approach as-
sociates constructivism with an emphasis on agency, set over and against
something loosely termed *structure*. The difference between constructivism
and certain versions of liberalism has consequently been obscured.[2] This
book consequently better specifies the processes at work in the social construction of state action by putting roles front and center.

The book can also be placed alongside a number of recent works in constructivist IR—broadly understood—that address the issue of how state identities and roles are reconstructed in the wake of historic events and significant shifts in the international order. Each rejects as oversimplified the
realist notion that state action is determined by relationships of material
power. Paving the way, Jeffrey Legro argued that the strategies great powers
follow result from struggles to define the national interest, understood as a
collectively held set of ideas about a state's role in the world.[3] Similarly, Andrew Oros has examined the emergence and historical development of Japan's "security identity" as a pacifistic international actor.[4] More recently
and from a more consistently constructivist standpoint, Patrick Jackson has
detailed how West Germany was "civilized" after 1945, the rhetorical com-

monplace of the "West" furnishing German policymakers with a powerful resource with which to secure Germany's position in the Western camp.[5] Finally, Ayşe Zarakol has detailed the effects of "stigma" in the interactions of states that find themselves on the wrong side of the insider/outsider dichotomy that structures international society.[6] In sum, it would not be going too far to identify these studies as a new genre of constructivist IR theory—and a generative one at that. This book adds to this body of scholarship.

To judge the appropriateness and evaluate the implications of the conceptual approach the book develops, it investigates the evolution of British foreign policy since 1945. Britain represents a puzzle in today's world. It has spent much of the past six decades declining relative to other powers and worrying about that decline. Yet Acheson's barb still cuts so deep because it goes against the unquestioned assumption in Whitehall circles that Britain remains a major world power with an independent voice in international affairs and the capabilities to back it up. As the equally clichéd phrase goes, Britain "punches above its weight." How should this state of affairs be understood? The book shows that British foreign policy is not the expression of an essential British identity; rather, Britain has time and again cast itself into—and crucially been cast into by important others like the United States and France—a prominent role in international politics. In short, without American support for Britain's internationalist orientation and France as a peer with a similar set of foreign policy dispositions, it is unthinkable that Britain could carry on quite the expansive foreign policy it has in contemporary international politics.

In this book I trace the roles that have emerged for Britain to play in world politics in four key episodes in its postwar international relations: the Suez Crisis of 1956; the Skybolt affair of 1962; Britain's second application to the EEC between 1964 and 1967; and the Falklands War of 1982. This book therefore simultaneously represents a serious work of theory-construction and an equally serious piece of historical research. My interpretation of Britain's changing role in the world not only engages with the dominant historical narratives found in the literature on Britain's international experience since 1945 but also provides a reconsideration of many of its by-now-familiar themes. The book is thus aimed at an audience beyond the narrow one of IR scholars and theorists and will be of value to international historians. That said, I beg their forgiveness for the long conceptual exegesis in chapter 2 and the inevitably limited choice of case studies addressed thereafter.

The book has its origins in a conversation I had as a history undergraduate considering doctoral study in International Relations, a discipline then entirely alien to me. While chatting with an IR doctoral student whose name I unfortunately do not remember to get a better sense of what the subject was all about, I was asked what topic I might propose if I did decide to switch track. I picked the only sure ground I had: UK foreign policy. "What is Britain all about in world politics?" I replied. "Why don't we just make up our minds? Are we really committed to Europe or not, best chums with the US until the end, and all that?" This book represents my answer.

That meeting is also noteworthy for setting me on a specific theoretical path. After pitching my gut response, which was something to the effect that I didn't think Britain would be the same type of country if we did make a choice—would somehow no longer be as much *Britain*—the student suggested that I read a new book he had just finished reading: Alexander Wendt's *Social Theory of International Politics*. *Social Theory* duly became the first IR book I ever read—an unwise choice, on reflection, since I barely understood a word of it. But I later came to understand that I did not think that the notion of state "identity" captured everything about Britain's predicament that interested me and that I was quite uncomfortable with the mode of explanation that remains predominant in IR—two themes that are prominent in what follows. This book, then, seeks to come to grips with UK foreign policy, on the one hand, and to make a statement about constructivism as an approach, on the other.

I owe thanks to a large number of people. First, my doctoral supervisor, Fritz Kratochwil, suggested that thinking about roles rather than identity might be a profitable endeavor. As usual, he was not only correct but far ahead of his time. Fritz's influence runs throughout the book, sometimes hidden, often much less so; it is a sincere pleasure to acknowledge his impact on my thinking. If this book in some small way progresses the disciplinary project he helped set in motion a quarter of a century ago, it will have been worth all the effort. If not, I will simply have to try again.

Christopher Hill offered the valuable suggestion that I apply to the European University Institute in Florence, one of the best decisions I ever made. I hope this book repays the faith he has showed throughout my career this far as well as his friendship. Richard Little and Chris Brown were fantastic examiners, and their comments have enriched this project as it has made the very long transition from dissertation to book manuscript. Richard has also gone above and beyond in support of my career, leaving me truly in his debt.

Thanks also go to Jamie Gaskarth, Oliver Daddow, and Ian Hall for accepting me as a legitimate scholar of UK foreign policy. Dave Allen, another member of the group, did likewise before his untimely passing. I hope he would have enjoyed this book. He is sorely missed.

At the EUI, I was fortunate to receive guidance and advice from Sven Steinmo, Pascal Vennesson, and Rainer Bauböck. Sincere thanks also go to a number of friends, both in Florence and elsewhere, who either offered comments and criticisms or read sections of the project as it developed: Nanning Arfsten, Andrew Glencross, Irial Glynn, Majda Idrizbegovic, Niklas Rossbach, Joel Van der Weele, and Fernando Veliz. Alun Gibbs deserves a special mention for acting as a private tutor in the philosophy of the human sciences, a discussant on the issue of the state of contemporary organized sport, and a friend.

It is a pleasure to thank a group of scholars who made me very welcome within American IR, academically and socially: Jon Acuff, Jack Amoureux, Alexander Barder, Jon Carlson, Harry Gould, Jarrod Hayes, Eric Heinze, Dan Levine, Dan Nexon, Laura Sjoberg, and Michael Struett. Brent Steele not only is a true friend but also promoted my work better than I ever could. This book would not exist without him. I thank those people at the University of California who showed me kindness after I landed unexpectedly on their doorstep. Bob Huckfeldt did me a great service in organizing a research position at the Institute for Governmental Affairs at UC-Davis for 2009–10. Bob Taylor accepted me as a political scientist, even if a barely recognizable one. Vicki Smith made me feel welcome among the Davis sociologists, where I was much more recognizable, as did Eddy U and Michael McQuarrie. At Berkeley, I thank the Center of British Studies, under the directorship of Ethan Shagan, and Institute of European Studies, for two years of breathing space in which I pursued this project. Ron Hassner was also extremely generous with his time and advice.

Although the book was completed before I began a lectureship at the University of Sheffield, I thank my former colleagues for making me feel at home. I am particularly grateful to Garrett Brown, Inanna Hamati-Attaya, John Hobson, Jonathan Joseph, Nicola Phillips, Nasos Roussias, Matt Sleat, Hayley Stevenson, and Rhiannon Vickers.

Most scholars are lucky to have one mentor of the standing of Fritz Kratochwil, but I have had the benefit of guidance from four. Our discussions rarely touch on the material included here, but I owe Jack Gunnell a very great debt for his gift of insight into the history and philosophy of political science (and his cherished friendship). Mark Bevir, who kindly invited me to Berkeley, has shown me more assistance than could ever be expected or repaid. Special words of thanks go to Patrick Jackson, who suggested that I submit my manuscript to the University of Michigan Press. The experience has been an entirely pleasurable one, with Melody Herr a good part of the reason.

Parts of chapters 1 and 3 were previously published as "The Roles States Play: A Meadian Interactionist Approach," *Journal of International Relations and Development* 15, no. 3 (2012): 370–92. Sections of the conclusion formed part of my chapter, "The New Labour Governments and Britain's Role in the World," in *British Foreign Policy: The New Labour Years,* ed. Oliver Daddow and Jamie Gaskarth (Basingstoke: Palgrave Macmillan, 2011). I am grateful to Palgrave Macmillan for permission to reproduce these sections. Parts of chapter 4 appeared as "Role-Playing and Identity Affirmation in International Politics: Britain's Reinvasion of the Falklands, 1982," *Review of International Studies* 37, no. 4 (2011): 1599–1621. I thank Cambridge University Press for permission to reuse it here.

To anyone I have missed, my apologies: your help was much appreciated.

Finally, I thank my family: my sister, Clare, and her growing family; my wife and best friend, Stephanie Mudge, a better scholar than I'll ever be; and Leighton and Julian. I now understand why people acknowledge their children for making it all worthwhile. I hope this book is worth the move from sunny California to snowy South Yorkshire. The book is dedicated to my parents; they know why.

Foreword

IN THIS BOOK, David McCourt takes on a cutting-edge theoretical debate within IR constructivism about the role of "ideational" factors broadly (and somewhat imprecisely) conceived, addressing that debate both on the conceptual level *and* empirically by illustrating the explanatory productivity of a micro-interactionist take on the relevant issues. He delineates three ideal-typical modes of interaction—role-taking, role-making, and alter-casting—and engages in careful historical reconstruction of the ways that these mechanisms combine and concatenate in specific situations to produce outcomes that seem, both to the parties involved and to the informed researcher, perfectly reasonable and even inevitable under the circumstances. It is those "circumstances," the thick social contexts within which state officials interact, that McCourt's analysis unpacks and lays plain; the result is an outstanding demonstration of the explanatory benefits to be gained by moving beyond "norms" and "identity" and that duality of "agents/structures" in trying to ascertain why, in this instance, Britain has not made a fundamental reorientation in its foreign policy since 1945 despite a decline in its relative material capacity.

As a theoretical intervention, McCourt's book is an outstanding example of the recent wave of constructivist IR scholarship that seeks to move beyond the early call of "Norms and ideas matter!" by going back to original philosophical and social-theoretical sources to craft precise tools and techniques that are methodologically congruent with an explanatory strategy that seeks case-specific insights rather than nomothetic generalizations. Initial constructivist calls often posed misleading oppositions, such as norms/ideas *versus* material interests, and then sought to evaluate which kind of factor made more of a difference to outcomes. Conceptually, this approach is a problem because the sources on which constructivist IR scholars drew are more or less unanimous in pointing out that social action, as meaningful action, simply cannot be properly discussed as stemming from purely "material" factors; any identification of a "material interest" or a "material capacity" has always and already, if surreptitiously, smuggled in some set of meaning-making practices and some kind of cultural or historical tradition in terms of which the "material" factor is made meaningful for the actors involved. Hence, Mc-Court's recovery of the micro-interactionist roots of the concept of "role" stands as an important corrective to the misleading dichotomies of earlier scholarship, since a role is neither material in the sense of being completely nonsocial nor ideational in the sense of existing in the subjective consciousness of a particular individual or a set of individuals. Rather, roles are *social* facts, *social* arrangements, and as such instruct actors what do to in particular circumstances—circumstances that may themselves be any combination of "material" or "ideational" factors that are deemed *relevant* in context. So the question is not whether ideas or material factors explain Britain's foreign policy since 1945 but how particular combinations of role-taking, role-making, and alter-casting combine with available historical and cultural materials to generate the puzzling outcome: the persistence of a great power orientation in British foreign policy long past the point at which Britain had the conventional military might to sustain such an orientation.

McCourt's empirical chapters cash in on the promise of this explanatory strategy. In each chapter, he reconstructs how state officials from Britain and elsewhere engaged in role-taking, role-making, and alter-casting; this approach allows him to make plain why Britain did not change its basic foreign policy orientation when it might have been expected to do so according to IR approaches that focus more purely on military and economic factors. From the micro-interactionist perspective that McCourt adopts and develops, action is *joint* action; hence, explaining why Britain does what it does involves not reconstructing Britain's motives or the motives of the representatives of the British state but tracing how a course of action comes to be over time. The empirical outcome may be well known to scholars of British foreign policy or causal observers of British politics, but the explanations—the reasons *why*—are novel and insightful. A better explanation of the foreign policy of an important global actor, made possible through an innovative theoretical apparatus is perhaps precisely the definition of progress in the social-scientific study of world politics.

Patrick Thaddeus Jackson
Series Editor, Configurations
Professor of International Relations and Associate Dean
for Undergraduate Education in the School of International
Service at the American University, Washington, D.C.

Introduction

THIS IS A BOOK ABOUT British foreign policy since the end of the Second World War—about the adjustments UK policymakers have and have not made in response to Britain's relative decline in power over the period.[1] To that extent, it is a work of international history. It is also a book about how to understand state action in international relations—about how foreign policymakers come to recognize what is appropriate and possible for them to do in world politics. To that extent, it is a work of international relations theory. Specifically, it is a contribution to social constructivism,[2] one that stresses the importance of social roles in the construction of international politics. These two elements intertwine, finally, in a practical goal: to highlight trends in Britain's recent history that can inform contemporary political practice—in particular, problems related to the task British leaders face in navigating a shifting global order. This book thus seeks to draw wider conclusions about the sources of state action in international relations that pertain beyond the British case.

The main theoretical claim of the book is that state action in international politics is fundamentally role-based. That is, the sphere of possible action within which leaders engage in foreign policymaking is a function of the expectations that emerge about the appropriate behavior of their states in world politics. These expectations take the form of roles such as *ally, great power, alliance leader,* and others. Crucially, what behaviors these roles impart in any given instance are an effect of the specific interaction in which the role emerges. In other words, what social roles mean in terms of appropriate behavior is negotiated by states with other international actors. A secondary claim, then, is that roles should be a key part of how IR scholars go about explaining what states do in international affairs. This is particularly pressing, although not exclusively so, for constructivists. Constructivists—a varied group I will disaggregate later in this introduction—have usefully brought to the attention of IR scholars the "social" origins of state action, but they have almost entirely dismissed the importance of roles in favor of the more problematic notion of "identity."[3] At the same time, in search of legitimacy they have by and large neglected to claim causal explanatory status for their findings. In this book I will move counter to these trends, favoring roles over identity and offering an explicitly causal and explanatory account.

The main empirical argument of the book is that British foreign policy since 1945 has been based on the emergence of a role in its international interactions over the period, a role that I term *residual great power*. Although it quickly became clear that Britain was not in the same rank as the United States and the Soviet Union after the end of the Second World War in terms of material power, British policymakers have nonetheless viewed their state as continuing to have a prominent part to play in world politics and the country as requiring the diplomatic and military capabilities to play that part. Rather than view this tendency in terms of some innate British identity or sense of self, the case studies in this volume trace the expectations attached to Britain in relation to the *residual great power* role over four key episodes of its international history. The most important expectations, it shows, were largely those held by two powers: the US and France. Britain's international history and consequently its place in world politics today cannot be understood by looking at Britain alone.

These, then, are the main elements of the book in broad-brush strokes. In the remainder of this introduction, I discuss the puzzle of Britain's postwar history before assessing the problem of its contemporary foreign policy and the type of approach the problem requires. I then turn to the constructivist research agenda and its emphasis on state identity, using the shortcomings identified to justify a resort to roles. I then address case selection and identify the sources consulted. A plan of the book completes the introduction.

THE PUZZLE

Contemporary Britain represents a puzzling example of state behavior in international affairs. Despite more than half a century of relative decline, the UK remains a prominent member of international society. Britain retains a seat at the top table of international diplomacy, including a veto in the UN

Security Council. It backs up its diplomacy with highly professional and well-equipped armed forces that rank it in the top five of military powers. It also has an independent nuclear deterrent.[4] In recent years, moreover, it has deployed its forces to fight in Iraq and Afghanistan, provided air and naval support to NATO operations in Libya, and maintained other long-term commitments.[5] Britain's institutional bases of power, meanwhile, are used to protect purported interests that are distinctly more global in character than might seem appropriate to a nation of its geographical position and population as well as size and economic capacity, as the UK's recent military deployments suggest. Somewhat counterintuitively, therefore, and in contradiction to Acheson, Britain still appears to play a role in international affairs incommensurate with its geopolitical reality.

What is puzzling about Britain "punching above its weight"[6] is that it contradicts the traditional historical wisdom on Britain's international history since 1945: following the Suez Crisis of 1956, the withdrawal from "East of Suez" in 1968, and eventual UK entry into the European Economic Community (EEC) in 1973, Britain was thought to have settled in favor of a purely European outlook. This standard interpretation is found in a number of histories of postwar British foreign policy, and when they were written in the early 1970s, those assessments seemed apt and likely to remain so.[7] The British economy had been sluggish in comparison to its European neighbors and especially to the US and Japan, and the UK had consistently slipped down the world rankings of GDP per capita. Perhaps as worrying was the declining specialness of the "special relationship" with the US, which was thought to be at a low ebb from U.S. president John F. Kennedy's assassination in November 1963, as Britain's usefulness to its more powerful ally appeared to decrease.[8] Britain was also a newcomer to the European project and was keenly aware of that fact.[9] Postimperial readjustment was thought complete.

Yet more than thirty years later, there is something dissatisfying about the conclusion that post-1945 British foreign policy can be understood solely in terms of the readjustment from an imperial to a European power. Like early histories of Britain's postwar foreign policy, which blamed British policymakers for being too slow in adjusting to the country's diminished status, hankering after an imperial role rather than settling down to the difficult task of readjusting to new circumstances, there would seem to be more to Britain's postwar experience than can be explained by the country's postwar decline.[10] As a number of revisionist historians later showed, postwar policymakers adjusted to Britain's relative decline in material power through innovative strategies aimed at conserving British influence and freedom of action where feasible.[11] This took the form of a "Bevinite consensus": a shared opinion, named after postwar Foreign Secretary Ernest Bevin, that Britain remained a power of the first rank in international affairs and must retain the capabilities commensurate with that status.[12]

The Bevinite consensus was grounded not only in the conviction that Britain was still a prominent international player—even though, as political geographer Peter J. Taylor has noted, "Everybody understood full well that without the economic resources of a great power Britain could not carry out the political role of a great power"[13]—but also on the specifics of strategy for retaining that position. Labour's response, which jettisoned any pretense of a "socialist" foreign policy, had two parts. "The first was to align with the USA as the new hegemonic power and become a junior partner in the grand project."[14] Although this was, as Taylor stresses, "a real drop in status . . . , it seemed to be the only feasible way of maintaining a world role in 1945." The second response "was to be found in the 'new politics' of atomic power:"[15] Britain must have the Bomb.

The historical debate over postwar British foreign policy was therefore unenlightening.[16] Judgments about success and failure masked complete agreement that for better or worse, Britain's leaders had not adjusted to their country's reduced circumstances because they were almost unanimous in considering Britain still a great power.[17] Despite the changeover of government, IR scholar Stuart Croft has noted, "British foreign policy under the Attlee governments was characterized . . . by the same foreign policy conceptions as had dominated Churchill's National government."[18] Although two distinct groups emerged in the Foreign Office, divided by their views on the potential for co-operation with the Soviet Union, Croft goes on, "For both groups, Britain—as a *superpower*—had to be directly involved in the construction of a new global order."[19] The question was not, then, whether Britain would regain its power and influence, as historian John Kent makes clear; rather, "it was question of finding the means to achieve such ends."[20] Even as it dawned on UK policymakers that Britain's power base was not going to recover, the commitment to Britain as a great power retained its hold: the means changed over the period, from Britain as a four-power manager to the leader of a "third force" to America's leading ally in a two-power bloc, but the end remained the same.[21]

The key question is why this conception of Britain's place in international affairs retained such force as Britain's economic decline continued after the war. This draws us into the realm of theoretical inquiry. Numerous features of British foreign policy since 1945 can be explained using existing theories and theoretical approaches in IR—no approach is an island. First, a structural realist account would characterize Britain's cultivation of a special relationship with the US—one of the two great powers in the postwar order—as a form of "balancing" behavior.[22] However, a comparison with another postimperial power, France, illustrates the limitations of this explanation. Both emerged victorious in 1945, but each had clearly fallen to a rank below the new superpowers. From the perspective of structural realism, therefore, because the two countries retained largely comparable capabilities, they should have behaved in a broadly similar manner. Yet in several fundamental respects, British and French foreign policy have diverged since the war. In relation to their behavior toward the US for example, from Suez onward, Britain has aligned itself with the wishes of Washington wherever possible; in contrast, especially during the 1960s, France has attempted to lead a resurgent Europe as a potential counterweight to the US.[23] The question then turns on whether the surface form of foreign policy is considered important.[24] If it is, then we must accept that a structural explanation omits much of value for understanding the formulation of foreign policy.

Other theoretical approaches illuminate further important aspects of Britain's trajectory. A classical realist approach, for example, might suggest that Britain's postwar foreign policy has been par for the international political course: the desire to maintain large and capable armed forces, the attempt to gain prestige and influence on the world stage, and the aim of internationalizing certain values speak to realism's traditional concerns of power and its preservation.[25] Liberal scholars would in turn focus on Britain's support for international law and institutions, especially those of a liberal economic nature. Alternatively, from the perspective of Andrew Moravcsik's version of liberal theory, they might stress the economic interests of various domestic groups in an open international economic order.[26] A Marxist approach, broadly defined, would also be far from voiceless: Britain's actions are unsurprising in light of the global economic interests of the country's capitalist elite. This would also draw attention to the influence of the press, the academy, and think tanks on the formulation of UK foreign policy.[27]

But these approaches would be less useful at explaining the particular foreign policy actions UK foreign policymakers have taken beyond these broad tendencies. What specific elements of Britain's international position have policymakers prioritized? Why, for example, has Britain retained such reluctance to fully engage itself in the project of European integration as well as a consensus on the centrality of the transatlantic relationship? My aim is not, then, to argue that IR has nothing to say about the disjuncture between Britain's actions and its decline but to suggest that something rather valuable is left out of these approaches: a fine-grained account of the social sources of British action. For this reason, I draw on social constructivism, which— sometimes more accurately than others—has come to be associated with the more historical, interpretive and constitutive forms of theorizing in IR.[28] This leads me to reexamine the social constructivist theoretical toolbox for ways of explaining where foreign policy options come from and hence why they are subsequently enacted. Before I turn to these questions, I first explain why this task is pressing and what type of analysis the book represents.

THE PROBLEM: BRITISH FOREIGN POLICY IN THE TWENTY-FIRST CENTURY

The challenges British policymakers face are substantial. The UK is tied into an American global order many commentators view as being in its twilight.[29] The rise of China, India, and Brazil and the resurgence of Russia signal the genuine reemergence of a multipolar world order in which the voice of the West will no longer carry the preeminent weight it has for the past three cen- turies and that may become correspondingly less capable of facing up to global threats such as climate change.[30] Britain's relative decline, once a question worthy of historical debate, has become a truism.[31] At the same time, British foreign policy displays a strong conservative streak: policymak- ers are reluctant to promote the transformations in the institutional archi- tecture of Britain's international relations that will become necessary to ac- commodate these changes, such as further progress toward European integration and institutional change at the United Nations.[32] British officials remain trapped in a remarkably limited discursive space, their freedom of action narrowed by the need to "win" in their interactions with the EU, place a "special relationship" with Washington over specific foreign policy goals, and achieve "leadership" in international affairs wherever possible, to name only the most salient tropes.[33] Taken together, these developments suggest important limits on UK policymakers' degree of agency in dealing with the pressing international problems of the day.

This book is directed principally at the question of state agency. I do not, however, attempt to assess whether Britain has agency in world politics or, if not, how it can be acquired. The agent-structure dichotomy that lurks in the background of these questions has worn out its usefulness: most scholars now accept that action cannot be understood in terms of either agent or structure taken alone.[34] We should begin instead from Marx's dictum: Man makes his own history, but in ways not of his own choosing.[35] Britain can act but is not the sole author of its fate. Similarly, we can also dispense with the ideational/material dichotomy from the outset: the idea of the "rise of the rest" borders on the overly materialistic, undervaluing the ideational and discursive elements that shape how material forces impact the everyday of global politics.[36] World power is shifting eastward, but foreign policies still must be designed and put into effect, and important analytical tasks in assessing their varied bases therefore remain. Finally, the type of knowledge of politics that would be gained from trying to gauge a state's agency in abstract terms is overly technical—even if we knew for certain how shifts in power affected the behavior of states in general, we would still be left with the question of the practical application of that knowledge in specific instances.[37]

In this book, I seek to understand the actions of states (in this case, Britain) in world politics in a different sense, one that can be termed practical-moral. Assessing state action from a practical-moral perspective, the task is to recognize the origins of the options from which foreign policymakers choose and of the political strategies leaders can pursue. The key question is why do states do what they do in their affairs with one another in specific instances? Thus, it is imperative to stress the historical and context-dependent nature of international political practices. Doing so, in turn, requires accepting that states, like individuals, are products of social forces and therefore can be understood using the tools of sociology and social theory. Crucially, although social life appears orderly, even automatic, it is anything but: a stable social order is the contingent and ever-changing outcome of countless mutually coordinated "joint actions" by participants.[38]

This book, then, seeks to develop a means of understanding state action that is attuned to the practical logics within which foreign policy is carried on and international social life maintained and hence to its fundamentally social and therefore moral origins. Such "realities" of international life as shifts in economic power are not thereby disregarded, but the question of what they mean and for whom is the central focus.

BEYOND IDENTITY

The status of constructivism as a paradigmatic alternative in IR was won on the back of repeated demonstrations by early constructivist scholars that taking state interests as given, as do rationalists, comes at considerable analytical cost.[39] What states have an interest in doing, as Martha Finnemore, Jutta Weldes, Richard Price, and others have shown, depends on social context—it is socially constructed. Practically, this has come to mean that state interests derive from either what is appropriate and typical—that is, the "norm"—or from what has been termed a state's "identity."[40] There has consequently emerged within constructivism an accepted notion that states socially construct their interests in international affairs at least in part on the basis of their identity.[41] As Finnemore notes, before we know what we want, we have to know who we are.[42]

Before questioning this assumption, it is important to disaggregate constructivism, a rather loose theoretical container, to properly situate my contribution.[43] One of the effects of the identity agenda has been to foster a division between, broadly speaking, constructivism as a contribution to "mainstream" IR—understood as rationalist, neopositivist, and focused on certain problematics such as the origins of state interests in an anarchical world—and constructivism as a more far-reaching critique of the mainstream, able to problematize notions such as interests and even the state itself.[44] Commentators such as Emanuel Adler, Ted Hopf, and John Gerard Ruggie have consequently distinguished "modernist," "law and jurisprudential," "narrative-knowing," and "postmodernist" constructivisms (for Adler), from "norms-based," "systemic," and "societal" constructivisms (for Hopf), and "neoclassical," "postmodernist," and "naturalistic" constructivisms (for Ruggie).[45] In each, divisions over analytical foci sit alongside a principled metatheoretical distinction: between rationalism and reflexivism in Robert Keohane's almost overly prophetic terms.[46]

My approach crisscrosses these boundaries: it is explicitly non-neopositivist but equally explicitly social scientific while stressing the importance of narrative knowing, which is often considered nonscientific.[47] The book also engages norm-based, systemic, and societal constructivisms while accepting the substantive focus of none of them—norms, the international system, or domestic societies. In this, the book accords with the spirit of the early constructivists such as Finnemore, Weldes, Audie Klotz, and Christian Reus-Smit whose main aim was the creation of empirical knowledge of world politics.[48] But it also accords with the aims of a new generation of constructivist scholarship that seeks to rediscover the critical potential of constructivism in social science IR while moving away from the study of norms, culture, and, most important here, identity, toward "practices" and "relations" in world politics.[49] I elaborate further on this movement and the relationship of my work to it in chapter 1 and in the conclusion. In short, my approach sits within mainstream constructivism but highlights how constructivism itself is better understood as an interstitial space in the field, between the rationalist-neopositivist mainstream and critical alternatives, rather than a research agenda settled on any specific concepts once and for all.

The essence of the identity agenda in IR with which I take issue is that foreign policy is an outward expression of the state's "self," just as human behavior is an expression of the individual self. British policymakers adopted the Bevinite worldview after 1945 and have subsequently maintained it—for example, because it gives life to Britain's international identity. Britain's "ontological security," in other terms, has come to be bound up with "a certain idea of Britain."[50] The idea that identity explains action is straightforward and intuitively plausible. But it is also problematic and fraught with ambiguity. We can see why by assessing Hopf's impressive study *Social Construction of International Politics*.

Hopf opens with the following gambit: "Every individual in society has many identities."[51] Each identity, he goes on, "has associated with it a collection of discursive practices, including a language with a vocabulary, written or verbal, and characteristic physical behaviors, such as gestures, dress, customs and habits."[52] Hopf is correctly stressing the way in which individuals behave differently in different social situations. Understood in this way, the same person might have an "identity" as an American, a New Yorker, a Christian, and a Yankees fan, for example. In this he echoes Alexander Wendt, for whom "we all have many, many identities, and this is no less true of states. Each [identity] is a script or schema, constituted to varying degrees by cultural forms, about who we are and what we should do in a certain context."[53]

The problem with this gambit is that it conflates the concept of identity with that of "role." Hopf's approach thus illustrates a wider tendency in the identity agenda in constructivism to sideline roles in favor of identity as well as some of the problems to which this tendency leads.[54] Roles and identity have become almost equated—if roles are mentioned at all. In their recent guide to constructivist research methods, for example, Klotz and Cecilia Lynch treat the two concepts as identical: the index to their volume reads

"Role(s): *See* identity."[55] Elsewhere Mlada Bukovansky defines roles as "corollaries of broader and vaguer identity conceptualizations,"[56] and she too uses the terms interchangeably. Jeffrey Legro identifies three ideal-type identities to explain changes in ideas about a state's international identity.[57] Yet these identities—*hermit, trustee,* and *rebel*[58]—could surely more accurately be described as social roles.

The use of the term *identity* in this way is, of course, common in both everyday language and among scholars.[59] It is not my intention—and it would be pointless even if it were—to argue that this usage is in some final sense wrong. Rather, if we want to use these terms in social scientific analysis, there are important reasons to make clear distinctions between the social groups and types with which we identify (Yankees fan, American, Christian, and so forth), our individual identity (or who we are), and the social roles we play. This is critical if these concepts are to be used to explain state action and not merely represent neat ways of describing or characterizing it.[60]

The first reason to stress the conceptual distinction, then, is because there is no such thing as a presocial identity. Identities are as much a product of as an input to the action of states and individuals in international and domestic life. In other words, identity- or self-based analyses suffer from an endogeneity problem. Identities are formed in social interaction; their ontological condition is one of the day-to-day and minute-to-minute stabilizations of the process, practices, and relations that construct them. There is no identity, or role, as a Yankees fan without the practice of following the baseball team called the Yankees, and those practices are reproduced in contexts such as Yankees games. It is not surprising, then, that some constructivists have stretched the concept of identity to "social identity" to cover the inherently social aspects of state action.[61] Also not surprising is constructivists' recent interest in practices, habits, relations, and configurations, all of which were included in Hopf's definition of identity but are worthy of analysis on their own terms.[62] This book forms part of that movement, which seeks to more accurately understand how action is socially constructed.

Second, distinguishing between identity and role is crucial because the privileging of identity over role displays the common tendency to believe that we have produced our social world rather than the other way around.[63] For this reason, attempts to characterize what constructivism is tend to boil down to Wendt's notion that "anarchy is what states make of it."[64] Not only is this merely trivially true—there are no structures without agents engaging in practices that uphold them—it may be more true for some states than others. For the majority, this idea is a gross oversimplification of the extent to which they can truly shape their international environment. It is not for nothing that many examples in IR of identity clearly influencing state action have focused on powers at the peak of their capabilities, notably the United States. This is like noting that the strongest and coolest kid on the playground tends to get her way. Why another kid suddenly wants to wear certain types of footwear, then, has less to do with his identity than with the expectations that make up the social role of *normal kid,* like not wearing uncool footwear. Explanations based on the first child's identity would not only be partial but would actually choose the wrong person to study, as it is in interaction with the cool kid that the normal kid discovers he wants new sneakers.

Every individual in society, I argue, has one identity. But all individuals play numerous social roles over the course of their lives. Being an American, a New Yorker, a Christian, and a Yankees fan are part of an individual's identity; they are what makes someone who they are. As Friedrich Kratochwil has argued, identity can then be understood as the story that knits together the different aspects of an individual's identity over the course of his or her life.[65] But in specific contexts, these identifications take the form of expectations about appropriate and likely behavior, which are not identities properly understood but social roles. In chapter 2, therefore, I develop a constructivist approach to state action in international politics that is based on social roles, not identity, and can thus circumvent some of the problems with the identity agenda in IR constructivism while preserving its central insights. I also explicitly defend its causal explanatory credentials against the traditional equation of constructivist accounts of world politics with "constitutive" theory, "understanding," and generally noncausal approaches. I then demonstrate its empirical advantages vis-à-vis theoretical alternatives in the empirical chapters that follow.

THE RESORT TO ROLES

A role, political scientist James Rosenau has observed, is "defined by the attitudinal and behavioral expectations that those who relate to its occupant have of the occupant and the expectations that the occupant has of himself or herself in the role."[66] Use of the concept is common in everyday life, including roles such as "father," "wife," or "professor." We have an innate sense of social order as fundamentally role-based. To conceptualize international politics in terms of the roles nations play, therefore, is to suggest that there are sets of expectations in the international sphere that are sufficiently coherent to explain the foreign policy of the states that play those roles, just as roles explain individual actions in everyday life.

A number of consequences follow from this discussion of identity. First, when the role concept is invoked, there is a common emphasis on action: the expectations that constitute roles focus on what the actor will or will not do in a particular situation. If we can go some way toward understanding those expectations and how they are communicated to their actors, then action is cast into a good deal more light. Second, roles are inherently social concepts: their meaning and content exist only within specific contexts and institutions. A *husband,* for example, does not occupy the role without a *spouse.* Here counterroles and socialization processes become crucial, as do relevant "others."[67] Also implied here is that another social context, like work, might override the husband/spouse roles, supplanting them with *colleagues* or *boss/worker.* Third, this example also highlights the importance of the practices and institutionalized authority relationships constitutive of a legitimate union and its corresponding behaviors.

Despite the intuitive power of the role concept and its frequent use in everyday speech, however, roles have not been (explicitly) placed as central to IR theory. Identity serves as constructivism's watchword—its version of "power" for realists, "security" for neorealists, or "institutions" for liberals. Nor does it come in a close second, with "norms" and "culture" the front-runners for that honor. The reason, it can be surmised, is the difficulty with using roles in social scientific research.

That said, roles implicitly have been commonplace in IR theory. In the realist tradition, there has been a common focus on the expectations attached to the behavior of the *great powers*—a social role.[68] This preoccupation links realists of the classical tradition and power-oriented English School theorists to the more rigorous systemic theorizing of the neorealists.[69] The presence of balancing behavior, for example, is often explained by positing it as a feature intrinsic to the international system. In the anarchical environment, survival-seeking states are compelled to form alliances and build up their capabilities to balance power against potential hegemonic states.[70] Their role in the sense of the predominant expectations about their behavior is to follow the logic of the international system and balance. Elsewhere, so-called hegemonic stability theorists also make strong claims about the expected behavior of great powers—specifically, those who have over-come this propensity toward a balance of power and become global or re-gional *hegemons*, another status that could also be understood as a social role.[71]

However, the concept of role itself does little, if any, theoretical work in these approaches and is heavily undertheorized (see chapter 1).[72] Not only are the expectations attached to the position not viewed as intersubjective in nature, they are derived instead from exogenous models of interaction. In this view, states have roles only to the extent that they have a status as a player in the game of international politics: they have the role of *great power,* and from this all else follows. Even if it occasionally seems accurate, this view does not sit well with the ontology of role-playing. Similar problems attend two further approaches and justify the attempt to rethink roles in interna-tional politics.

The first approach emerged in the subfield of foreign policy analysis (FPA), particularly with the work of political scientist Kal Holsti.[73] Holsti de-fines roles as "the policymakers' own definitions of the general kinds of deci-sions, commitments, rules and actions suitable to their state, and of the functions, if any, their state should perform on a continuing basis in the in-ternational system."[74] In line with the initial definition outlined earlier, therefore, Holsti sees roles as consisting of the expectations about state ac-tion held by those in positions of control: the decision makers. Holsti's defi-nition rests on an analytical move that disaggregates the origins of roles: on the one hand, "role prescriptions" are the expectations placed on state ac-tion that emanate from the external environment, a result of the expecta-tions of significant others; on the other, "role conceptions" are policymak-ers' beliefs and expectations relating to the role of their states.[75] As is clear from Holsti's definition, he accords priority to the self-conceptions of deci-sion makers regarding the roles their states should play. Role conceptions have been the central tenet of the research agenda inspired by Holsti's work, a development that might have been expected given that the agenda has taken root within FPA and not within mainstream IR theory.[76]

As Wendt points out, however, the Holstian research agenda has not re-sulted in a widespread acceptance among IR scholars of the importance of roles in international politics.[77] The reason is that role conceptions grasp only part of the power of the role concept. In privileging the point of view of decision makers, role conceptions do not take full account of the expecta-tions about state behavior that emanate from the international sphere.[78]

The second approach to consider, then, is that of Wendt himself. For Wendt, "Role should be a key concept in structural theorizing about the international system."[79] Wendt claims that "the culture of an international system is based on a structure of roles,"[80] which is to argue, in contradistinction to Kenneth Waltz, that the structure of the international system is, at least in part, made up of ideas and not merely material elements.[81] What defines the structure of the system is the shared knowledge that exists between states about their behavior toward each other, which is a function of the "role structure" they exhibit.[82] Anarchy, in this reading, is thus a particularly powerful belief that the lack of a world government results in the only role available being that of *enemy* to every other state. But in Wendt's view, three roles are characteristic of three "cultures of anarchy": (Hobbesian) *enemy,* (Lockean) *rival,* and (Kantian) *friend.*[83]

This rather idiosyncratic definition is essential for Wendt's structural social theory of international politics, but it, too, has its limitations. It represents a remarkably spare vision of the structure of international political life and is thus far removed from the historical and social contexts within which roles emerge as well as, crucially, the language of international political life constructivists should place central to their analyses.[84] In the same way that the use of Waltz's theory is problematic in relation to foreign policy, therefore, Wendt's approach is only partially suitable if the intention is to analyze the nature and content of a specific state's role in international relations, including how that role changes or evolves over time.

In this book, I put forward an approach to state action based on the concept of social roles, which I term *micro-interactionist constructivism.*[85] This understanding of foreign policymaking is fleshed out in depth in chapter 1. For readers more interested in the historical sections of the book than the theoretical and who thus might want to skip to chapter 2, I argue that foreign policymakers come to recognize the boundaries of acceptable and therefore possible action because social roles structure the interactions of states in international affairs in much the same way they do for individuals in everyday life. Drawing on the symbolic interactionist social psychology of George Herbert Mead, together with his interpreters in sociology, I contend that state leaders take the role of the Other in their international interactions: that is, they view situations from the perspective of other states, putting themselves into their shoes.[86] British leaders can be seen to have taken the role of the United States and France to a degree downplayed in the literature on UK foreign policy since 1945. On that basis, they then try to "make" a particular role in a given situation—framing their behavior in certain ways to make it fit. This, in turn, may involve "alter-casting" others into complementary roles. Foreign policy action, I show, is coordinated in response to the expectations that make up social roles, which are communicated in interaction. This takes us beyond agency versus structure and into the mutual coordination of actions that is a more complex but realistic picture of social life.

A NOTE ON CASE SELECTION AND SOURCES

The empirical chapters of this book assess the changes and continuities in British foreign policy over the course of four prominent events: the Suez Crisis, the Skybolt affair, Britain's second application to the EEC, and the Falklands War. The selection of these events is pragmatic: as in all theory-driven exercises, choices and cuts must inevitably be made, although almost any aspect of Britain's foreign relations could highlight something important about the roles the country has played over the period and how they have changed. There are, therefore, a number of important episodes neglected, in particular, the granting of independence to India in 1947, the withdrawal from East of Suez in 1968, the first and third applications to Europe, and Britain's involvement in a series of wars and interventions since the end of the Cold War. Each would be worthy of extended treatment. The conclusion discusses the justification for stopping in 1982 yet making claims up to the present. Here I briefly defend the decision to begin in 1956 rather than 1945.

At the time of the Suez Crisis, more than a decade after the war, the disjuncture between Britain's material power and foreign policy orientation became clearly apparent. Although Britain had been weakened by the Second World War and found it self much diminished vis-à-vis the US and the Soviet Union, its extensive engagement in international politics in the postwar years meant that its presence at the postwar councils was taken for granted. This book thus takes the existence of the Bevinite consensus—a vision of Britain's role in the world that emerged in the immediate aftermath of the war and that led the Attlee government to oversee the significant restructuring of British foreign policy—as its starting point and addresses the puzzle of its longevity. Why did it not come under greater scrutiny both from within Britain and beyond, as the 1940s and 1950s progressed? How the consensus emerged in the tumultuous years after the end of the war, with specific focus on the part played by the US and other states in its construction, would make a valuable addition to this study—or, indeed, a book in its own right.[87] But although interesting and pertinent to the story, given the acceptance of the Bevinite consensus in the historiography of the Britain's postwar foreign policy and early Cold War history, and given that the puzzle the book addresses truly begins after the emergence of that consensus, it makes more sense to begin instead with Suez.[88]

There are also strong reasons for the four cases chosen. First, the prominence of the Suez Crisis in Britain's recent international history means its inclusion requires little justification. While historical accounts of the crisis—in which Britain colluded with France and Israel to invade Egypt in response to President Gamel Nasser's nationalization of the Suez Canal Company in July 1956—abound, few explanations have been considered authoritative. At the same time, the notion that Suez represented the end of Britain's great power status seems both true and quite unenlightening given the puzzle of British foreign policy on which this book is based.[89]

Second, when it erupted in the early 1960s the Skybolt affair brought to the fore a number of important expectations attached to Britain's role in the world. It centered on a crisis in US-UK relations caused by the American cancellation in late 1962 of a nuclear weapons system—Skybolt—promised to Britain in the late 1950s. The affair highlighted inherent tensions in UK-US-European relations with regard to nuclear policy and Britain's independent deterrent and more broadly between the "Atlanticist" and "Europeanist" elements of British foreign policy. Although historians now deem the incident less of a crisis than has been traditionally thought, Skybolt offers a useful perspective from which to view the longer-term results of Suez, which is often considered the key episode in Britain's postwar experience, and the effects of the Cold War context on the development of Britain's role.

Third, Britain's second application for membership of the EEC in 1967 represents the moment when the British political establishment swung decisively in favor of entry into Europe. Whereas the Labour Party had opposed entry during Britain's first attempt earlier in the decade, both parties supported the second application in 1966–67, meaning that it has much to tell us about the role of "Europe" in Britain's international reorientation.

Fourth, the 1982 Falklands War between Britain and Argentina is another important example of Britain's postwar adjustment in that it seems, as has been often noted, entirely out of place in the 1980s: a colonial war far from British shores. Beyond prestige politics and Britain's desire to protect its subjects, despite their distance from London, the Falklands War illuminates numerous themes of British foreign policy in the early 1980s—in particular, relations with those who supported and made the expedition possible, the United States and Britain's European partners. Again, the incident also offers several historiographical debates with which to engage, including the war as a point of national regeneration, and the war as a historical anomaly that tells us little about Britain in the world in the 1980s and beyond.

The sources consulted reflect the emphasis of micro-interactionist constructivism on the identification of spaces of possible action in foreign policy formulation and the centrality of international interaction to that process. First and foremost, I analyzed public documents that give a sense of the discursive space created during each of the episodes chosen. Parliamentary debates, official speeches, and other public declarations of the relevant ministers were of paramount importance. Also useful here was the recently digitized *Times* online archive. Second, I consulted archival sources in the UK to gather a comprehensive account of the diplomatic interactions in which British policymakers engaged. In addition, given the centrality of the US to the cases, the *Foreign Relations of the United States* series proved invaluable. Finally, I drew on memoirs and biographies of the British and non-British policymakers concerned. Once again, I sought to reconstruct the discursive space rather than to discern private beliefs and motivations.

PLAN OF THE BOOK

The book comprises seven substantive chapters. Chapter 2 develops a *micro-interactionist constructivist* account of state action, drawn from a reading of symbolic interactionism and an engagement with the current approaches in IR. The problems with these approaches do not spring entirely from the work of their authors but come from the underlying theories in sociology from which they borrow. A symbolic-interactionist-inspired framework can overcome these shortcomings. I then outline a historical interpretive methodology.

The four subsequent chapters analyze salient episodes in Britain's postwar experience. Chapter 3 assesses the Suez Crisis of 1956, which, along with the 2003 invasion of Iraq, is now typically considered the most important event in Britain's international relations since the Second World War. Here, Britain's pretensions to playing the *great power* role structure the interaction, alongside relations with France and the United States, actors that will be prominent in the subsequent cases discussed. Chapter 4 focuses on the 1962

Skybolt affair, which highlights important bases of Britain's international relations at the dawn of the 1960s, particularly with regard to its relationship with advanced nuclear technology and transatlantic relations. Chapter 4 then turns to Britain's second application to the European Economic Community, between the coming to power of Harold Wilson's Labour Government in October 1964 and Charles de Gaulle's eventual veto of Britain's membership in November 1967. Chapter 5 analyzes the 1982 conflict between Britain and Argentina over the Falkland Islands, which put to a severe test the military posture left after many of the decisions taken regarding East of Suez. The conclusion discusses the study's most important insights in both theoretical and empirical terms.

CHAPTER ONE

The Roles Nations Play

"We are the victims of an illusion which leads us to believe we have ourselves produced what has been imposed on us externally."

—EMILE DURKHEIM[1]

IN THIS CHAPTER, I present a role-based approach to the analysis of state action in international relations; I then use this approach in the remainder of the book to explain Britain's puzzling maintenance of an expansive foreign policy orientation long after its decline from world power. I call this approach *micro-interactionist constructivism.*[2]

Theorizing state action from this perspective entails three tasks for this chapter. The first is to explore what roles are and how they work in social life. This step is crucial, since although roles are a familiar notion, using them to explain foreign policy raises numerous rather thorny problems at the level of social theory. I begin, therefore, by contrasting two traditions of thought within sociology—micro-interactionism and structural-functionalism—that make extensive use of the role concept but do so in distinctly different ways. Juxtaposing these two approaches to social explanation draws out the value of a micro-interactionist account based on symbolic interactionism in general and the work of George Herbert Mead in particular.[3] Put briefly, a micro-interactionist perspective on the nature of social roles holds the promise of moving us away from overly abstract structural accounts of state action[4] and toward a relational and practice-oriented approach that offers fine-grained and context-specific explanations for why states engage in specific foreign policy actions.

After making clear the value of a micro-interactionist reading of roles, the chapter then develops a conceptual vocabulary that can be used to analyze state action in world politics from this perspective. To this end, I outline a parsimonious set of concepts drawn from symbolic interactionism—"role-taking," "role-making," and "alter-casting"—and elaborate on this framework by contrasting it with alternative approaches, particularly identity- and norms-based constructivisms and rationalist bargaining approaches.[5] In contrast to these approaches, a role-based micro-interactionist approach highlights the way that state identities and preferences emerge and social norms come to influence state leaders only within unique interactions in world politics. Interaction is an inherently dynamic, role-based process of orientating action to the behavior of others; identity-, norms-, and preference-based explanations are therefore necessarily limited at best, since by downplaying the subtle processes through which state actions are matched to the expectations of others, they beg further crucial questions: How do states come to know what they want, what they should do, or what they want to do?

The third task is to outline a set of methods and a methodology under-pinning them appropriate to micro-interactionist constructivism.[6] The choice of roles as research object does not determine the way in which they must be studied; depending on what we want to get from our research, methods as diverse as large-n statistical analyses, game theory, and small-n quali-tative methods might be appropriate.[7] My aim here, however, is to explain foreign policy decisions in as much detail as possible. Consequently, I de-fend a historical interpretive method.[8] This approach is inductive rather than deductive and is sensitive to the microlevel dynamics of role-playing in international relations. But it is also leads to causal explanations of foreign policy as long as our understanding of what it means for action to be caused and behavior explained is expanded beyond what is typical in the social sci-ences.[9] In short, a role-based approach explains foreign policy by making clear how states come to define their options in interaction with others, which is a function of the role requirements that emerge during interna-tional interaction that render some options more "live" than others.

ROLES AND THE SOCIAL SOURCES OF (STATE) ACTION

Roles are fundamental to the architecture of social life.[10] Although largely un-aware of it, roles structure many aspects of our daily interactions, from gen-eral roles like *father* and *wife,* which can endure for many decades, to specific roles like *waiter* and *customer* that can span the duration of only a brief interaction. A common example is the classroom, made up of the roles *student* and *teacher* and their narrowly defined associated behaviors. As Alexander Wendt remarks, "When I step in front of the classroom I could in theory take the role of opera singer, but that would be costly."[11] Rather than sing, individuals playing the teacher role engage in actions such as lecturing and assigning work, which both flow from and constitute the role of teacher itself.

As an initial definition, roles can be understood as "clusters of normative behavioral expectations directed at the behavior of position-holders."[12] These expectations lead those who play roles to behave in patterned and often quite predictable—although not predetermined—ways. But while this definition captures the key aspects of roles, it also leads to myriad further questions that require conceptual investigation: What are "expectations," and how do they relate to observed action? What does it mean to "occupy" a "social position"? How can we be certain of its effects? These questions emerge even before we attempt the shift to the international level. What are roles when we move beyond the individual to the group? Are they ideas in the heads of individuals? Or positions within discursive spaces? Again, how can we be certain of their causal effects?

Conceptualizing roles for empirical analysis thus requires a coherent vision of roles that encompasses ontological, epistemological, and methodological elements. Rather than pick and choose from approaches in cognate disciplines, I contrast two opposed approaches from sociology—structural-functionalism and micro-interactionism—and, in making the case for the latter, draw out its unique understanding of role-based social action.

Structural-Functionalism and Micro-Interactionism Compared

Structural-functionalism is associated with the later work of Talcott Parsons, whose thought dominated US sociology during the 1950s and 1960s.[13] From a Parsonian perspective, roles are general behavioral patterns that form the basic units of social systems.[14] The power of this conception lies in the view that social action is explicable without taking into account every attribute of the actors in a system—that is, individual human beings, what they actually do, their specific acts. What is needed instead is an understanding of the behavioral patterns in the shape of principal "roles" that the system requires to perpetuate itself and the way in which those roles relate to the successful functioning of the system. Parsons identifies three functional role requirements: that social systems be compatible with the needs of their main actors; that actors abstain from deviant activities that threaten the system's continuation; and that systems support cultural patterns that underpin the first two requirements.[15]

Figure 1 presents this approach in diagrammatic form. It illustrates the parsimony of the structural-functional approach as well as its impersonal nature. The circles represent sets of expectations that structure social situations from this perspective, not human individuals, who were notably absent from the approach.[16] The figure also illustrates the "substantialist" nature of this approach: roles, like the human agents who play them, are considered to exist prior to the interaction or "transaction" between individuals.[17] The rejection of substantialism in social science, however, forms part of the recent movement toward practices and relations in IR theory. A micro-interactionist reading of roles, then, is explicitly antisubstantialist.

Structural-functionalism represents one way to conceptualize what roles are and how they work in international politics. Indeed, it already underpins two of the most important theories of international relations, those of Kenneth Waltz[18] and Alexander Wendt.[19]

Waltzian neorealism is a structural-functional theory in the Parsonian mold.[20] The unit of analysis is not real states in world politics, and the theory does not purport to explain any specific states' foreign policies, echoing Parsons's rejection of the individual and the act as the basis for a structural theory of society.[21] Rather, the basic unit of neorealism is "quite simply the role expectation of self-regarding behavior":[22] the role of *enemy* to every other state. Given certain basic assumptions about the international system—that it is anarchical and the units seek to survive—states can be predicted to engage in one particular behavior in international affairs: power balancing.[23]

Paradoxically perhaps, as a result of its status as the bible of neorealism's paradigmatic competitor, constructivism, Wendt's social constructivist theory of international politics should also be considered strongly Parsonian because of its close engagement with Waltz's substantive claims about the structure of the international system. Wendt seeks to show that because the structure of the international system has ideational as well as material elements, the lack of a supranational government in world politics does not make inevitable a Hobbesian "war of all against all."[24] Rather, by enacting cooperative practices over time, states can change the "role structure" of the international system[25] to a less conflictual "culture of anarchy" that includes roles such as *rival*[26] and even *friend,*[27] as the creation of zones of peace or

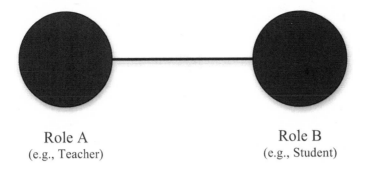

Role A
(e.g., Teacher)

Role B
(e.g., Student)

Fig. 1.   A simple two-role social system from a structural functionalist perspective

"security communities" such as the transatlantic area demonstrates.[28] "Anarchy," in Wendt's felicitous phrase, "is what states make of it."[29]

Expanding on these theories in the development of a more self-consciously role-based account of foreign policy from a structural-functional perspective would thus follow a clear lineage. What counsels against such a move, however, is that structural-functionalism has long since fallen from favor in sociology. It was criticized for representing an overly rigid vision of society and an oversocialized conception of the individual, who in this viewpoint becomes something of a structural dupe.[30] A related critique can be leveled against Waltz's and Wendt's structural theories of international politics: neither approach deals with the question of precisely *how* states know how to act in accordance with the role expectations emerging from the international system in any specific instance.[31] Beyond being ahistorical and somewhat arbitrary, the structural roles of *enemy, friend,* and *rival* Waltz and Wendt outline are too abstract to provide fine-grained accounts of the foreign policies of specific states. This is because their theories do not include a means by which the expectations that constitute these roles are transmitted to state decision makers or an account of how expectations become actions.[32] But as Martin Hollis and Steve Smith note,

> No role could possibly be specified in enough detail to make all decisions automatic. . . . There are some specific duties of a role, some dos and don'ts which set limits to what may be attempted. But there is also an area of indeterminacy, governed only by a broad duty to act so as to be able to justify oneself afterwards.[33]

Yet despite these shortcomings, those in IR interested in roles have not questioned structural-functionalism itself, instead descending from the social to the cognitive level to develop a psychological perspective on role-playing.[34] Foreign policy role theorists, following Holsti, have thus focused on the "role conceptions" of decision makers, understood as their "own definitions of the general kinds of decisions, commitments, rules and actions suitable to their state, and of the functions, if any, their state should perform on a continuing basis in the international system."[35] The resort to the cognitive reduces the theoretical power of roles since they are truly interesting theoretically only insofar as they are properties of social contexts and not things in the minds of particular actors.[36] Viewing roles in cognitive terms, therefore, removes what is distinctive about roles vis-à-vis other ideational approaches, such as those focusing on "ideas," "belief-systems," and "operational codes."[37]

There are, however, sociological alternatives to structural-functionalism to which those wary of structuralism could have turned. In fact, as Steven Lukes has noted, "Every [structural] macro-theory presupposes, whether implicitly or explicitly, a micro-theory to back up its explanations"—a mechanism or set of mechanisms, in other words, through which structures underpin behavior.[38] Scholars could then have drawn on another tradition of thought in sociology, the "micro-interactionist" tradition,[39] which evolved as a response to the indeterminacy of structural approaches à la Parsons and has viewed roles as critical elements of social action.[40] With a lineage running from American pragmatists such as Charles Houghton Cooley, John Dewey, William James, Charles Sanders Pierce, and George Herbert Mead through their interpreters in sociology itself, particularly Herbert Blumer and the symbolic interactionists[41] but also others such as Erving Goffman[42] and Harold Garfinkel,[43] and also including the work of European philosophers and social theorists such as Alfred Shutz[44] and phenomenologists Edmund Husserl[45] and Martin Heidegger,[46] the micro-interactionist sociological tradition is united by a focus on precisely the context-specific microlevel drivers of social action from which structural-functionalism chooses to abstract.

Micro-interactionist approaches, despite their variety, thus retain the social—and hence noncognitive—nature of action while not abstracting entirely from the individual human being. They problematize the most basic elements of social existence: How do individuals know how to behave in interaction? How, for example, can Wendt be sure that playing the role of opera singer in the classroom would be costly? In developing a role-based approach to state action, therefore, I turn to the micro-interactionist tradition. Since not all micro-interactionists view roles as central to interaction,[47] however, I draw specifically on symbolic interactionism and the work of Mead in particular.

Role as Perspective: An Invitation to Symbolic Interactionism[48]

Symbolic interactionism has its roots in the thought of the Scottish moral philosophers and the American pragmatists, Mead chief among them, with the term itself coined by one of Mead's students, Herbert Blumer.[49] For Blumer, symbolic interactionism is based on three simple premises: "human beings act towards things on the basis of the meanings things have for them"; the meaning things have is fundamentally a product of interaction; and, finally, interaction conveys meaning through a process of interpretation.[50] The affinities here with IR constructivism are immediately apparent; constructivists also stress the inherent meaningfulness of social and political life and the necessity of interpreting what individuals think is going on as a preliminary to explaining why certain actions are thinkable and hence doable.[51] The specific potential of symbolic interactionism, however, lies in its distinct perspective on social action, developed over several decades of theoretical and empirical inquiry, which helps avoid common pitfalls in constructivist research, including viewing constructivism as straightforwardly privileging either agency or structure; overly intersubjectivizing constructivism at the cost of the merits of objectification; and equating constructivism with "constitutive theorizing." By stepping away from the terms of the debate in IR, therefore, it is possible to address these misunderstandings from firmer ground.

This can be done by discussing the four key concepts symbolic interactionists use to cash out the basic premises of their approach—"role," "self," "symbol," and "object."[52] Together, they conceptualize what for symbolic interactionists is the most basic element of social reality: human interaction. For symbolic interactionists, the social is not a neutral context or background against which action takes place but an ongoing accomplishment of individuals. The common invocation of preferences, desires, expectations, language, meaning, identity, norms, institutions, and all of the other aspects cited in the social sciences as essential for explaining human action is underpinned by a primary ontological condition: individuals coming together and engaging in mutually oriented action. Individuals' ability to engage in social interaction is an ongoing achievement. As Jon Levi Martin notes, "Keeping the nonproblematic nonproblematic is a problem for actors and requires their continual readjustment and mutual susceptibility."[53]

Roles are central to this process. For symbolic interactionists, roles are neither sets of fixed rights and duties that must be acted out nor "ideas" inside people's heads. Both of these conceptualizations play down the importance of interaction—viewing the "social" as merely a context within which to act out understandings of what to do formed outside of it. Mead's most important contribution to philosophy and social psychology is to show how individuals come to know what is expected of them. For him, people recognize expected action through the process of "role-taking":[54] looking at their own position from the viewpoint of those with whom they are interacting. The symbolic interactionist usage of the term *role* is thus very different from the everyday use of the word, with its connotations of functions, rights, and duties. It can therefore appear confusing. Role-taking does not mean role-playing, since the whole point is to question how role-playing (behaving in ways that correspond to the expectations that make up roles) is possible in the first place. Role-taking in a Meadian sense means "perspective-assuming."[55] Roles are perspectives taken during interaction from which the individual interprets what actions are expected, appropriate, necessary, and hence possible.[56]

The example Mead uses to illustrate this understanding of roles is the game.[57] To recognize what actions are expected of them, players in games "take the role" of other participants. That is, they assume the perspective of the other players, interpreting their words, gestures, and bodily and facial expressions in search of clues as to what the situation calls for. In baseball, for example, the batter considers his moves by taking the role of a variety of others: the pitcher, the outfielders, or teammates. Another perspective is what Mead terms the "generalized other"—the organized perspective of a group of others.[58] In baseball, "the team is the generalized other in so far as it enters—as an organized process or social activity—into the experience of any one of the individual members of it."[59] From these perspectives, the batter gleans expectations about the upcoming action. In baseball, role-taking most obviously tells the batter to try to hit the ball, but the game may be poised so that a bunt is a better option than a swing for a home run.

With time, of course, what is expected of the baseball player becomes second nature in many situations, and it becomes less meaningful to talk of explicit moments of role-taking than of habitual behavior—actions engaged in as a matter of routine.[60] But this is an empirical question. At important moments of action, role-taking is a necessary element of knowing what to do. "If there is a chance for a double play," for example, Baldwin notes, "each player must know how the others will contribute to making it,"[61] and doing so requires role-taking. In Mead's words,

> [The batter] must know what everyone else is going to do in order to carry out his own play. He has to take all of these roles. They do not have to be present in consciousness at the same time, but at some moments he has to have three or four individuals present in his own attitude, such as the one who is going to throw the ball, the one who is going to catch it, and so on.[62]

The notion of "role-taking" demonstrates that role-based behavior is essentially an active process: what individuals are expected to do while playing a social role is not handed to them, they must figure it out. Figure 2 represents this alternative understanding of how roles work. The squares now represent human beings, as indicated by the stick figure, and the process is a dynamic interpersonal one, in contrast to structural functionalism.[63]

Most individuals are adept at putting themselves in other people's shoes and grasping expected behavior. This is not to say that role-taking is always successful or that the results of role-taking will be conformed to in every case. It is not my intention to present a rosy picture in which people cooperate easily and never miscommunicate or have diverging notions of different situations.[64] Yet simply because role-taking is not always successful does not mean that it is not occurring. Otherwise, both hostile *and* friendly intentions would be essential—either individuals get along or they do not—and negotiation or compromise would be denied as an assumption. The existence of coordinated action—whether cooperative or conflictual—is better explained by a perspective that holds both successful and unsuccessful mutual orientation of action as theoretically plausible than one that assumes away genuine interaction. A symbolic interactionist approach therefore represents a more sophisticated understanding of the place of roles in interaction than does the structural-functional alternative. But before taking this definition of roles to the international level, three further concepts make clear how role-taking and social interaction in general are possible.

The first is the "symbol." Role-taking is based on the human ability to share meanings, to see similar situations in similar ways, which is possible because interaction is symbolic. A social symbol is a "vocal or other kind of

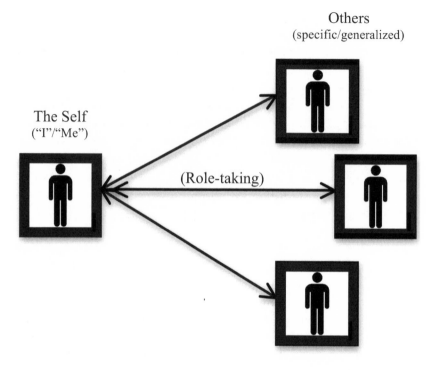

Fig. 2.   Role-taking

gesture that arouses in the one using it the same response as it arouses in those to whom it is directed."[65] Wendt illustrates this point with the example of the "first encounter."[66] Two individuals, meeting for the first time and sharing no "stocks of knowledge,"[67] gesture in ways familiar to themselves— "my smile means I have friendly intentions"—not sure that their meaning is shared. Interaction becomes meaningful only when shared symbols emerge by which each are certain that they are understood—when the smile has become accepted as meaning friendliness.[68] The most important set of symbols, of course, is language itself, but much communication also contains nonlinguistic elements such as gestures. Gilbert Ryle's famous distinction between a twitch and a wink is the typical example: the difference between them is that the twitch is a symbol, existing only in context to refer to a meaning already shared—"I'm joking."[69] Linguistic and nonlinguistic symbols nonetheless both denote shared meanings so that individuals know how to "go on."[70]

This symbolic nature of interaction is belied by structural functional-ism. The actions of individuals are fundamentally shaped by the meanings they share, and the motivations and signaling of their desires, on which rational choice approaches in particular focus, are in fact derivative of these meanings. The meanings individuals act on also preexist alter and ego. If they meet on a narrow bridge, for example, it is commonly polite for both to make a gesture of passing sideways or to wait for the other and gesture them to pass. Little about what they actually do, therefore, follows from the sim-ple desire to cross the bridge. What is crucial is that the role of *bridge crosser* and its associated behaviors of politeness emerge only within the bridge-meeting interaction itself and are not objects tied to alter or ego. The ex-pected actions cannot then be reduced to properties of the "mind" but exist only within an emergent relationship in interaction structured by shared symbols.

How then do things become symbols? A second key concept elaborates on the way in which symbols enable social interaction: the "social object." A social object, for symbolic interactionists, is a symbolically designated phys-ical object.[71] Although physical things exist all around us, "for the human being, they are pointed out, isolated, catalogued, interpreted, and given meaning through social interaction."[72] Heidegger's discussion of the mode of being of "equipment" and of the hammer in particular are illustrative in this regard. Heidegger terms that mode of being "ready-to-hand" and argues that a hammer's physical aspects—its weight, shape, and so forth—have meaning only to the extent that they relate to an object's use: too heavy, too light, too big, too small, or just right for the task.[73] The question is not, there-fore, whether "things" exist, as critics of social constructivism often fre-quently and mistakenly suggest, but how they exist, for what purposes, and how their characteristics relate to those uses. Crucially, this requires a shift in analytical focus from essential qualities of things to the configurations and relations within which things have meaning—to how they are used in concrete human practices.

Together, then, the concepts of "symbol" and "social object" form the basis of a symbolic interactionist approach to social action that is much richer than the abstract world of structural functionalism. Without the abil-ity to share meaning, interaction would not be possible, since there would be no background set of understandings against which it could be oriented. Ev-ery interaction would be instead a coincident set of separate actions. The Weberian example of a crowd of people all opening their umbrellas at the same time is paradigmatic here.[74] Although done concomitantly, it is not an example of social action since it is not meaningfully oriented toward the actions of others; it is a simple utility maximization strategy to avoid getting wet. Social interaction, again, is not merely a neutral "context" of human action for symbolic interactionists; it is the ontological basis of human life.

The final key concept of social interaction to discuss is the "self." For Mead, both self and society are fundamentally products of interaction. The self is not an ultimate foundation for individuality—the "essence" of a person once all his or her social commitments are removed and the basis of agency. Rather, the self can be considered an agent only because it becomes a social object in interaction: through role-taking, the self perceives as meaningful its different gestures, actions, and orientations because it acts toward itself in the same way as it acts toward other social objects, be they chairs, hammers, or whatever.[75] By assuming the perspective of others, the self appraises potential action by looking back on itself, so that actions are made to fit the situation.[76]

The self can become a social object in this way because for Mead the self is composed of two elements: the presocial "I" and the social "me":

> The "I" is the response of the organism to the attitudes of the others; the "me" is the organized set of attitudes of others which one himself assumes. The attitudes of the others constitute the organized "me," and then one reacts towards that as an "I."[77]

This distinction is designed to grasp human action as an inherently interpretive process: a constant task of interpreting the words and physical gestures and countenances of others and of thereby adjusting behavior to the expectations, constraints, and possibilities of specific social situations gained from that interpretive process. Although Mead retains scope for volition, however, it is clear that the "I" for the most part depends on the "me." Only through the interactive process does a sense of individuality become possible. Indeed, Mead says, "When we are completely absorbed in doing something, there is no Self."[78]

Together, the concepts of "role," "self," "symbol," and "object" are the building blocks of a symbolic interactionist account of social action, including its sophisticated understanding of the place of roles therein. In the next section, therefore, I conceptualize state action from this perspective.

MICRO-INTERACTIONIST CONSTRUCTIVISM

Non-neopositivist work is often presented as being opposed to the search for parsimonious explanations of world politics in favor of complex context-specific interpretations.[79] Yet while it is true that non-neopositivists take context more seriously than their neopositivist counterparts, it is not the case that parsimony itself must be abandoned along the way. The conflation of parsimony with neopositivism in fact entails another conflation—that of disagreements over ontology and epistemology, or the complexity of the social world and the extreme subtlety of our knowledge of it, with those over methodology and method, or what forms of analysis and specific techniques are most appropriate for studying social life, including, crucially, the use of concepts. Complexity in the world is then considered to necessitate complexity in our approaches to its study. This misunderstands the role of concepts and concept formation in social science, where a degree of parsimony might be valuable and is in any case inevitable. As a result, while in the following section I defend the choice of a non-neopositivist methodology, in this one I develop a micro-interactionist constructivist analytical framework that aims to be relatively parsimonious conceptually.

I defend conceptual parsimony in similar terms to those laid out by Kenneth Waltz.[80] Waltz stresses that the measure of a theory is its usefulness— that is, what it tells us about international politics, not its relationship to the "real world," complex or not. This is because in Waltz's understanding, theories do not represent the world but rather construct an analytical model of a sphere of social life that presents a world to us. Waltz was thus quite clear in pointing out that theories should not be too realistic; if they are, they lose the abstract nature that makes them useful. The example of a map of scale 1:1 is the standard illustration here.[81] The orienteer does not need to know everything about the terrain he or she is trying to navigate, only the most salient features, like recognizable buildings, peaks, and gradient changes marked with contours. The key issue is whether the map has indeed included all the relevant features: if it leaves out a ravine, for example, the orienteer might find him- or herself in an unfortunate situation. Similarly, a Marxist conceptual tool kit focused on class analysis will only tell us so much about certain international interactions where class simply is not a relevant analytical category given the nature of the events in question.

All theories are therefore parsimonious to some degree, since their creators face the question of where to draw the line between including more of experienced reality with gaining more usefulness through abstraction—the threat of doing violence to experience being an unavoidable danger.[82] Parsimony is therefore relative and should not be discounted out of hand. The important question, rather, is whether the approach I put forward has analytical purchase in relation to its empirical object—here state action in international relations—and hence whether it could be improved by including more elements drawn from the micro-interactionist tradition in sociology. Would, for example, my approach be more useful if it drew explicitly on the Goffmanian notion of "framing" or other aspects of Turner's highly complex synthetic model of social interaction, which blends aspects from thinkers from Mead to Schutz?[83] I argue that the concepts of role-taking, role-making, and alter-casting represent a coherent vision of role-based social interaction and can therefore be confidently considered sufficiently complex for my purposes. They draw strength from the micro-interactionist tradition from which they are taken and which other scholars following in my footsteps could draw.

After describing the concepts of role-taking, role-making, and alter-casting, I assess how well the approach deals with the domestic-to-international scale shift; in what way it relates to approaches rooted in the concepts of "identity" and "norms"; how it confronts the agent/structure divide; and finally, given certain similarities, in what way a micro-interactionist approach is distinct from a formal game-theoretic approach. In each case, I seek to stress how the methodological choices I make concerning how to study roles are related to the micro-interactionist approach to what roles are.

Micro-Interactionist Constructivism: Basic Concepts

Following Mead, the primary concept of micro-interactionist constructivism is "role-taking."[84] Decision makers are not empty vessels, filled with the knowledge of exactly what to do in any given situation, as both structuralists and proponents of identity- and norm-based constructivism seem to infer. Rather, by imaginatively "taking the role" of others or stepping into their shoes within interactions like crisis-bargaining, summits, or intergovernmental conferences, decision makers grasp the expectations attached to their own state's role. In other words, through role-taking, state leaders come to recognize the scope of their foreign policy options. The main way decision makers do so is by assessing what the officials of other states actually say and do in diplomatic exchanges. Even when others are not physically present—like when foreign policy is discussed in small groups around the executive or in parliament or the public sphere—it is still meaningful to talk about role-taking because doing so captures the process of objectifying the state's self and viewing appropriate behavior from the perspective of others.

While meaningful action depends on assuming the perspective of others during interaction, however, the concept of role-taking does not by itself account for everything that is going on. What is left out is a sense in which the decision makers in question make strong choices concerning what action to undertake and do not merely carry out the will or conform to the expectations of others. The second concept of micro-interactionist constructivism therefore is "role-making."[85] Role-making is "the process wherein the person constructs activity in a situation so that it fits the definition of the situation."[86] Role-making is particularly important in international politics because "defining a role and having it accepted by other actors remain basic objectives of states."[87] Indeed, IR scholars have often focused on this type of activity by the so-called *great powers,* which are defined as countries that can act in the world independently of other powers—that is, countries that can make their role as they choose.[88] However, this idea neglects the fact that most states are not great powers, that they are strongly influenced by the expectations of others, and that this is grasped through role-taking.

The final concept is "alter-casting." As typically described in social psychology, alter-casting takes the form of a negotiation during interaction between ego and alter.[89] Once the individual has interpreted his or her appropriate behavior based on the process of role-taking, the next endeavor is to get this role accepted by relevant others. They seek to "cast" a certain "alter" onto the other—an alter that accords with their particular vision of themselves. In such situations, the others are trying to do the same thing, and the actual roles taken, therefore, are determined when the roles each is seeking to play correspond to the best fit or one beats the other into a corner through successful rhetorical strategies.[90] Wendt discusses this process with reference to the example of Gorbachev's Perestroika, during which the USSR attempted to alter-cast the US into the role of "friend" helping to integrate a former enemy into the international system.[91]

These three processes do not take place in an interaction "three-step."[92] Interaction is diachronic and intensely fluid, and there are feedback loops between each process. Moreover, conceptually, role-taking is the most fundamental, since without the ability to assume the perspective of others, no meaning could be shared and the self consequently could not become a social object. Nonetheless, it is useful for the sake of clarity to present them as if they occur sequentially. Individuals "take" the perspective of others, on the basis of which they grasp the "space of possibles" concerning their course of action. On this basis, they "make" roles for themselves that are subject to modification through further rounds of role-taking. Both the state in question and the others with which it interacts attempt not only to convince each other of the worth of their definition of their own role but also to "cast" them into appropriate corresponding roles. Although particular interactions will differ from this model of interaction to greater or lesser degrees, this relatively parsimonious framework provides a useful way of analyzing state action.

In the remainder of this section, I flesh out this conceptual framework by considering its implications from a number of different directions that place in sharper relief the value of a symbolic interactionist take on roles and social action.

Role-Taking, State Centrism, and the Problem of Corporate Agency

The imputation of roles to states is contentious. State-centrism is frequently attacked in IR—deemed indicative of wider problems in the discipline, including its reification of the sovereign nation-state, the way in which it tends to limit international relations to Europe after 1648, and hence its in-built pro-Western bias.[93] The implication is typically that we should move beyond the state in our scientific imagination as a preliminary to moving beyond it in practice.[94] Even below this maximal position, however, the argument that state action can and should be conceptualized in role-based terms seems to make several contestable assumptions about the nature of the state: that it is a unitary actor and even that it can be personified, which are problematic in analytical terms. Addressing the "roles nations play," therefore, raises the question of the nature of the state itself.[95] How, in short, does a micro-interactionist constructivist deal with the issue of the state?

A defense of a state-centric micro-interactionist approach begins by suggesting that states can be understood as role-playing actors since they are corporate agents.[96] At base, states have some governing apparatus that endows certain individuals with the power to make authoritative decisions on behalf of the state, a power others in society do not have. Thus, "in the last analysis," individuals make decisions: particular presidents, generals, kings, and decision-making bodies ultimately decide to make war or peace, sign treaties, or lower tariffs, and so on. States can therefore be viewed as role-playing actors because individuals have the power to take the role of other states and engage in role-making and alter-casting on behalf of their states. However, making the obvious point that states have the machinery to engage in role-taking does not settle the relevant issues at stake, as the "last analysis" argument ignores the fact that although individuals do all of these things, they do not do them as private citizens but rather as officials of the state. The problem of corporate agency thus involves more substantive ontological and epistemological claims about states and social action that must be teased apart.

In so doing, I follow Bartelson, who highlights a fundamental tension in how IR scholars typically consider the nature of the sovereign state in international relations.[97] Bartelson begins by noting that each of the three main approaches to the question "What is the (sovereign) state?" end up in either circular arguments or a problematic regress. The issue of the state's identity, he shows, rests on answering the logically prior question of what makes the state identical to itself. Three main answers are typically put forward. First, there are those who view the state as ontologically given, a set of rights and duties based on sovereignty and the continuity of the state from government to government.[98] The problem with this account is that it is largely ahistorical and leads to a regress toward some mythical founding moment that presupposes the authority to found the state that is the exactly what was sought to explain the identity of the state. A similar problem haunts the second approach—that is, the social constructivist perspective that views the sovereign state in institutional terms. It exists because people think it exists.[99] While adding a useful historical dimension, there still lurks the specter of a hidden foundational authority. A final approach views the state as a discursive rather than institutional fact or a priori.[100] From this perspective, the state is not essential but is a product of the contingencies of political discourse; it is impossible to move beyond the state because of the stickiness of language. Here, too, is the problem of where the foundational power to "speak the state" originated.

For Bartelson, the problem with finding an adequate answer to the question of what makes a state a state lies not with these approaches to the sovereign state as a specific historical type or with particular sovereign states but with the notion of "identity" itself—with the question of what it means for something to be the same as itself. The issue here is whether there is some-thing essential to anything—be it a sovereign state or human being—just by virtue of that thing itself. For Bartelson, such identity is a fallacy, as identity can only be understood within a context of difference. In other words, for something to be what it is, there has to be at least the possibility of it being something else, and that difference has to be imminent in its very being. "In the final analysis," Bartelson suggests, "what is proper to identity is the abil-ity to enter into a relationship to oneself, and to be different from oneself as a condition of oneself."[101]

If, logically speaking, nothing can be identical to itself only by virtue of itself, then the question of what something is becomes one of the relational configurations within which it is embedded. This is drawn from Hegel's dis-cussion of the dialectic relationship between the master and the slave: both depend fundamentally on the other to be what they are.[102] Consequently, it is meaningful to talk of "identity" only as a relationship between something and something else. It is nonsensical, for example, to talk of a slave in the absence of a master, and vice versa. This fundamentally "with-other-ness" of identity is what makes identity "a profoundly contradictory concept."[103] Identity is self-referential in most uses of the term; it is used to assert the ex-istence of something at the same time being invoked to explain that thing's existence. As Bartelson makes clear, therefore, as "type"—that is, the sover-eign state—"the kind of state identity which figures as an object of theoreti-cal controversy in International Relations theory is nothing but a fiction dreamed up by contractarians and their historicist successors in order to conceal the facts of conquest and the ignoble origin of all law."[104] As to what Bartelson calls "token" states—that is, specific states such as Britain, France, and so forth—these are claims to there being something essential and im-mutable to Britain (for example, as a political community), a notion with which historians and social theorists from Benedict Anderson on have al-ready dispensed.[105]

In simple terms, then, the invocation of "identity"—either as type or, for us here, token—does not do much in terms of explaining state behavior in international politics. "Existing accounts of state identity are therefore best understood as expressive of the same identity they seek to describe and ex-plain, since the very possibility they share in common, namely that of con-ceptualizing the state as if one stood outside it, presupposes precisely that kind of difference which it integral to its proper identity."[106] Only a dia-chronic analysis of how identities are constructed with others—that is, one concerned with their construction over time—can claim to do much in terms of explanatory work. To do that, one would need an understanding of social interaction that does not see interaction as merely a neutral background for the performance of preformed identities or selves. This makes clear that adopting a micro-interactionist approach results in the need to make an important corrective to recent theorizing in IR on the relationship between state "identity" and action in international politics.

Before doing so, a final implication to be drawn from Bartelson's discussion is that the domestic/international dichotomy that underpins IR theory is itself misleading in that all politics is international politics in the sense not of relations between preconstituted "nations" but as the politics that lies at the roots of the establishment of such realms—the original Greek meaning of *politics* as relating to the formation of walled communities being key here.[107] This is why Jackson can argue, in all seriousness, not only that Alexander Wendt is right to say that "states are people too" but also that "people are states too."[108] If nothing can be identical to itself only by virtue of itself, and it is meaningful to talk of identity only within the context of relations to difference, it follows that identity is also only meaningful to talk about as sets of practices and uses. It is here that the value of symbolic interactionism again becomes apparent. Human beings—and by extension human groups, such as states—are themselves therefore social objects, which is precisely what a Mead-inspired approach asserts. This means that human groups of whatever type can only be grasped within the configurations and relations within which they can be what they are.

Identity, the Social Self, and Practical Reasoning

A micro-interactionist approach to state action offers a way of overcoming this deficiency within the identity-agenda in constructivism without falling into the trap of structuralism, the original reason Hopf rejected roles.[109] It allows the notions of identity and roles to be separated conceptually yet combined as part of a more complete perspective on the social construction of international politics. It does so by remaining silent on the notion of "identity" itself as a way of trying to explain action. Identity becomes *explanda* rather than *explanandum:* as Kratochwil notes, "identity" is best understood as that notion of sameness which gives our lives coherence, despite the many roles we play over the course of them.[110] Instead, it places central the social emergence of the "self." From a micro-interactionist perspective, the self is an important aspect of social interaction since individuals engage in reflective action that entails the objectification of the self through role-taking. But again, the crucial point is that self is a product of interaction, not its agent. As Blumer makes clear, the self is not the same as something like an ego: "The self, in the form of a process of self-indication, operates in the course of the act and cannot be reduced to, or collapsed into, an initial agent such as an ego."[111] Again, the aim is to understand the mutual orientation of action rather than some fundamental and somewhat mysterious psychological basis.

Consideration of Hollis and Smith's explanation of why people conform to the expectations that constitute social roles is useful in that regard:

> The constraint on the obedient actors [from a role] lies in the normative expectations upon them, reinforced by sanctions. "Normative" refers not to what is normal or usual but what is required, in the sense that failure to perform the role is given to criticism, censure, and penalty.[112]

Most IR theories focus on "constraint," "sanctions," and "penalties" when trying to understand why states do what they do. But roles also influence action through the desire to avoid "censure" and "criticism." That is, role-players *reason* out the best way to conform to the role's expectations: "The leading idea [of a role-based approach to action] is reasoned judgment, not of computation."[113] Practical reasoning is, then, precisely the essence of role-based action from a micro-interactionist constructivist perspective.

Practical reasoning is also the essence of foreign policy decision making. As Wendt notes, by taking the role of the other, a state can choose "from among the available representations of the Self who one will be, and thus what interests one intends to pursue, in an interaction."[114] This characterizes how foreign policy proceeds. Leaders' initial question, "What should we do?" takes the form of an outlining of options, followed by a discussion of the pros and cons of each in relation to conceptions of a state's proper place or sense of self in world politics. But the options themselves do not emerge from thin air; rather, they follow from a process of taking the roles of others—either through interpreting the words and gestures of others in face-to-face diplomatic interaction or through asking hypothetical questions in the absence of others during domestic-level discussion and debate, both public and behind closed doors.

A symbolic interactionist account does therefore not "black-box" the state: domestic disagreement does not mean that role-based dynamics are not at play. Quite the opposite: they are the discursive vehicle through which role-taking and role-making are made apparent. The approach does not prioritize domestic institutional arrangements, including partisan alignments, but it does not prevent these arrangements from being an important aspect of foreign policy. Even if different parties or domestic groups support different visions of a state's "self" in international affairs, those visions must be meaningfully related to the expectations of others through role-taking.[115]

A symbolic interactionist account of roles in international politics therefore incorporates into its purview identity, in the form of the self, and a more complex understanding of the social through its focus on role-taking in interaction. It has space for norms as well in the form of Mead's notion of the "generalized other."

Social Norms and the Generalized Other

The issue of exactly which others a state takes during a given international interaction is an empirical one, not an issue of theory: frequently, it is a specific other state during bilateral diplomacy or group of states in multilateral forums. In both of these cases, then, roles are taken in face-to-face contact. The US, for example, takes its role from the large number of other states and nonstate actors that make up its wide diplomatic networks; other states (for example, the smaller South American states) are primarily regional in orientation and consequently have more limited numbers of significant others. In those cases, role-taking is mainly conducted with familiar others with whom interaction is frequent. There is also, however, what Mead termed the "generalized other."[116] This represents the perspective of the whole or a specified part of the individuals involved in a social interaction and can thus be considered Mead's corollary to the notion of social norms.

For Mead, interpersonal interaction and the taking of the roles of specific concrete individuals are not sufficient for the development of the self in the fullest sense. The individual must also "in the same way that he takes the attitudes of other individuals toward himself and toward one another, take their attitudes toward the various phases or aspects of the common social activity . . . in which . . . they are all engaged."[117] This is an important phase in the development of the child to adulthood—adults are capable of doing it, while children are not. The developed individual can generalize the attitudes of numerous others to be able to act in the different social projects in which he or she is engaged at any one time without feeling the insecurity or embarrassment that comes from not knowing how to behave. Rather than a vision of norms as internalized behaviors, taking the role of the generalized other shows how these internalized behaviors work in practice. They work through a process of imaginatively considering possible choices and their hypothesized outcomes based on precedents in related yet different social settings and time periods.

Mead's discussion of the emergence of self in society has, however, been criticized by some who consider it to ignore the macrolevel forces influencing human behavior. Presenting a structural vision of society was indeed not Mead's principal aim, and the voluntarist overtones of the process of role-taking do seem to downplay issues of power and coercion. But nothing about his discussion of the emergence of the self in social interaction should be taken to mean that Mead viewed the wider of social setting of interaction as unimportant. Indeed, he notes quite clearly,

> It is in the form of the generalized other that the social process influences the behavior of the individuals involved in it and carrying it on, i.e., that the community exercises control over the conduct of its individual members; for it is in this form that the social process or community enters as a determining factor into the individual's thinking.[118]

As Hollis and Smith similarly note, "If one thinks of role-players as stewards of their offices, working chiefly in the permissive area between what the role definitely requires and what it definitely forbids, then the manipulative aspect of power is more readily understood."[119]

More recently, scholars have recognized this element to Mead's work as part of a drawing out of his larger social theory.[120] Thus, although it remains the case that the strengths of an approach that draws on Mead lie not with macroprocesses of international political culture—that is, the general form of what Wendt terms the "culture of anarchy"—but with how such forms are translated into the actions of concrete individuals within interaction, micro-interactionist constructivism enjoys the strength of an approach that can coherently combine identity, norms, and roles into its conceptual vocabulary.

Role-Taking, Rationality, and Social Interaction

Given the stress placed by a micro-interactionist constructivist approach on "gesturing" and "indication" and the similarities of these notions with those of "signaling" already familiar in IR, some readers may legitimately wonder why the same empirical phenomena cannot be incorporated into rationalist models of state behavior. It is imperative, therefore, to draw a clear distinction between a micro-interactionist constructivist account of interstate interaction with a rationalist approach to bargaining. In short, what is it about interaction that a bargaining approach does not or cannot capture?

Consider a disagreement between two states, A and B, over an international issue C, where A and B are unaware of each other's preferences regarding how to solve the issue. Analyzed in this way from a rationalist perspective, C represents a "signaling game"[121] and would focus on the problems related to incomplete information and the inability of either A or B to make clear signals about their preferences regarding the outcome and then to engage in the making of "credible commitments."[122] A rationalist analysis would seem to offer a strikingly similar type of approach to a micro-interactionist account, which would itself stress the importance of role-taking—assuming the perspective of the other—and role-making and alter-casting, each of which would be considered part of what is going on in interaction but not sufficient to explain action. However, a micro-interactionist interpretation has a fundamental conceptual advantage over a rationalist account, over and above the challenges posed to a game-theoretic analysis by the complexity of social life.[123]

From a micro-interactionist perspective, the reasons C would be an event necessitating crisis "bargaining" would be role-based: they would be the emergent roles, defined in relation to each other and the roles of other important parties to the dispute, including the "international community," that actually produce the preference orderings a rationalist account would merely assume. A problematic circularity that afflicts rationalist accounts of interaction is thereby avoided by the adoption of a Median approach: only if A and B had somehow been able to change their preferences would it be meaningful to talk of a rational "solution" to C. Yet since A and B would be players of a different "type" if endowed with different preference orderings—they would in fact be D and E—such a move would represent a change to the game's initial setup, making it a far less crisis-prone game. This would have to be rejected as less a "rational" assessment of the causes of the crisis than an ad hoc pseudo-explanation, since the outcome would be *presupposed* in the assumptions made in the game's initial setup.

From a Meadian perspective, in contrast, A and B's observed actions would not follow preset preferences "revealed" during the crisis but instead would represent dynamic responses to the expectations of the roles that emerged within the specific context of the interaction. Exposing the circular reasoning underpinning a rationalist approach thus makes clear the benefit of presenting historically rich and contextually thick reconstructions of interactions within which the interests and identities of the actors involved are created and re-created, rather than thin and context-free "games" in which players enter with preferences formed and leave with identities unchanged. A micro-interactionist constructivist approach thus does far more than provide actors with preferences for rationalists to utilize, as constructivist-rationalist "division of labor" arguments recommend.[124] It presents a powerful and logically distinct viewpoint on interaction that suggests that states have few context-free utility functions. Rather, what states view as appropriate and necessary is tied to the relational roles they play, roles that emerge within and structure their interactions in international affairs.[125]

METHODS AND METHODOLOGY

Alexander Wendt has given voice to a popular sentiment in IR after the constructivist turn by cautioning scholars against becoming obsessed with epistemological questions.[126] This could be broadened to philosophical questions more generally, since epistemological questions are, quite frequently, not epistemological at all but ontological or methodological in nature—distinguishing clearly among these areas has not always been top priority in the discipline.[127] However, despite Wendt's quite justified view that IR theorists should stick to world politics rather than philosophy, it is important not to gloss over the full metatheoretical and hence philosophical implications of choices relating to research goals and the conceptualization of research objects. In particular, Patrick Jackson's distinction between methodology and methods is important. Methodological choices (that is, those concerning "the logical structure and procedure of scientific enquiry")[128] have consequences regarding concrete methods (appropriate techniques by which data can be generated and analyzed, such as ethnography, archival research, textual analysis, surveying, statistical analysis, and so forth).

In this section, therefore, I develop a methodology and set of methods for the micro-interactionist constructivist analysis of state action. The aim, once again, is fine-grained analysis of British foreign policy since 1945, not the discovery of general patterns of state behavior applied to the British case. This approach traces microlevel processes underpinning state action on the basis of a theoretically sophisticated model of interaction using what I term a historical interpretive approach. While I use the term *interpretive,* this approach is neither "merely" interpretive nor just an exercise in "constitutive theorizing": it explains elements of social action better than alternatives and does so in a way that can be meaningfully termed "causal." It thus promises to highlight important aspects of UK foreign policy decision making—or of such decision making by other international actors it might be used to analyze—that would escape attention from alternative perspectives.

Logics of Social Action and the Functions of Norms

The most common way of connecting what might be termed "ideational" concepts such as roles to observed behavior within political science has been the "logic of appropriateness."[129] It is useful, therefore, to begin by assessing the logic of appropriateness and its suitability for underpinning a micro-interactionist account of state action in international relations.

The logic of appropriateness is defined in explicit contrast to the "logic of consequences," which posits that actions taken by individuals or groups are designed to achieve certain preconceived ends—to get what those individuals or groups *want*.[130] Rational choice models provide the clearest example of this type of reasoning: people act for instrumental reasons, with goals resulting from rational ends-means calculations.[131] According to logics of appropriateness, conversely, action is intended to fit the social situation in which an actor finds him or herself: action is still intentional, but what the actor has an "interest" in doing is determined with reference to a number of norms that govern appropriate behavior. From this perspective, the logic of consequences is actually just one form of norm-governed behavior, a specific logic of appropriateness that privileges cost-benefit calculations over considerations such as manners or custom.

The logic of appropriateness represents one way of grounding a micro-interactionist approach. Indeed, it would seem particularly apt since the approach outlined here draws specific attention to the way in which action follows from the process of role-taking and is hence designed to fit social situations. Yet the notion of the logic of appropriateness is in many ways misleading, as Hopf and others have demonstrated. It focuses overly on the interpretation and following of expected behaviors, when behavior is frequently more habitual than this approach suggests.[132] While useful for situations in which norms are explicit and hence little reason exists to quibble over the "real" reasons behind observed actions, logics of appropriateness struggle to conceptualize behavior when individuals are guided not by explicit norms but by behavioral habits or less tacit understandings of appropriate conduct.[133] In those cases, how do we know why an agent acted in a certain way?

To conceptualize this habitual aspect of behavior, Hopf therefore distinguishes what he terms "logics of the everyday" from logics of appropriateness, which he has more recently named the "logic of habit."[134]Adler and Pouliot and others have also shown that international political life has its own "practical logics"[135]—patterned ways of doing things that are neither appropriate nor inappropriate but just *are,* almost as ends in themselves.[136] However, these logics, too, are, in fact, merely "logics of appropriateness" attuned to more habitual action. Hopf admits as much when he states that the distinction he makes between logics of the everyday and logics of appropriateness is made not on ontological grounds but on methodological grounds.[137]

Logics of "appropriateness," "consequences," the "everyday," "habit," and "practice" are therefore better thought of as ways of describing different modes of behavior. Their differences relate to the degrees to which norm-based behavior has been internalized[138] and not to some fundamentally different forms of human experience. As such, the best that can be said of them is that they characterize behavior rather than fully explain it. Again, the notion of role-taking makes clear how behavior can be patterned to fit the expectations of others. A methodology, however, requires something more: a set of fundamental choices regarding how the social world is and how we can gain knowledge of it across social science practices. In contrast to proponents of these logics—March and Olsen, Hopf, and Pouliot and Adler—such knowledge cannot be gained by reference to named "logics" of social action.

At this point, it is useful to recall the tale of an Englishman in India who, having been told that the world rested on a platform which rested on the back of an elephant which rested on the back of a turtle, asked . . . what did the turtle rest on? Another turtle. And that turtle? "Ah Sahib," came the reply, "after that it is turtles all the way down."[139]

The issue of whether it is possible to explain action by reference to social norms then turns on the issue of whether or not norms go "all the way down."[140] That issue rests in turn on what norms are, how they work, and their consequences for the way in which we should understand social action.

Two functions of norms are typically distinguished: their "regulative" and "constitutive" functions.[141] In their regulative sense, norms affect behavior by making explicit what one ought to do in a particular situation, or at least one's limited choices. But it is never possible to say for certain that a particular norm identified resulted in the observed action, because other norms often require competing responses. "Walk on the right" might, for example, be overridden by the norm of politeness to pregnant women if the right is the more dangerous path. Norms are therefore both overlaid and often underpinned by other social norms. If the aim is to present a full explanation of social action by reference to norms, then in theory, these norms themselves would require identification and explanation. This is clear because norms also work in a second way. Underpinning their regulative function is the fact that norms also constitute the social world with which actors engage, including its legitimate players, its rules, its taboos, and, notably, its roles. Discerning this second aspect of norms has been one of the central focuses of the social constructivist research agenda in IR.[142]

As noted in the introduction, different strands of constructivism are marked off by how they deal with this condition and by the specter of infinite regress and epistemological nihilism seemingly portended by the fact that norms are always based on other norms. Many so-called mainstream constructivists,[143] for example, have downplayed the constitutive aspects of norms, probably because if norms are viewed as having constitutive as well as regulative features, the roles and identities of states are themselves socially constructed and are not just intervening variables between the international system and state interests.[144] Things such as norms, identities, and roles, then, would not be considered causal according to the classical precepts of social science.[145] Although the language of variables is consciously avoided here, what would in mainstream approach be the independent variable (for example, the role) would have to be considered deeply bound up with the dependent variable (state action in international politics). This would entail a rejection of the strict separation between subject and object required, and there would be seemingly no potential for independent and empirically verifiable knowledge.

The issue of an adequate methodological underpinning for micro-interactionist constructivism therefore turns on the question of whether norms only constrain or regulate, and, as a corollary, whether it can be said that roles cause action, and, if so, how?

Roles, Rules, and Causation

The micro-interactionist account of state action I develop in this book makes claims about world politics that are explicitly causal in nature. It explains by making clear how foreign policy options present themselves to foreign policymakers within interaction—that is, though role-taking. It thus rejects the regulative/constitutive distinction as disregarding a crucial third function of norms: as facilitating state "strategies." In so doing, it also rethinks what it means to use the terms *cause* and *explain* in IR theory.

This perspective shows that what states want to do does not come out of thin air as the will of an essential initiating agent or ego, from the structure of the international system, or from some exogenously given preference: it emerges within social interaction, which is a role-based process. The explanatory work, then, is done by the specification of a space of possible action and the emergence of one most appropriate policy strategy and lack of other "live" options. Crucially, explanation does not suggest that other options were impossible and the outcome consequently was predetermined; it focuses instead on the dynamics of foreign policy choice. This type of explanation, which I will discuss later under the Weberian label "singular causal analysis," does not sit particularly easily with the predominant approach to causal analysis in international relations today. We are left, therefore, with the problem of reconciling—or not—the prevailing understanding of causation with this a micro-interactionist constructivist account. This requires taking a closer look at the predominant approach itself.

As Jon Levi Martin has recently noted, "For too long, the social sciences have attempted to invent and defend their own criteria for explanatory success."[146] These criteria are based on an understanding of causation that downplays how individuals view their world but offers a third-person perspective on action in response to questions posed of the social world in the form of "why" X happened—a perspective that is backed by the cultural strength of the notion of "science."[147] This vision has further key attributes: first, it subsumes particular actions or events to general ones; second, it uses abstract concepts that are alien to the world as experienced by the actor that is the object of research; and third, it then links abstractions via constraint. In a withering critique of this predominant notion of causation, Martin argues that the result is "a [social] science in which statements are made about the connection of imaginary elements in an imaginary world, and our justification is the hope that these will explain no case but rather an unknown portion of every case."[148]

The aim of causal explanation as commonly practiced in social science is to posit the "efficient'" causes that made an action result in outcome X. It attempts not to capture the desired event in all its complexity but rather to isolate the most important elements of it, especially those that pertain to causal laws, since it is through the identification of laws that every case can be explained.[149] In a similar way to an apple falling off a table according to the laws of gravity, therefore, if it can be shown that states attack others when they feel threatened, for example, not only is a particular attack explained, but general and cumulative theoretical knowledge of international politics can be generated. Once again, the central ideas are "subsumption" under a law, "abstraction" from any specific case, and "constraint" on agency.

By rejecting a holistic view of events in favor of causal explanations thus understood, neopositivist accounts of social action leave out information essential to understanding international politics. Efficient causes may not exhaust the elements necessary to account for international political action. In fact, a narrow focus on efficient causes alone ignores three other classes of "causes" distinguished by Aristotle—the "material," the "formal," and the "final"[150]—which our modern understanding of explanation, and particularly that adopted in the social sciences, has demoted to noncauses. While efficient causes are "the primary origin (arche) of change and rest,"[151] according to Aristotle, the "material" also constitutes a cause in the sense that it is the "existing thing out of which something comes to be, e.g., the bronze of the statue . . . (physics)."[152] A "formal" cause, conversely, "is the formula (logos) of what-it-is-to-be."[153] And a "final" cause "is the end. This is that for the sake of which, e.g. health of walking; for why does he walk? In order, we say, to be healthy, and in so saying we think that we have given the reason (aition)."[154] Hence,

> Aristotle's scheme incorporates the matter (the locus for change); the form, or structural organization which is realized in the matter; the agent, or the efficient cause, which brings that information about; and (in some cases at least) the goal, or final end, towards which that process tends.[155]

The crucial point here is not that we should revert to earlier understanding of cause in a simple manner—that is, of course, impossible. Nor is it that each class of causes Aristotle delineates must be integrated as a sort of causal checklist to achieve full explanation of social action.[156] Nor, finally, is it that a role-based approach can be neatly slotted into any one of the three other forms of cause Aristotle distinguishes. The aim is not, of course, to return to a classical context long lost. Rather, it is to follow a number of scholars in IR and beyond in showing how narrow the conception of cause held as paradigmatic in contemporary social science really is.[157] This then leaves us with a stark option: try to alter the predominant understanding of causation, or admit a clear divorce between explanations and something else, such as "descriptions" or even just "enlightening tales" or "fables."[158]

The latter path has been taken by a number of scholars. Some postpositivists, for example, reject causation as having dangerously "technologizing" consequences.[159] Other non-neopositivists have defended a rejection of causation by instead proclaiming a rigid distinction between "understanding" and explanation and supporting the search for the former rather than the latter.[160] In their classic statement, Hollis and Smith argue that explanatory and understanding-based approaches to international politics are doing different things, "telling different stories":[161] explanatory accounts, on the one hand, recount the story of an event, or state of affairs, from the position of a detached observer[162]—the "view from nowhere";[163] on the other hand, an account that seeks understanding tells the story from the inside and is concerned with interpreting the meanings of events for individuals.[164] Hollis and Smith conclude that these stories do not preclude one another but refrain from offering suggestions about how or when they might fruitfully be combined, implying that they should remain separate.

Alexander Wendt goes further than Hollis and Smith by arguing that there is no necessary zero-sum element to the issue.[165] Wendt contends that constitutive understanding of events or states of affairs themselves *are* explanations but that they are of a different type. He makes this argument on the basis that the zero-sum nature of the way in which the question has been posed is based on a perceived misunderstanding of the natural sciences and what scientists do. The direct comparison between positivists and natural scientists is false: natural scientists are not entirely detached from their subject matter. In fact, most explanation undertaken by both natural and social scientists is constitutive in that it is explanation through the use of concepts. Scientists do not merely try to understand why things are the way they are but also seek to ascertain what there is and how it comes to be that way. Wendt thus concludes that there is "no fundamental epistemological difference between Explanation and Understanding."[166]

I side with Wendt here, not least because social scientists from Kuhn onward should have accepted Wendt's observation that the common understanding of causation is only one of many gross distortions of actual practice in the hard sciences.[167] In moving beyond "both constitution and causation," however, it is useful to highlight the dictionary definition of "explain" as "to make plain." As such, explanation is not to be directly opposed to the notion of understanding, since the nature of explanation is not at base a philosophical question but a social one about the relationship between two individuals, A and C, such that A could "make plain" to C why B did something, while B would recognize more or less the explanation A had offered for his or her actions.[168] As Martin makes clear, however, the origins of the common understanding of causation in the social sciences in the French insane asylum in the late nineteenth century actually hides within it an authority relationship whereby the explainer knows better than the subject why he or she did what he or she did. At the same time as A explains to C, therefore, A deliberately silences B.[169] Although we might with good reason remain skeptical of the claim that policymakers know all the reasons for their actions, no theory of state action in international relations should thus disregard what policymakers think and say is going on in international politics.

A micro-interactionist analysis, by contrast, offers a different form of explanation that does not follow the subsume-abstract-constrain model. In many ways, a role-based approach to causality resembles the way in which institutional analyses explain. It rejects the notion of cause as constraint but does not rely on a simple "both/and" solution to the false dichotomy of constrain or enable. To see why, it is useful to return to the metaphor of the game and add a third way in which norms exist within the game: as strategies used by players in their attempts to excel at the game. As Martin notes, "We take seriously the metaphor of the game, we find by rules [i.e., norms] we refer not only to the formal prescriptions, whether regulative or constitutive, but also to a larger set of shared understandings and expectations that establish a sense of appropriateness."[170] Crucially, breaking the prevailing norms can be a strategy for success—doing something the other team could not possibly have expected.

Rather than reject the game metaphor because enable-and-constrain contrasts with the predominant understanding of causality, therefore, we should accept that social life does not come ready-made and that this is exactly the key point made by the game metaphor. Again, the stability of the form of games—the predominant ways in which they are played—like institutions, is an achievement of social life. "Rather than the regularity of social life being a law that constrains, that is, the cause of individual actions, it is the outcome of actions undertaken by actors with some sense (presumably imperfect) of the expectations others have and the likely reactions to confirmation and nonconfirmation of various expectations."[171] Rules and laws are not understood here in the "causal" sense first formulated by Hempel and since made foundational to neopositivist social science.[172]

A micro-interactionist approach does not therefore seek causes in terms of constraint or as an occurrence subsumed under a causal law. Nor does it seek causes that are abstract—that is, those that would not be understood by role-players (here, foreign policymakers). Once again, the intention here is not to offer explanations of action over and above the understandings of those actually doing the acting. Two issues are raised at this stage, however, that warrant further discussion: the place of motivations and beliefs in a micro-interactionist constructivist account of foreign policy. These issues are important since scholars typically draw on one or the other or both when offering firsthand explanations of social action: either observed action is considered to follow from subjectively held beliefs, or it follows from phenomenologically felt motivations. I address the issue of beliefs in the following section; I address the issue of motivations here. In short, motivations are bracketed from the analysis from a micro-interactionist constructivist perspective because although it is entirely reasonable to assume that role requirements are felt phenomenologically, proving it is another matter.

The motivations to which actors feel impelled to respond—including emotions such as feelings of shame, fear, and anger—are responses to the felt requirements of roles. The communication of these motivations is possible because—as a symbolic interactionist approach makes clear—perception and apperception (that is, the perception of one's own person as perceiver) are inseparable in interaction. As Martin notes, "The process whereby the actor takes in information about the world . . . is not merely relative to this person's position . . . , it actually provides the actor information about his or her own position."[173] In other words, "We find the appropriateness of an action in the qualitative nature of the experience being in that position—that is, having a set of relations."[174] Martin goes on, "To the extent that action is social it involves not only sets of relationships of mutual orientation but also the distillation of imperatives—felt motivations—from these sets of relationships."[175] Motivations are therefore implied by a micro-interactionist constructivist account of foreign policymaking.

However, micro-interactionist constructivism does not rely on motivations to back up its explanatory claims; instead, it bases its knowledge claims on the identification of a space of possible action and a particularly "live" political strategy. It brackets motivations for three related reasons. First, gathering sufficient evidence to prove that certain motivations and not others caused action offers far less in terms of explanatory payoff versus time spent in engaging in empirical research than can be justified. Mapping out spaces of possible action on the basis of role-taking is itself a time-intensive activity: attempting to grasp the scope of expected actions requires close analysis of a discursive space and the interpretation of the requirements of the social roles that emerge within international interaction. It is not altogether clear how much empirical evidence would be needed to prove that those role requirements were then translated into motivations felt sufficiently strongly by policymakers to explain their actions to a high degree of satisfaction. Second, motivations may themselves be misleading, as there are frequent examples when role requirements go against what individuals want to do, like paying for a coffee in a coffee shop.[176] If we had to rely on felt motivations rather than role expectations to explain action, we might find no evidence that the consumer wanted to pay—except for the fact that she did pay. Third, motivations have associations of getting to the "real reasons"—or efficient causes—behind action that constructivism in general seeks to bring into doubt.

The attempt, then, to link role-based expectations to felt motivations and then to the specific actions of individuals is simply not needed and is not relied on in a micro-interactionist constructivist approach. Rather, my approach can be better illuminated by reference to Weber's notion of "ideal types," "singular causal analysis," and his search for what he termed "adequate causation."[177]

Role-based interaction as relied on here is an ideal type in the Weberian sense: role-taking, role-making, and alter-casting are objectifications of certain processes characteristic of experience, put together to form a model of how social interaction "works" between states in international politics. The key facet of ideal types here is what they do for researchers: allow them to cut into reality in a way that is not true or false in some ultimate sense but is more or less useful.[178] The standard of appraisal is not falsifiability, since ideal types cannot thus be falsified, but pragmatic agreement that the ideal type highlights something important about social life: here, hopefully, the improvement of a role-based constructivism over identity-based constructivism and rational approaches to interaction in world politics.[179] As Kedar stresses, "Ideal types postulate certain interconnections between concepts and/or phenomena considered to be capable of throwing new light on social reality."[180]

The persuasiveness of a micro-interactionist constructivist account, consequently, is sought on the basis of what Patrick Jackson has termed a "disciplined imagining" of the likely outcomes of the ideal type role-based interaction rather than hypothetical alternatives. The aim is to think through the ways in which the unique concatenation of expectations emerged within the specific context of a given international interaction, how these expectations were communicated to policymakers through the ideal typical processes of role-taking, and how certain role-making and alter-casting strategies were subsequently employed. Appraisal proceeds by assessing the strength of the account relative to available alternatives. As Jackson notes, "For an analyticist [using a Weberian ideal-type] to claim that some factor is causal is to claim that we cannot imagine the outcome having occurred in its absence."[181] Again, ultimate timeless truth is not at issue. "Instead," Jackson continues,

> an analytical elaboration of the logical consequences of a particular set of definitions and depictions would provide a frictionless, artificially pure account of objects and processes—what Weber called a "utopia" . . .—which is intended less to predict actual concrete outcomes and more to provide a conceptual baseline in terms of which actual outcomes can be comprehended.[182]

Other causal factors such as misperception or successful or unsuccessful framing strategies may be relevant, which I have deliberately left out of the approach developed here. But if the micro-interactionist account I have put forward is to be considered fruitful, it will offer new ways of understanding British action in international politics that could not have been developed without the ideal-typical framework it imposes. Crucially, then, we need to consider these accounts not mere noncausal "stories" but genuinely causal in the Weberian sense of adequate causation.

Martin concludes his attack on the common-sense understanding of causation in social science by charging that "there is a tradition of social analysis, inspired by economics, that is able to explain every bit of social action quite satisfactorily, with one exception—what people are trying to do in the first place."[183] Micro-interactionist constructivism reverses the direction of priorities: it seeks to understand specific social actions by explaining what actors are trying to do in the first place. The final task of this chapter, then, is to explain how it goes about doing that in more concrete terms.

A Historical Interpretive Method

The method employed in the following chapters is historical and interpretive in nature. It is historical in that it represents an approach that considers the meaning and value of history and historical knowledge as more important than is typically the case in political science. Approaches drawn from the discipline of history often do better than those in political science in explaining—or making plain—the essential elements of actions and events in international relations.[184] The method employed in these empirical investigations is also heavily interpretive. The interpretive nature of role-based social interaction has been stressed throughout this chapter. However, the label "interpretivism" as it is currently employed within political science does not square with the intersubjective, relational, and practical elements of role-playing.

To address the importance of an adequately historical methodology—and what such a methodology would look like—it is useful to contrast the type of account of Britain's role to be utilized here with a deductive account based on a reified role. A deductive operationalization would require the derivation of hypotheses about what might prove or disprove compliance with a role uncovered at a particular point. The "salience" of a role-based behavioral requirement to the coherence of a particular identity—that is, the proposition that people are more likely to fulfill the requirements of a role if it is considered salient to their identity—offers a clear example here.[185] These hypotheses could then be tested in the empirical case study of British foreign policy since 1945. Such an approach would make the focus of the research a predetermined role and its influence on behavior, explained on the basis of the logic of appropriateness, instead of the form and nature of roles as they develop in and hence help create a given historical context. This highlights a problematic tendency in political science to view history and the historical episode simply as a case of some phenomenon or class of events—for example, wars or revolutions.[186] Yet history is not simply a laboratory in which to test hypotheses in search of potential causal laws.[187] History does not appear for use as a ready-made data set; rather, history is in many ways constituted by present political projects and cultural forms of remembering.

This critique of deductive practice is informed by the work of Andrew Abbott, who has clarified what those cases do in the majority of works in social science.[188] Abbott argues that the people, events, or classes of things deemed a case of a particular phenomenon often do very little in analysis, with the result that the examples chosen to highlight general trends lose their complexity and narrative order.[189] In fact, he argues, an implicit narrative argument—which is often thought to typify what historians do—is brought into nearly all social scientific approaches to correct for this loss. Abbott's aim is to explode the myth that the "population/analytic" (that is, large-N) approach as superior to the single historical case since it alone can provide explanations with a clear and scientific logical standard without resorting to narratives.[190] Explicitly historical approaches, in the sense of a narrative, in fact have a number of advantages vis-à-vis large-N studies. "The single (historical) case study," Friedrich Kratochwil has noted,

> focuses right from the beginning on the issue of delimiting the case by providing a narrative "plot" and examining its coherence and "followability" critically. Here getting the context right and making judgement calls as to the important dimensions that develop throughout the observation is the actual puzzle.[191]

Consequently, the intention in the following studies is not to analyze the workings of variables and indicators in the cases treated as particular examples of more general types of event but to draw from the historical episodes chosen evidence that supports or disproves accounts based on a conceptual model of role-based social interaction. The aim, then, is to provide better explanations of those episodes than, on the one hand, historical narratives that lack theory and, on the other, causal accounts of the type critiqued earlier.

The method used is also heavily interpretive, but it does not rely on beliefs and hence differs from the interpretivist approach in political science, particularly that associated with the work of Mark Bevir and Rod Rhodes.[192] The interpretivist's antinaturalist stance does not accord with a symbolic interactionist perspective on roles, which views the expectations that constitute roles not as subjective beliefs but as intersubjective contextualized meanings that emerge only within interaction. The reasoning here resembles that in the case of motivations: it is indeed quite likely that actors frequently believe that their chosen actions are the best response to role requirements, as Bevir and Rhodes stress. But explanations of action cannot be based on belief alone. The explanatory weight should be placed on the active process of interaction and the mutual construction of social situations—which is fundamentally role-based.

A micro-interactionist constructivist account thus retains then both respect for human meaningfulness normally associated with interpretive approaches focused on meanings and the beliefs of purposive human agents, with an enthusiastic embrace of the faith in objectification and concept-driven analysis central to political science as a project. As Blumer noted,

> Adhering to scientific protocol, engaging in replication, testing hypotheses, and using operational procedure . . . do not provide the empirical validation that genuine empirical social science requires. They give no assurance that premises, problems, data, relations, concepts, and interpretations are empirically valid. . . . [T]he only way to get this assurance is to go directly to the empirical world—to see through meticulous examination of it whether one's premises or root images of it, one's questions and problems posed for it, the date one chooses out of it, the concepts through which one sees and analyzes it, and the interpretations one applies to it are actually borne out.[193]

The following empirical analysis therefore begins from these concepts and compares them to the empirical reality of Britain's foreign policy in a number of key episodes since 1945. To take the example of the Skybolt Crisis, the analysis uses archival data and printed primary and secondary sources to reconstruct the interaction between British decision makers and important others, particularly the United States. What positions did British leaders "take" from the US? What were the major features of the role British policy-makers tried to make? Did Britain try to alter-cast the US into helping maintain the British nuclear deterrent, and if so, how? Alternatively, was Britain subject to insurmountable alter-casting pressures, either from the US or others? In line with the intersubjective nature of the theoretical framework, therefore, I argue that these role dynamics are to be found in the discursive activities and actions of the decision makers themselves rather than in the overt reference to some genuinely objective "role." Rather, the core concepts outlined previously—role-taking, role-making, and alter-casting—structure the interpretation of the events.

These statements are not intended to imply that everything in each event counts as an aspect of one of these processes or as part of the role dynamic as a whole: the theoretical framework would thus be true by tautology and hence largely trivial. Although the tendency might be to simply describe in narrative form the episodes and claim that they represent Britain's role being played out, doing so would serve only to depoliticize and dehistoricize an approach that has as its central aim the desire to focus on political dynamics and history. Interpretation remains, therefore, an argumentative technique; the claims made are open to counterclaims regarding more appropriate interpretations. This is the basis of many critiques of historical methodologies' "narrative explanations": there is no independent standard against which knowledge claims can be judged, so one interpretation is as good as another. In the final analysis, my interpretation of Britain's changing role will not be correct in any absolute sense. The only true test of validity lies in comparison with other possible interpretations.

CONCLUSION

I began this chapter by contrasting two traditions of thought within sociology and the distinct ways in which they each view the role concept and its place in social action. The structural-functionalist approach, which abstracts from individuals or states to generalize about behavioral patterns, is insufficiently attentive to the concrete drivers of action to tell us much about the social sources of particular states' foreign policies, despite its continued prominence within IR theory. The micro-interactionist tradition, conversely, has significant promise as an alternative way of understanding action, one with particular affinities to IR constructivism. I then turned to the development of a relatively parsimonious conceptual vocabulary drawing on this tradition—an approach focused on role-taking, role-making, and altercasting. During interaction, foreign policymakers consider their potential foreign policies by viewing their states from the perspectives of others—specific others within the interaction as well as the "generalized others" of particular groups or even the whole international community. Micro-interactionist constructivism offers a more complete understanding of foreign policy action because it does not appeal to something essential—a social norm, an exogenously given preference, or an identity—to explain the resulting action. Each of these forms of explanation only makes sense against a background of role-based international interaction.

In the final section, I addressed metatheoretical questions, arguing that roles do cause action, but not in the way we currently understand that term. I consequently followed Martin, who notes that "if our explanation for why people do something resolves around an appeal to causal process that have shaped them in a certain way, our work boils down to 'they did this because they are what they are.'"[194] In other words, a narrow understanding of explanation does not allow us to get at some of the most important—and surprising—aspects of international politics: why states actually do what they do. Through the role-based process of interaction, foreign policies options are outlined, with one being more live than the others. The final step was to outline a historical interpretive approach that can uncover this process. I use this approach in the following chapters to detail the way in which Britain's role in international relations shifted over the postwar period through in-depth analyses of the Suez Crisis, the Skybolt affair, the second application to the EEC, and the Falklands War.

CHAPTER TWO

The Suez Crisis, 1956

FOR MANY COMMENTATORS, the Suez Crisis of 1956 represents the most significant episode in British foreign policy since 1945. Although Britain struggled on much diminished as an international political force after the war, the attempt of Anthony Eden's government to use military means to reverse Egypt's nationalization of the Suez Canal Company—an attempt the British undertook in collusion with France and Israel and against the wishes of the United States—revealed in stark terms Britain's decline from great power status. Before Suez, British leaders could feign an independent role in world affairs based on a special relationship with the US, a worldwide network of bases and political commitments, and a sphere of influence in the Middle East; afterward, Britain's inability to act alone was made abundantly clear, since it was the withdrawal of American diplomatic and economic support that led the British into a humiliating retreat.[1] Never again would British policymakers risk a clear rift with Washington. Suez was "the Lion's last roar."[2]

As is often the case, such historical judgments contain a kernel of truth: Britain's role as a *great power* was at stake, and that fact led the Eden government to make a series of fateful decisions many would come to regret.[3] However, such judgments also leave important questions unanswered. If Britain was no longer a great power, why did its leaders not recognize that fact and avoid confrontation over Suez? Conversely, if Britain was still a great power in 1956, why did its chosen response not succeed? This chapter analyzes Britain's actions during the crisis from a micro-interactionist constructivist perspective with the aim of providing a more fine-grained explanation than these historical characterizations permit. I argue that British policymakers came to use force over Suez because a political space opened up within which such action was thinkable and doable. In turn, that space opened up because of the emergence of a role for Britain that I term *residual great power*—a role, crucially, co-constituted with France. But at the same time that American diplomacy seemed to cast Britain and France into this role, the US role as *alliance leader* led Washington to restrain its allies when they chose to use force.

The chapter begins by reviewing the historical background of the crisis, both outlining its most salient features and illustrating what is puzzling about the episode. The chapter then assesses opinion within Britain regarding what was at stake in the nationalization of the Suez Canal Company. It focuses in particular on the Eden government's role-taking interactions with France, which facilitated role-making as a power capable of using force alone if necessary to reverse nationalization. The third section describes this role and analyzes further the expectations constituting it. The chapter then turns to the role Britain took from the United States, which did not show the depth of feeling that would later lead Washington to take drastic measures to hinder French and British military action. Next, the chapter addresses world opinion, mirrored in increasingly hostile opinion within the UK, that Britain's actions were shameful and outdated, beliefs that ultimately led Britain to back off. The concluding section contrasts the explanation with possible alternatives.

THE SUEZ CRISIS—HISTORICAL BACKGROUND AND PUZZLE

The Suez Crisis was sparked by Egyptian president Gamel Nasser's nationalization of the Suez Canal Company on 27 July 1956.[4] Nasser's actions were met with shock by canal users and nonusers alike, but they struck a particularly raw nerve in Britain and France, which relied heavily on the canal and had financial stakes in the company that ran it.[5] Britain also used the canal for troop movements to its military presence in the Middle East and Asia, an area that Britain referred to as "East of Suez."[6] Both countries had aspirations to continued political influence in the Middle East as well. For Britain, this aspiration took the form of the Baghdad Pact,[7] a putatively anticommunist alliance; France's interest centered on the consequences of Nasser's action for French Algeria.[8] Consequently, when Eden was informed of nationalization, he declared that Nasser "must not be allowed to get away with it."[9] Military planning was immediately initiated should Nasser not give up control peacefully.[10] Similar decisions were made across the Channel, backed in both cases by bellicose public opinion.

Egypt's nationalization of the Suez Canal also had implications for other countries, most important among them the United States.[11] Nasser's actions constituted an explicit response to the withdrawal on 17 July 1956 of American financial support for the Aswan High Dam hydroelectric project, on which the general had staked much prestige.[12] Nasser's move therefore had a Cold War rationale, with the question of to which superpower patron Cairo would turn for arms and aid drawing the Soviet Union into the events. Britain and France's possible responses to nationalization were thus constrained by this Cold War context. In addition, Britain, France and America's responses to nationalization cannot be separated from the conflict between Israel and the Palestinians and the wider tensions in the Middle East. The powers were party to the 1955 Tripartite Declaration, in which all three pledged to come to the others' aid if they became the victims of aggression, whatever its origin.[13] Any attempt to tell the story of Suez must, then, do justice to its inherently transnational character; this was far more than a simple two-player bargaining scenario over an insignificant stretch of water.

An intense round of meetings among British, French, and American officials in the days after nationalization led to a shared strategy focused on the establishment of international control of the canal, the details of which were to be worked out at a users' conference in London on 16–23 August.[14] Allied unity, however, was only paper-thin: while disturbing for America, Nasser's seizure of the canal was not sufficient grounds for military redress. Only a visible sign of obstructionist behavior would warrant the use of force. For the Europeans, by contrast, nationalization alone was sufficient to require military reversal.[15] This fundamental disagreement set the pattern for the Suez interaction as it progressed. For Britain and France, for example, the London Conference sought to discuss possible courses of action with like-minded governments; for America, the goal was to allow calmer heads to prevail. The majority of world opinion was more accommodating of what seemed a legitimate nationalization of a domestic asset, with opinion in many ex-colonies like India opposed to what appeared to be British and French imperialism.[16]

The London Conference failed to secure agreement regarding internationalization of the canal, as Britain and France had hoped, and instead issued a declaration of support for international control that affirmed Egyptian sovereignty. With Anglo-French military planning ongoing and the US engaging in alliance restraint, therefore, diplomacy continued—first in the form of a mission to Cairo under the direction of Australian prime minister

Robert Menzies, tasked with persuading Nasser to give up control of the canal, then via a second conference in London that sought to create an association of canal users, a middle ground between Egyptian control and internationalization.[17] At the same time as the users' association was being discussed, however, diplomacy shifted to the United Nations, which the Western powers had up to that point avoided for fear of getting bogged down in interminable legal discussion. Unsurprisingly, Russian opposition and American prevarication prevented passage of a Security Council resolution that might offer a pretext for war.[18]

In mid-October 1956, Eden and his close advisers considered calling off military preparations.[19] Diplomatic pressure appeared to be moving Nasser closer to acceptable terms, and domestic opposition to British and French responses was increasing.[20] But on 14 October, Eden held a secret meeting with French general Maurice Challe and minister of labor Albert Gazier at which France offered to collude with Israel in creating a pretext for the invasion of Egypt.[21] Israel would invade Egypt; Britain and France, recognizing the threat to the canal and international peace and security, would demand that both sides withdraw from the area; if Egypt refused, as was inevitable, British and French forces would "restore peace." Eden was "thrilled at the idea."[22]

The Israeli operation began on 30 October, with British and French military action beginning two days later. In the US, President Dwight Eisenhower was furious. Although Secretary of State John Foster Dulles began to suspect that French-Israeli collusion had taken place—possibly with British involvement—Ike was taken entirely by surprise at what appeared a premeditated plan.[23] He was particularly disbelieving of Britain's involvement, since London did not share France's close relationship with Israel and had longer-standing relations with the Arab world; US leaders simply could not believe that the Eden government would jeopardize Britain's position in the region through cooperation with Israel. Washington's ire was also aimed at the timing of their allies' move. Intervention in Egypt weakened Western moral authority precisely when it should have been enhanced in the face of Soviet action in Hungary, which would result in thirty thousand deaths. The US consequently withdrew support for its errant allies, backing two UN resolutions condemning Israeli action, both of which Britain and France vetoed.[24] Shortly thereafter, a General Assembly resolution in support of Egypt passed overwhelmingly, further isolating Britain and France.[25] Concern was even voiced that the latter might be forced to leave the organization. At the same time, Soviet threats to intervene heightened the threat of war.[26] Military action was halted on 6 November, after a run on sterling—with Washington blocking Britain's access to the International Monetary Fund—convinced the British to agree to a cease-fire, to French annoyance.[27]

The chief puzzle here is why British policymakers considered military action a necessary and appropriate response to nationalization. British troops had only recently been removed from a previous base in the Canal Zone under an agreement negotiated by Eden himself.[28] Moreover, the Suez Canal Company's concession, signed in 1876 for ninety-nine years, was only twelve years away from lapsing. British and French dominance of the canal, at least in its current form, was soon coming to an end. Why risk war? A subsidiary puzzle is why Eden and his inner circle also believed Nasser's actions justified underhanded diplomatic moves and military collusion. In Anthony Nutting's words, "Why did Eden take action that was, at the same time, morally indefensible and politically suicidal?"[29] These questions cannot be answered without an analysis of the actions of France and the United States. Why did France also consider military action necessary and appropriate, and why did the US not only not share this view but disagree to such an extent that it was prepared to withdraw vital economic support from Britain to bring its allies to heel?

Britain, France, and the Making of the Suez Crisis

The British public reacted to news of the nationalization with shock and outrage. The *Daily Herald* proclaimed it "A Time to Resist," while the *Daily Mail* urged the government to reoccupy the Canal Zone immediately.[30] The *News Chronicle* asserted in no uncertain terms, "The British government will be fully justified in taking retaliatory action."[31] Members of the government and the opposition struck a similar tone. This sense of outrage did not, however, spring from some transhistorical and essential British "identity," nor did British preferences "reveal" themselves unproblematically after nationalization—two counterexplanations for Britain's response that will be considered later in the chapter. Focusing on identity or preferences alone removes exactly the process of constructing Suez as an international crisis, which a constructivist account should naturally privilege. Rather, Britain's actions were caused by the emergence in interaction among Britain, the United States, and France of a political space within which the most appropriate response for the Eden government relied on the use of force. This political space was the context-dependent outcome of a particular rhetorical construction of the meaning of the Suez Canal, of Nasser and his actions, and of the relations among Britain, France and the United States to each other and to the events, relations that can best be grasped in role-based terms.

First, the British government did not view the Suez Canal and the Suez Canal Company as normal Egyptian assets. The financing for the construction of the canal had come from Britain and France, and its purpose was to benefit world trade, not the Egyptian people.[32] The canal was thus what Eden termed early in the crisis an "international waterway." As he told members of Parliament on 2 August, "The industrial life of Western Europe literally depends upon the continuing free navigation of the canal as one of the great international waterways of the world."[33] This rhetorical move had several important implications. It suggested that Nasser could not legitimately take the canal into Egyptian possession because it was not Egyptian. As Jack Jones argued in the House of Commons,

> There was the naïve suggestion from this side of the House that "It is, of course, their country." Of course it is. It is also said, "It is their Canal." It is not. Nobody took a bucketful of soil away from the cutting of the Canal. The earth is still there, on the embankment . . . and the water in the Canal has come from the seven seas—the Egyptians never put it there.[34]

Although Jones's argument is bizarre in retrospect, he gave voice to a feeling that the canal was not Egyptian in any fundamental way, a view that ran counter to Nasser's professions that "the Suez Canal could never be nationalized because the Suez Canal is ours, our soil [and] an inseparable part of Egypt."[35] For Eden, following this logic, *nationalization* was "a wholly inappropriate word to apply to Colonel Nasser's action. . . . [W]e shall have to coin a new and hideous word. . . . What Colonel Nasser has done is to 'de-internationalise' the Canal."[36] In this view, nationalization was simply illegitimate.

The description of Suez as an international waterway fudged the question of whether nationalization was in accordance with international law. It quickly emerged, however, that Nasser had acted legally. Even so, as historian Donald Neff notes, "When [Eden] received the official legal report from the F[oreign] O[ffice] lawyers, he became incensed, ripped it up, and threw it in the lawyer's face."[37] Both the British and the French saw the issue as political: What did Nasser's move mean for their positions in the Middle East? Britain thus downplayed the legal aspects throughout the crisis. As Eden told Eisenhower on 27 July, "We should not allow ourselves to become involved in legal quibbles about the rights of the Egyptian Government to nationalize what is technically an Egyptian company, or in financial arguments about their capacity to pay the compensation offered to them."[38] Eden played up the political threat Nasser posed instead of addressing nationalization's legality.

In this regard, the prime minister repeatedly stated both privately and publicly his conviction that the Egyptians could not be trusted to run the canal effectively. As he wrote to the president in his first letter after nationalization, "Apart from the Egyptians' complete lack of technical qualifications, their past behaviour gives no confidence that they can be trusted to manage it with any sense of international obligation."[39] Alongside the continued closure of the canal to Israeli shipping, the sudden seizure of the canal was Eden's main example here. As he stressed during the first tripartite meeting, "This is the end. We can't put up with any more of this. By this means Nasser can blackmail us, he can put up the canal dues, he'll run it very badly, this will absolutely stifle our trade."[40] Of greater moment than the act of nationalization itself, however, were Nasser's plans over the short to medium term. The Egyptian leader represented a threat to Britain's entire position in the Middle East, it was claimed. As Eden professed during the first meeting with US and French officials after nationalization,

> Failure on the part of the Western Powers to take the necessary steps to regain control over the Canal would have disastrous consequences for the economic life of the Western Powers and for their standing and influence in the Middle East. . . . Failure to hold the Suez Canal would lead inevitably to the loss one by one of all of our interests and assets in the Middle East and, even if we had to act alone, we could not stop short of using force to protect our position.[41]

Because Nasser was the figurehead of the pan-Arab movement, a rise in his prestige would lead to the ejection of Western influence in the entire Middle East. The only way to prevent this, Eden concluded, was "to seize the canal and take charge of it again."[42]

This construction of Nasser as an existential threat to Britain and France and their interests in the region was made meaningful, finally, by frequent associations of Nasser with Hitler and of UK opponents to war with the "men of Munich."[43] Nasser's book, *The Philosophy of the Revolution,* was paraded as his *Mein Kampf.*[44] Labour Party leader Hugh Gaitskell told members of Parliament on 2 August that Nasser's actions were "all very familiar. It is exactly the same as we encountered from Mussolini and Hitler in those years before the war."[45] The theme was repeated by proponents of military force throughout the crisis, and the implications needed little elaboration. Eden told the House on 12 September, for example, that "there are those who say that we should not be justified in reacting vigorously unless Colonel Nasser commits some further act of aggression. That was the argument used in the 1930s to justify every concession that was made to the dictators."[46]

These meanings and associations attached to the act of nationalization emerged within a dynamic international interaction involving not only Egypt, Britain, and France but also the United States and many other interested states around the world. Accounts that look only at British interests, preferences, and identity; the psychology of Britain's leadership; or the structure of Britain's bureaucracy miss out in this fundamentally social aspect of the crisis.

Eden's initial response to the crisis was to facilitate role-taking by calling for a series of meetings with officials from France and the United States, proving that the meaning of Nasser's actions for Britain did not come out of nowhere. As Eden told Parliament, "I am sure that the House will feel with me that it is necessary and desirable that full time should be taken with our Allies for all the aspect of this international problem to be considered."[47] Opposition questioning was kept to a minimum, with the House strongly behind the prime minister in seeking the opinion of important others. Gaitskell stressed that "this is not our affair alone."[48] Hinting that seeking the advice of other parties might cool talk of war, he went on to stress that "it would be ridiculous to treat ourselves as though we were the only Power involved. It is essentially a matter for all the maritime powers of the world, and we must act in concert with other nations."[49] It can be assumed that emotions in Britain, related to a sense of Britain's self, inclined Eden and his colleagues toward the use of force. But more important in terms of whether such force would be used is the way in which the Suez Crisis unfolded in the interaction that followed.

At the first meeting of the tripartite powers on the evening of 27 July, attended by Eden and his close advisers (including foreign secretary Selwyn Lloyd, French foreign minister Christian Pineau, and American chargé d'affaires Andrew Foster), each expressed astonishment and displeasure at the events. Echoing Eden's construction of the canal as fundamentally non-Egyptian, Foster noted that "it was intolerable that a great international waterway should be completely under the domination of any one country, without international control."[50] It seemed, therefore, that the parties agreed on the need for strong action. Yet it was also clear from the outset that Britain and France were closer to each other on the central issues than either was to the United States. Foster told the meeting that he "didn't have much to say" and "was there only to listen" to the opinions voiced by others.[51] By contrast, a true meeting of minds occurred between Eden and Pineau over the significance of nationalization and the range of appropriate responses.[52] In terms of the expectations about appropriate responses to nationalization, Washington was placed differently vis-à-vis Nasser's action than were Paris and London. The mutually constitutive role-taking, role-making, and alter-casting dynamics between the British and French governments underpinned their militaristic response and the maintenance of that course of action despite strong and growing opposition.

French policymakers thus offered justifications for the strength of their reaction that resembled those of their British counterparts. The French shared the view that the question of Suez was of a political rather than moral, economic, or legal nature. As Robert Murphy, undersecretary of state for foreign affairs, reported back to Washington on 29 July, France was faced not with a "juridical question but [a] political one."[53] Indeed, French declarations were if anything even more bellicose in tone than the British utterances. French bellicosity was related to the country's position in North Africa. Whereas Nasser represented a general threat to Britain's position in the Middle East, his potential predominance in the region held a more specific portent for France: turning the tide in the ongoing war in Algeria against the metropole. This translated into a stronger conviction in the French public discourse that force was appropriate. As a result, Murphy went on, "France attaches greatest importance to [the] effect [of Nasser's action] on North Africa. If Nasser succeeds [it will be] completely useless to fight there."[54] Finally, France agreed with Britain's assessment on the implication of nationalization for the Western position in the Middle East in general. The French prime minister, Guy Mollet, "was convinced that if Nasser is successful all Western positions in the Middle East and North Africa will be lost within the next 12 months," Dulles told Eisenhower on 2 August.[55]

From the outset, then, through their words, countenance, and actions, French leaders bolstered Britain's understanding of the Suez Crisis. "The

French were ready to go all the way with us," Lloyd told Gladwyn Jebb, British ambassador to Paris on 29 July. "The mood was one of extreme urgency," the French ambassador to London, Jean Chauvel, had stressed, "since it was thought that the effect of Nasser's action in Algeria would be so serious if counter-measures were not taken immediately that the whole position might well collapse."[56] French support for the British position included the question of the use of force. The first meeting of British, French, and US officials concluded "with the firm assurance by M. Pineau that a French Armoured Division . . . could certainly be made available together with a brigade of paratroops."[57] French leaders were even willing to remove troops from the fight in Algeria to send to Egypt and to place French troops under a British commander.[58] This willingness persisted until the ignominious 6 November cease-fire: despite growing opposition to British and French military preparations, Anglo-French cooperation remained strong. Eden reported to the cabinet on 3 October that he "was impressed by the vigour of M. Mollet's Government and their uncompromising attitude toward the Suez situation. They were determined that Nasser's actions should not go uncorrected."[59]

Britain and France's expectations regarding Suez, in the form of their respective social roles, then, were co-constructed: the strong reactions of both governments and publics reinforced the understandings of their appropriate roles through the process of role-taking. This does not mean that either the British or French governments had to respond with force. Rather, the construction of a political space within which force was seen as legitimate and hence politically actionable would have been impossible for each absent the other. Again, this was because Britain and France were positioned similarly within the situation Nasser's action had created, and they consequently went about making similar roles. The next task is to discuss the expectations that made up these roles in greater depth.

The Residual Great Powers

Naming operative roles and outlining the general expectations that constitute them outside of particular contexts comes at an analytical price, since what actually causes action is the expectations that emerge in specific instances. It is nonetheless necessary at this stage to characterize the role that emerged for both Britain and France in broad terms before continuing the analysis of what expected behaviors constituted it. I call this role *residual great power*. This term is chosen to emphasize the way in which Britain and

France co-constructed the traditional *great power* role over Suez. The existence of *great powers* has been an important feature of international politics since at least the Congress of Vienna, and they are central to realist and English School theorizing.[60] For both, *great powers* enjoy a unique degree of freedom to act in support of their preferences within a specific sphere of influence. For the latter in particular, the great power role also prescribes unique responsibilities to states—for example, in upholding the norms of international society.[61] During the Suez Crisis, Britain and France made—and cast each other into—the role of a state that had the right to engage in military action in defense of its economic and security interests, which could also be portrayed as international interests.

It is, of course, traditionally argued that Suez highlighted the *end* of Britain as a great power, a role that France had already lost following its occupation during the war and the loss of French Indochina. "The Suez Crisis marked the end of Britain and France as world powers," Neff argues. "The countries entered the affair as colonial giants and emerged from it as faintly disrespectable second-raters."[62] Constructivists, moreover, are skeptical about essentializing features of the international system such as its principal roles since those roles change over time. Therefore, I use the qualifier *residual* to emphasize that the reality or unreality of Britain and France's great power pretensions is not at issue here; rather, I am concerned with the ways in which a specific set of expectations emerged for Britain and France that can be best characterized—and nothing more—with the use of this prominent ideal type. Beyond this spare definition, the task remains to interpret the expectations attached to the role of *residual great power* as it emerged for Britain during the Suez Crisis.

Nasser's action positioned Britain and France alongside the United States as the powers that could legitimately be expected to respond on behalf of the international community. In addition to the Tripartite Agreement, which committed Britain and France to keep the peace in the region, the association of Nasser with Hitler had this connotation, since in the 1930s, Britain and France had failed in their duties as *great powers* to stand up to Germany in a timely manner. Other leaders supported this historical lesson. Belgian prime minister Paul-Henri Spaak wrote to Eden on 21 August, for example, "I do not wish to hide from you that I am haunted by the memory of the mistakes which were committed at the outset of the Hitler period—mistakes which have cost us dear."[63] Such statements implied that Britain and France were the type of powers on whose interests nationalization encroached in a way that was not the case for, say, the Scandinavian countries.

It is also instructive that the notion that Britain's response was justified by its *great power* position was invoked at various times by proponents of force. As Hugh Fraser noted in his 2 August speech in the House of Commons, "I am quite certain that it is the duty of a great Power, especially of a Power such as we are, with our friends in the Middle East, to move with the French alone, if we are driven to it."[64] This meant that

> if other nations will not take the lead in this matter, we ourselves must take the lead. . . . I further believe that it is necessary, if we cannot get unanimity between ourselves, the Americans and the French, for us to join hands with the French on this issue. . . . This is the point of no return. It is vital that the Middle East, and the West and the world, should know that if Nasser is not prepared to accept the principle of an international waterway, of an international agency for the carrying out of that international authority, then he must firmly be told that all means will be used to enforce our will.[65]

Viscount Hitchingbrooke, a member of Parliament and a strong proponent of the use of force throughout the crisis, continued to argue in these terms on the eve of military action by Britain and France. For him, Britain and France were "acting on behalf of peace and order" as well as "the maintenance of the great international waterway and free passage for the ships of all the world."[66]

Even after Britain had engaged in collusion, UK policymakers still justified their actions in terms of Britain as a qualitatively different type of international actor from most states, justified in taking the Suez matter into its own hands—a viewpoint indicative of *great power* expectations. As Eden wrote to Eisenhower on 5 November, "If you cannot approve" of Britain's action, "I would like you at least to understand the terrible decisions that we have had to make. I do want to assure you that we have made [them] from a genuine sense of responsibility, not only to our country, but to all the world."[67] In discussion with Murphy, Chancellor of the Exchequer Harold Macmillan used a common tactic in British foreign policy discourse—arguing that Britain would become "just another European country" if it failed to engage in certain actions characteristic of a *great power* and of its own more powerful past.[68] "Macmillan indulged in much graphic dissertation on British past history," Murphy reported, "and stressed that if they had to go down so the Government and he believed [the] British people would rather do so on this issue than become another Netherlands."[69] Or, as Eden wrote to Eisenhower on 6 September, "It would be an ignoble end of our long history if we tamely accepted to perish by degrees."[70]

In addition to practical and unspoken support for their mutual *residual great power* roles given by Britain and France, others, including Menzies, supported British action on precisely these grounds. The Australian prime minister wrote to Eden shortly before British operations began to express his personal opinion that "it may prove a healthy reminder to Nasser that though he may imagine that the great powers are powerless the facts are that they are not unwilling to defend their legitimate interests which include [the] vital commercial lifeline through the Canal."[71] Menzies saw Britain and France as still the types of states that could take the law into their own hands when the situation demanded it: "What many people fail to understand is that [the] best way to avoid a major conflict is to be completely firm about smaller ones."[72]

From a micro-interactionist constructivist perspective, therefore, the central aspect of the Suez Crisis was the co-construction of mutually supportive sets of expectations by France and Britain in the form of *residual great power* roles. This goes well beyond apportion of blame to French leaders for originating the notion of collusion with Israel. Rather, it shows how the Eden government's conviction that nationalization represented a problem requiring a particular form of solution, removing control of the canal from Nasser's hands and making it clear that he had been "defeated" and that the West had "won," was both created and sustained by the Franco-British interaction. A space remained open within the British political sphere for the use of force, and in that space, arguments like that of member of Parliament Patrick Maitland could have political purchase:

> I believe that we shall find in the days to come, perhaps soon, that the public is wholeheartedly relieved that at last there are Governments in Europe—indeed, in the world—who are prepared to take some action to defend an international interest.[73]

French support, once again, maintained this space. On 31 July, Pineau told British policymakers that "he wished to emphasize France's wholehearted support for Great Britain over the question of Suez. With the exception of the Communists, French public opinion fully supported us. Britain and France should go forward together and not allow themselves to be held up by United States waverings and reluctance."[74] This support—in the form of the co-constitution of *residual great power* roles—fundamentally underpinned Britain's actions regarding Suez between 27 July and 6 November 1956.

The United States, Western Leadership, and the Use of Force

The United States faced a difficult balancing act in the Suez Crisis between providing moral and diplomatic support for the cause of its allies and re-straining Britain and France from engaging in military action likely to arouse significant opposition to the West in the Middle East and beyond. The American position, too, was a function of its relations to the other states involved and the role-based expectations that emerged in the Suez interaction. The US role in the conflict was what can be termed *alliance leader:* when taking the role of others, it faced primarily expectations related to the Cold War and the question of international peace and security. Throughout the crisis, Britain and France tried to alter-cast the US into the alliance leader role. Both governments were aware that Washington did not share their material interests regarding the canal and were likely to be less favorable to the use of force. But there was no question of excluding Washington from the high-level discussions. When it became clear that the Eisenhower administration was not disposed toward military action, Britain and France remained convinced that they could contain any rift while securing US protection from Soviet interference. However, the combination of underhanded political maneu-verings with actions the US believed were politically inadvisable, to say the least, presented the Eisenhower administration with a choice: support its allies in a grave error of judgment or take drastic action to preserve peace. Eisenhower chose the latter.

The tripartite meeting set the pattern, with the British and French co-constructing their roles as *residual great powers,* able and justified in launch-ing a military attack to restore the status quo ex ante if need be, and the US as *alliance leader,* seeking to find a solution short of force. When news of na-tionalization broke, Secretary of State Dulles was on a visit to South America; Eisenhower therefore sent Murphy to "see what it's all about" and "hold the fort."[75] The choice of a lower-ranked official demonstrated that although the US would assume a degree of control over the collective response, the coun-try was simply less outraged than were Britain and France. Whereas military action had been the initial reaction of Paris and London, for Washington it represented only a distant possibility. As Andrew Foster told Lloyd and Chauvel, with the bellicosity of his interlocutors apparent, while America was eager to assess the options Britain and France would put on the table, "nothing of the foregoing should be construed as any carte blanche approval of such proposals as might now be under consideration."[76]

The Eisenhower administration thus remained noncommittal on the specific scenarios that might unfold. As the president wrote to Eden on 31 July, he "recognize[ed] the transcendent worth of the Canal to the free world" and the "possibility that eventually the use of force might be necessary in order to protect international rights"; nevertheless, he emphasized the need for the conference method to be employed before any military force could be considered. Otherwise, "Public opinion here and, I am convinced, in most of the world, would be outraged."[77] As it became obvious that the British and French governments were thinking in terms of military action first, diplomacy second, US policymakers and officials repeatedly made it clear that force was not an appropriate response to nationalization. As Murphy stated unequivocally on 27 July, "The question of military intervention does not seem to arise. It would depend on developments. For the present we believe it should be relegated to the background."[78] Dulles stated similarly on 1 August that US public opinion was simply not ready to back a military adventure that "could be portrayed as driven by imperialist and colonialist ambitions."[79] The secretary of state had already stressed to Eden that "the United States Government would not be in sympathy with any attempt to make the Egyptian Government rescind their nationalization decrees, or to regard them as inoperative, under the threat of force."[80]

This trend continued as the initial anger in Britain and France gave way to a calmer sense of determination. Eisenhower wrote to Eden on 30 July, "It is our basic view that Nasser should not now be presented with, in effect, an ultimatum requiring him to reverse his nationalization action under threat of force."[81] The president argued that it was "most unlikely he would back down and that war would accordingly become inevitable."[82] When discussing the details of the proposed conference on the Suez Canal problem at the seventh tripartite meeting, held on 2 August, Dulles argued that the tripartite powers should first reach agreement among themselves, then decide where the conference should be and what it should be for. If the Egyptians refused to cooperate with the conference and its conclusion, "she would be isolated in the eyes of world opinion."[83] The conference was crucial since

Egypt could not be isolated, but the American warned that "this would not be the case if other friendly Powers gained the impression that the conference was not a genuine attempt to reach agreement, but merely a pretext for the ultimate use of force."[84] For the United States, as the leader of the tripartite group and the Western alliance, force was not the answer.

However, while the US government's view that the use of force should be avoided was fixed as far as the White House was concerned, this position was not effectively communicated to Britain and France. As Nutting later recalled, Dulles "undoubtedly encouraged Eden to believe that, notwithstanding Eisenhower's cautionary cable, the United States was a lot more solidly behind Britain and France than was the case, or could possibly be the case, with a presidential election looming in three months' time."[85] As a result, during the early stages of the Suez affair, "appearances suggested more or less complete unity of purpose between America, Britain, and France."[86] Nutting lays much of the blame for this miscommunication on Dulles. During a 1 August meeting with Harold Caccia, for example, the secretary of state left the impression that "the Americans were entirely at one with us in considering it to be intolerable that the future management of the Canal should be in the sole hands of Colonel Nasser."[87] This was, of course, true. However, plenty of space remained for different interpretations of how Nasser's action could be overturned. "For Dulles to mislead his two allies at this stage," Nutting thus argues, "was as unwise and dangerous as were his later attempts to restrain Britain and France from forcing the issue."[88]

There was then no real unity of purpose. Indeed, what developed was an emerging opposition of purpose: Britain, France, and the United States each attempted to maintain the facade of togetherness, but Britain and France sought from the outset to overturn the nationalization, by force if necessary; the United States sought to restrain its allies from taking precisely that action. This was not then a matter of simple miscommunication. The British and French were well aware of the different emphasis Washington placed on Suez. As Eden cabled to Lloyd on 3 October, "I think we must never forget that Dulles' purpose is different from ours. The Canal is in no sense vital to the United States and his game is to string us along at least until Polling Day."[89] They calculated, however, that Dulles and Eisenhower would not stand in their way. Macmillan's comment that "Ike will lie doggo" is only one overquoted example.[90] It illustrates not just Macmillan's arrogance in referring to the US president in these terms but also the British certainty that the US would not oppose British-French action. "In separate conversations

[Eden and Macmillan] each said in substance they ardently hoped the US would be with them in this determination [to use force if necessary], but if we could not they would understand and our friendship would be unimpaired."[91] Outright opposition, including coercive diplomacy, did not enter the picture. Britain and France rested assured that the *alliance leader* would ultimately support their actions.

What turned out to be such wishful thinking was facilitated by US officials' words and deeds that led Eden and his government to believe that Britain's strong stance was if not correct, then understandable and hence justifiable. During a private discussion on 26 September, for example, Eisenhower told Macmillan that he was determined to bring Nasser down one way or another and to move beyond the UN, which, he noted, had "destroyed the power of leadership of the great powers," enabling "small nations like Egypt [to] do the most outrageous things."[92] The president "felt that the *great Powers*—U.S., UK, France and Germany—should get together to maintain order, peace and justice, as well as mere absence of armed conflict. . . . This is, of course, the old concert of Europe in a new form."[93] One could forgive Eden for sensing an alter-cast into the *great power* role from the direction of Dulles and Eisenhower.

Yet this transatlantic misunderstanding would seem to be as much a case of Eden and his advisers reading what they wanted to hear into their American counterparts' statements. Beyond mere rejections of force, there were simply too many instances of attempts by members of the US government to persuade their British counterparts that were ways to deal with Nasser that did not include the use of force. That process, in turn, required persuading British leaders that their sense of what the *residual great power* role required was inappropriate. At the same time, Britain and France were attempting to fasten the role of *alliance leader* onto America to garner support for their actions. Both alter-casting attempts failed.

Alter-Casting Failures

Eisenhower wrote to Eden on 8 September, suggesting "that when you use phrases in connexion with the Suez affair, like 'ignoble end to our long history' in describing the possible future of your great country, you are making of Nasser a much more important figure than he is."[94] From the American perspective, Nasser was no Hitler, and Eden would therefore be no Chamberlain in settling for a resolution without the use of force. During a meeting of US policymakers on 31 July, "Mr. Allen Dulles said that British comment is full of reference to Hitler's occupation of the Rhineland. A number of differences were cited."[95] The differences were clear to opponents in Britain, too. Richard Crossman, for example, argued, "It is quite ridiculous to compare Nasser with either Hitler or Mussolini, and those who do so are rather like the person who supposed that Goliath thought he was the fellow who was in danger and the likely victim of aggression."[96] In Crossman's eyes, Britain was the aggressor. If the proponents of force "should inquire in Asia and in Africa," he noted, "they would discover . . . that to many people in the world . . . the British Government seem to be indulging in hectoring and bullying behavior."[97]

The Americans were acutely aware of the depths of their ties with the British and the potential political problems that would accrue from opposing them openly. As Eisenhower told Dulles during his trip to London in early August, "if [you] can't persuade the British from their course, the news of the rift would come out right away." Dulles replied that "if separate communiqués were released, indicating a rift, the effect would be spectacular."[98] However, the desire to avoid a public break did not extend to backing the British in an ill-advised military adventure. When George Humphrey, Secretary of the Treasury, asked what the repercussions would be if Secretary Dulles returned from London with an obvious split with the British, the president replied that such an event would be extremely serious "but not as serious as letting a war start and not trying to stop it."[99] The prime American concern, then, was maintaining international peace. From this perspective, Eden's obsession with Nasser was unbecoming of a great power. Statements like those of Macmillan to Dulles on 1 August—"If the final result was to be the destruction of Great Britain as a first class power and its reduction to a similar status to that of Holland, the danger should be met now"; "If we shall be destroyed by Russian bombs now that would be better than to be reduced to impotence by the disintegration of its entire position abroad"—worried the president.[100] They showed that Britain's leaders were no longer making rational calculations in relation to Nasser's action and were acting in a way that was unbecoming of a *great power.*

The Eisenhower administration attempted to prove to Britain that in the case of Suez, the British had misunderstood the expectations attached to their role as a residual great power. The proper response of a great power to the Suez problem was to play the long game. "We have two problems," the president wrote to the Eden in early September, "the first of which is the assurance of permanent and efficient operation of the Suez Canal with justice to all concerned. The second is to see that Nasser shall not grow as a menace to the peace and vital national interests of the West." Whereas Eden saw the two problems as one and the same, the president believed that "these two problems need not and possibly cannot be solved simultaneously and by the same methods, although we are exploring further means to this end."[101]

Alternative courses of action were open to the Eden government. It is impossible to find some ultimate answer for why those paths were not taken. We can only examine how the argument in favor of peaceful resolution of the conflict was less powerful in the specific context of this crisis than the argument in favor of taking strong action, including the use of military force. Had Eden taken the former course, he would have left himself open to charges of appeasement, of failing to strike while the iron was hot, and of allowing Nasser to "get away with it." Eden could nonetheless have tried to make this role for Britain. The Labour Party would have supported his change of heart, but the opposition would have scored a mighty triumph should Eden have tried to reverse course.[102] Given the shape of the interaction as it unfolded, therefore, making the case for not using force would have simply been a more difficult political task than sending in the armed forces.

Instead both Britain and France attempted to alter-cast the United States into a particular understanding of the *alliance leader role* that would allow them to use military means. Throughout the crisis, in response to the lukewarm American reaction to Britain's steadfast opposition to nationalization, Britain and France tried to play up Nasser's threat to US interests in region in hopes of shifting US priorities from peace to the overthrow of the Egyptian leader. The European nations sought to subtly shift US expectations regarding the alliance leader role from restraining its allies to preserving the Western alliance by supporting them. In so doing, Britain and France played on two themes, both of them related to America's role as *leader of the West*.

The first theme was the vulnerability of the US position in the region should the British and French be displaced. As Pineau expressed to Murphy on 29 July, adding a little guilt into the bargain, the French "did not agree with the United States approach to this whole question," which was political rather than legal: "It was a direct result of the decision made by the United States Government not to finance the Aswan Dam. If Nasser were to get away with this, it would have incalculable consequences for the Western position."[103] The second theme, which became more prominent as the crisis unfolded and it became clear that the first theme had had little effect on the

United States, related to the potential for an emboldened Nasser to act as a stalking horse for Soviet influence in the Middle East and Africa. As Eden wrote to Eisenhower on 27 August,

> I have no doubt that the Bear is using Nasser, with or without his knowledge, to further his immediate aims. These are, I think, first to dislodge the West from the Middle East, and second to get a foothold in Africa so as to dominate that Continent in turn. . . . All this makes me more than ever sure that Nasser must not be allowed to get away with it at this time.[104]

Yet in spite of the effort expended, British and French alter-casting efforts did not persuade the Americans that supporting the use of force was an appropriate course of action. This failure caused much consternation in London and Paris.[105] As Roger Makins, the British Ambassador to the United Nations, cabled to London on 29 July, "Mr. [Herbert] Hoover [Jr., US Undersecretary of State] and his advisors [are] weak and irresolute in the face of this crisis, and are tepid about taking any vigorous action. (For what it is worth my French colleague received exactly the same impression from his talk with Mr. Hoover yesterday)."[106] The French felt betrayed by American inaction. Mollet told Douglas Dillon so on 31 July, suggesting to the American that "French opinion was particularly disturbed because they had the feeling that they were being abandoned by the US after the US had started the whole affair by their withdrawal from [the] Aswan Dam" project.[107] He was convinced that the US did not realize the full gravity of the situation.[108] Once again, this related explicitly to the French perspective on the US role in the crisis. Why was Washington favoring a small and troublesome country like Egypt over its Cold War allies? This was captured in a comment that appeared in the *Times* on 17 October in which a French right-winger "made a violent attack on the Americans for failing to assume the responsibility which leadership of the free world required." He continued, "Are they going to wait until the Cossacks are watering their horses in the Tuilleries [*sic*] fountains before making up their minds?"[109] The French felt more disappointed at their abandonment by the Americans than at Nasser's attitude.

Colonialism, World Opinion, and the Failure of Force

Mutual role-taking, role-making, and alter-casting by Britain, France, and the United States, with Britain and France in the role of *residual great power* and the US as *alliance leader,* occurred within the context of strong world opinion against the proposed British and French military action. Although other European states that depended on the canal gave Britain and France rhetorical support, including attending the London conferences aimed at creating an international body to oversee the functioning of the canal, many nations around the world saw the possible use of military force to reverse nationalization of the Suez Canal as colonialism, plain and simple.

British officials were not unaware of this viewpoint. Early on in the crisis, a set of studies were conducted of commonwealth attitudes regarding Nasser's action and likely diplomatic positions at the first users' conference—a clear example of *role-taking*—and found only lukewarm support for Britain.[110] New Zealand, the report stated, was "likely to give us complete support for the stand we have taken."[111] Australia was also considered likely to back forceful British action, although open division with the US was thought to present problems for the Australians, who were trying to forge closer ties with Washington in the security and defense sphere. Another report focused squarely on likely reactions to the use of force suggested condescendingly that Pakistan thought in a militaristic way and would therefore understand the resort to force.[112] India and Ceylon, however, were likely to be strongly opposed: "India is highly critical of U.K. and French 'warlike preparations.'"[113] The attitude of the South African government, the report continued, had been and was likely to remain "rather unsatisfactory."[114] The strength of opposition to the British and French line, therefore, was made clear to the government from an assessment of commonwealth opinion.

Consequently, British leaders were eager to make a role that walked a fine line between taking a stand on behalf of international agreements and principles, which could be portrayed as characteristic of a *great power,* and behaving in an overtly colonial manner, engaging in the forceful subjugation of weaker peoples. As Eden wrote to Eisenhower after issuing a 30 October ultimatum to Nasser, "I can assure you than any action which we may have to take to follow up the declaration is not part of a harking back to the old colonial and occupational concepts. We are most anxious to avoid this impression."[115] In public, Conservative member of Parliament Hugh Fraser stressed in the House of Commons that the rejuvenation of the entente cordiale facing down Nasser was not about "joining hands with bloodstained imperialists; it is not joining hands with men who are out merely for revenge. It is joining hands with one of the most honest Socialist Governments France has ever had."[116] French leaders, too, considered charges of colonialism similarly unfounded, with Mollet "affirm[ing] several times [to Dillon] that the question was not a local one and that France agreed entirely with the US that they should not be in a position defending the shareholders of Suez Canal Co. or of any outdated colonial rights."[117] However, such exhortations only proved the clear associations between what was happening on the ground and the colonial past of the protagonists; if it looked like gunboat diplomacy, it was gunboat diplomacy.

Outspoken support in Britain for military action by members of the "Suez Group" of Conservative members of Parliament reinforced the impression. Julian Amery's comments during the initial debate were typical: "There is a long gallery of tyrants, emperors and dictators who have paid with their lives for waking up and uniting the boldness of France and the determination of England," he told the House on 2 August.[118] "Colonel Nasser may find himself in that boat before long," Amery warned.[119] He continued by declaring that nationalization represented "an opportunity to redeem what has been lost and to re-establish British influence in the Middle East on firm and permanent foundations."[120] Such statements made the overtly colonial nature of Britain's actions tough to disguise. They were certainly clear to opponents of the use of force. As Secretary Humphrey told members of Eisenhower's cabinet, "It looked as though [the British] were simply trying to reverse the trend away from colonialism, and to turn the clock back fifty years."[121] Labour member of Parliament Desmond Donnelly stressed that rash action regarding Suez would ruin Britain's hard-fought postcolonial rehabilitation.

> In the years since 1945 we have established ourselves in a particular position as a former imperialist nation which has now become an anti-imperialist nation in many parts of the world. We have done more than any other single country to eradicate the old scars of imperialism. It would be a great tragedy if precipitous action by the British Government, urged on by any irresponsible elements on the benches opposite, were to prejudice the position which has been built up at so much cost and with so much hope.[122]

Konni Zilliacus was equally forthright in the Commons on 12 September. For him, it was plain that the Eden government was itching for a military confrontation aimed at allowing us to "bask in the glory of a sort of warmed-up

Neo-Disraelian imperial grandeur. The only thing wrong with that policy is that it comes from the wrong century."[123] The Suez Canal Users' Association (SCUA) should be renamed the "Nineteenth Century Club," he suggested.[124]

Many of those who did not believe Britain's actions were of a colonial nature still viewed them as inappropriate, invoking again the question of the expectations that accompanied the *residual great power* role. As Clement Davis, former leader of the Liberal Party, argued in the House on 2 August, "We hold a unique position in the world in our respect for the rule of law, and we, above everybody else, have insisted upon the value of international agreements and international associations."[125] For Davis and many others, Britain simply was not the type of power that disregarded the rule of law. From the earliest days of the crisis, then, the Labour Party line was that Britain should take the matter to the United Nations, which, they believed, was the proper approach for a true *great power*. In Davis's words, "We are signatories to the United Nations Charter, and . . . for many years in British policy we have steadfastly avoided any international action which would be in breach of international law or, indeed, contrary to the public opinion of the world."[126] The government must therefore tread carefully around the question of force, since Britain must not allow itself "to get into a position where we might be denounced in the Security Council as aggressors, or where the majority of the Assembly were against us."[127]

As a result of this difference of opinion, the initial degree of unity between the government and the opposition began to dissolve within a matter of days of nationalization. Again, this development followed explicitly from the respective understandings of the Conservative government and its Labourite and Liberal opponents regarding the requirements of the *residual great power* role. As William Warbey stated unequivocally in the Commons on 2 August,

> What we cannot do today in the modern world is to take up a viewpoint which says that any single nation or group of nations can arrogate to itself the right to exercise supra-national powers over any other country. That is no longer possible.[128]

He continued by telling his fellow members that they "should realize that the days of Disraeli, in which some of them still live, are past."[129] World opinion could not be disregarded as it had been in earlier eras. If force were used, he concluded, "we shall have three-fifths of the world, probably more, against us, not only in the Middle East, with the possible exception of Israel, but the uncommitted nations of Asia, of course the Communist countries, and possibly the United States."[130] Such isolation was not characteristic of legitimate action appropriate for a *great power*.

Another member of Parliament, James Griffiths, attempted to shame the prime minister in the House of Commons on 1 November by quoting from a speech Eden had made at the UN's Foundation Conference in 1945:

> At intervals in history mankind has sought by the creation of international machinery to solve disputes between nations by agreement and not by force. Yet no one here doubts that despite these earlier failures a further attempt must be made. . . . Great Powers can make a two-fold contribution: (1) by the support of this organization; (2) by setting themselves certain standards of international conduct and by observing them scrupulously in all their dealings with other countries. The greater the power any State commands, the heavier its responsibility to wield that power with consideration for others and with restraint upon its own selfish impulses.[131]

In the ensuing decade, Eden had not become anti-UN; rather, he believed that the "standards of conduct" and "responsibility to wield" great power did not mean that Britain should allow itself to be limited in its sphere of action. For Gaitskell, in contrast, it was not Britain's "business to decide on our behalf that we should take independent action, even if it be, or appear to be, from your point of view police action. There is nothing in the United Nations Charter which justifies any nation appointing itself as world policeman."[132]

The problem with taking the UN route, according to British policymakers, was that the UN was a potential quagmire of opposition from ex-colonial states. Military planning was continuing apace throughout August and September, and there was a strict military timetable—by September, when it became clear that the first London Conference had failed to achieve the desired results, potential delays caused great anxiety among British policymakers. Moreover, both France and the United States agreed with the British view that the matter should not be taken to the UN, with the Americans repeatedly advising the British against that approach lest it give the Russians an opportunity to score diplomatic points against the West. But in US eyes, avoiding the UN did not mean that Britain could disregard world opinion— that was what the two London conferences had been all about as far as Washington was concerned. The disagreement between the British and French on the one hand and the US on the other centered specifically on the question of what to do if Nasser made no more provocative actions. To the increasing domestic opposition in Britain, to the United States, and to the vast majority of the world, the answer was "anything but force." Denis Healey's speech in the Commons in the 2 August debate proved remarkably prescient:

> I think there is no doubt that this House, and, indeed, world opinion outside Britain, would fully support forceful action by this country, in conjunction with its Allies or even alone, if Colonel Nasser were to try to interfere with transit through the Canal by force. . . . On the other hand, Colonel Nasser has said he has no intention of doing this, and I think that, provided we make the necessary military preparations . . . there is little reason to doubt his word on this.[133]

> I believe that the only international framework in which a system can be worked out is the United Nations. . . . Let us not make a sort of Chauvinistic hullabaloo which only encourages other countries to twist the lion's tail. There is no pastime more attractive than twisting the lion's tail if one knows that it will make him roar and is almost sure that it will not make him bite.[134]

From a micro-interactionist perspective, in sum, Eden's decision to announce a cease-fire on 6 November was not the result of any single factor: not the run on sterling that led the initially bellicose Macmillan to recommend a cease-fire to the cabinet; not domestic opposition, with Gaitskell arguing that "the Government . . . have committed an act of disastrous folly whose tragic consequences we shall regret for years"[135] and even Labour MP Christopher Mayhew, no opponent of British military power, pronouncing that the "peace and the reputation of our country is safer in our hands than in theirs";[136] not public unrest, with citizens taking to the streets in opposition to military action; not even Soviet threats to intervene, including the use of the Bomb, if Britain did not withdraw. Rather, the decision was caused by the specific way in which all of these factors interacted with the role of *residual great power* as it emerged and shifted over the course of the Suez Crisis.

Thus it was not Gaitskell's calls for a change of government that made great political play but accusations that British actions "will have done irreparable harm to the prestige and reputation of our country."[137] Even domestic opposition could, perhaps, be tolerated—at least for a time—but threats to

Britain's membership in the United Nations could not. These threats became very real as Britain flouted repeated calls for a cease-fire. "Our friends," British ambassador to the UN Pierson Dixon cabled to London on 1 November, are "concerned at the possibility that our open defiance of the United Nations may be compounded to the point where we have no option but to leave the organization."[138] The effect "on the Commonwealth and on the whole of the network of Western alliances"—including the cherished Anglo-American relationship—"might then be disastrous."[139] American ambassador to the UN Henry Cabot Lodge Jr. stressed "to Dixon how serious the consequences for the UN and for Anglo-American relations would be if the UK were forced to leave the UN."[140] It was not just the threat of Soviet bombs that mattered, but Soviet threats in the absence of clear backing from Washington.

Finally, a cease-fire became politically feasible only after British and French leaders had concocted the notion of "police action" to describe what they were doing by occupying the Canal Zone. It was, of course, a fig leaf that masked a humiliating retreat, but it was essential for British leaders to be able to claim that their responsibilities as a *residual great power* in relation to international peace and security had been met.

CONCLUSION

This account of Britain's actions during the Suez Crisis can be contrasted with two counterexplanations: a rationalist preference-based explanation and constructivist identity-based one.

First, given the importance of misunderstanding and miscommunication during the crisis between Britain and France on the one hand and the US on the other, a rationalist bargaining approach suggests itself. As an incomplete information-signaling game in which Britain and the US were unaware of each other's preferences regarding the outcome—which would be taken as external inputs to the game—the crisis resulted from Eden's failure to signal his determination to bring down Nasser and Eisenhower's failure to signal his determination to prevent the use of force at all costs. Had either successfully communicated his preferences, strategies could have been changed to avoid the need for the US to force a cessation of hostilities, centered in all likelihood on the internationalization of the canal along the lines of Krisha Menon's proposal to appoint an international canal board to

work in coordination with Egypt over the running of the canal. The acceptance of this idea or something like it would have represented a solution to
the puzzle of why war was contemplated over the Suez problem.

Second, from a standard constructivist perspective, Janice Bially Mattern
offers an answer to the "Suez puzzle" with points of correspondence with my
micro-interactionist account.[141] For her, nationalization represented an ontological attack against the British self. While Britain could have "chosen to
accept [nationalization] as an inevitable concession to what was after 1954
in effect a newly-independent state striving to achieve a sense of national
identity,"[142] what Bially Mattern terms the British "Lion" identity could not
tolerate the blow to British prestige. The American self—the "Eagle," "the
identity that signified the U.S. as a proud and capable leader"[143]—was not
affected as strongly, and the US need to defend this identity outweighed alliance considerations. While Anglo-American relations had been strong since
1945, despite the transition of power between the two countries in the Middle East and elsewhere, the relationship almost entirely broke down over
Suez. For Bially Mattern, "It was the Lion/Eagle conflict that made the diver-
gence so divisive for the Anglo-American relationship."[144]

The value added of a constructivist account over a bargaining approach
is apparent in Bially Mattern's explanation. The sensitivity of constructivist
approach to the meaningful and context-dependent nature of social action
helps us to understand how and hence why the Suez "game" was set up as it
was in the first place rather than merely reading preferences off the declarations of British, French and American leaders as a rationalist perspective
would do. While persuasive, however, and as expected from the comments
in the previous two chapters, Bially Mattern's explanation, too, leads to further questions: in particular, why did the Lion/Eagle identities conflict over
Suez, and why did they require actions that brought Anglo-American relations to a unique nadir? Put another way, what was similar between the Lion
British self and that of the French—"le Coq," one might term it—that made
them react in similarly aggressive fashions and that rendered the British
identity less unique? This idea also relates to the element of the Suez Crisis
Bially Mattern considers puzzling. For her, the rehabilitation of Anglo-
American relations is the puzzle; here, however, the puzzle refers to the two
sides' actions regarding the Suez issue itself.

The value of a micro-interactionist constructivist approach becomes evident in that regard. A micro-interactionist approach suggests that the disagreement about Suez was caused by the respective roles that emerged for the

two parties during the conflict: whereas the Eden government wanted to affirm its "Lion" identity by making what might be termed a *residual great power*
role in the Middle East, a role that it had taken from France and that required
the reversal of Nasser's seizure of the canal by force if necessary, America's affirmation of its "Eagle" identity through playing the *alliance leader* role led
Washington to resist the strong pressure from Britain and France to support
Nasser's overthrow and to halt the US allies' military action.

CHAPTER THREE

The Skybolt Affair, 1962

ACHESON'S PRONOUNCEMENT THAT Britain had "lost an empire and not yet found a role" was not the only blot on the US-UK copybook in December 1962. Less than a week later, a transatlantic crisis broke that seemed to threaten the foundations of the special relationship, only recently repaired after the trauma of Suez.[1] The crisis was triggered by an American decision to cancel a nuclear missile system known as Skybolt to be purchased by Britain. UK resentment at the move was intense, as the deal had assumed significance beyond that of a mere arms sale. The degree to which Britain possessed a truly "independent" deterrent was at stake, as was the future of Western nuclear defense. Britain's negotiations over entry to the EEC also lurked in the background. The crisis ended with an American commitment to supply an alternative in the form of Polaris. Judgments about the seriousness of the affair vary: some observers have viewed it as the worst crisis in transatlantic relations since Suez,[2] while others have perceived little more than a storm in a teacup—a storm both sides whipped up to their advantage.[3] The episode is nonetheless one of the touchstones in Britain's postwar history, laying bare many of the most prescient expectations attached to Britain in the world at the beginning of the 1960s.

Despite the events of November 1956, Britain was still seeking to make a *residual great power* role in international politics in the early 1960s, but with very different expectations than had emerged in the Suez Crisis. Central here was the perceived need to possess a technologically advanced and notionally independent nuclear deterrent, in this case supplied by the United States. In this sense, Skybolt was less a real weapon than symbolic one, procured to maintain British prestige through its ability to underpin the *residual great power* role. These role-making attempts, however, clashed with the roles of two important others—once again the US and France. For the former, provision of a better nuclear delivery system was problematic for its role as *alliance leader;* for the latter, its role as *residual great power* was predicated on leadership of an independent Europe, of which Britain was attempting to become a member.[4] As in the case of Suez, therefore, Skybolt was a crisis precisely because different and conflicting expectations emerged concerning British foreign policy in relation to those of the United States and France. Unlike Suez, however, the Skybolt Crisis was resolved because the US supported British role-making attempts by supplying Polaris, which Britain accepted despite the missiles' potential negative effects on the attempt to join Europe.

The chapter begins by presenting the background to the Skybolt affair, identifying the chief puzzles, and discussing the ways in which commentators have traditionally used and understood the affair. The following three sections focus on the role Britain tried to make for itself, the role it took from the US, and the one it took from France. A short conclusion recapitulates.

THE SKYBOLT AFFAIR—HISTORICAL BACKGROUND AND PUZZLE

Although often described as the most serious crisis in postwar US-UK relations after Suez, the Skybolt Crisis was a brief affair, lasting barely two weeks in December 1962, with the majority of open confrontation taking place in the congenial environment of the Bahamas.[5] Recent historiography has thus downplayed its seriousness, pointing to the fleeting nature of the events, the ways in which both British prime minister Harold Macmillan and US president John F. Kennedy played those events to suit domestic political needs, and the likelihood of the final outcome.[6] At the time, many Americans perceived it as less than a crisis, since it came just two months after the Cuban Missile Crisis. Following that confrontation, an argument with old friends seemed like a small problem: as special adviser to the president Theodore Sorensen noted, "all problems did."[7] Nonetheless, the Skybolt affair dominated a meeting between the US and Britain at Nassau that had been scheduled to be a routine discussion of world affairs.[8]

While Britain and America had collaborated on nuclear weapons development through the Manhattan Program during the Second World War, the McMahon Act of 1947 halted cooperation, forcing UK policymakers either to authorize the abandonment of the nuclear project or to continue alone.[9] The British equated nuclear power with *great power* status. They also felt that since the atomic bomb had originally been a British project, it was a British birthright.[10] They thus pressed on, exploding a nuclear device five years later.[11] However, as the Cold War arms race continued apace and Britain's economy fared poorly, the country began to look for savings on nuclear weapons development.[12] This situation brought with it the seemingly un-avoidable choice of cooperation with another party. In reality, the choice was between the US and France, with France taking the first steps toward de-velopment of the *force de frappe*.[13] Anglo-French cooperation was thought to offer far fewer benefits to Britain than an arrangement with the US. Not only could transatlantic relations be augmented, such a deal brought access to the most advanced weapons systems and increased influence in Washing-ton. An agreement was consequently struck at Camp David in March 1960 for the UK to purchase an American missile, later known as Skybolt but at the time in the early stages of development.

An air-launched ballistic missile, Skybolt promised to prolong the life of the "V-Bomber" force that had been the backbone of Britain's nuclear deter-rent since the early 1950s, ensuring a meaningful deterrent capability at least until the mid-1960s.[14] Skybolt consequently also allowed the cancellation of the British fixed-site missile, Blue Streak, that officials believed Britain could no longer afford and no longer needed.[15] Under the terms of the agreement, the US would pay for research and development, with Britain obliged to pay for the missiles and the negligible costs of fitting them to the bombers.[16] Brit-ain also agreed to provide facilities at Holy Loch in Scotland as American Polaris-boat bases, an agreement would that would become contentious two years later.[17]. The Conservative government thus staked a large amount of prestige on the missile acquisition. However, policymakers acknowledged that the missile's chances of successful development at manageable cost were not entirely favorable and that Skybolt was consequently a dangerous basket to fill with Britain's precious nuclear eggs.[18] Rumors of cancellation were widespread in December 1960, when funding was reduced, and again in 1961, but each time development continued and British fears were temporar-ily allayed.[19] By the autumn of 1962, however, defense secretary Robert Mc-Namara considered Skybolt unworthy of further investment. As Kennedy explained, "We just don't think we're getting $2bn worth of security."[20]

Aware of the political problems that the missile's cancellation would cause the British,[21] McNamara recommended a round of meetings with them to discuss alternatives.[22] The question of alternatives constituted the substance of the disagreement. When McNamara visited London, he made a provocative statement to the press immediately after arriving: Skybolt had

failed a number of tests, and its future was under close scrutiny.[23] His statement served as proof that he had come to inform British officials that the
rumors of the weapon's cancellation were true.[24] The press reacted furiously,
and public opinion was dangerously hostile to the government's policy;
Macmillan even worried that his government might fall on the issue.[25] During the week prior to the Nassau meetings on 19–20 20 December, Macmillan and his colleagues came to the conclusion that Polaris was the only suitable replacement and that it must be acquired with no strings attached.
Moreover, Macmillan believed—or feigned to believe—that the US was morally obliged to supply Polaris given the agreement over Holy Loch.[26] The
Americans, however, saw the provision of Polaris as a commitment of a different order: Polaris promised Britain a highly sophisticated deterrent
throughout the 1970s, not a nuclear extension.[27] Concerns were also raised
about the signals such a deal would send to the Germans and the French,
both of whom might feel aggrieved at preferential treatment to the British or
entitled to US technology.[28] Moreover, the likely effects on the UK's chances
for EEC entry were entirely negative. Many in the State Department preferred progress on NATO cooperation to propping up Britain's independent
deterrent.[29]

Kennedy thus offered Britain the Hound Dog missile as an alternative,
but Macmillan refused.[30] Given the amount of criticism that Hound Dog
had received, "the virginity of the lady," he quipped, "must now be regarded
as doubtful."[31] Macmillan preferred to make a desperate play for Polaris,[32]
and he apparently persuaded Kennedy. Under the conditions of the subsequent deal, Polaris would be "assigned" to NATO under normal circumstances but would be available for independent British use in instances of
"supreme national emergency." The president's special assistant, Arthur
Schlesinger, described the plan as a piece of "masterful ambiguity."[33] The
press nevertheless argued that Macmillan had "sold" the British independent deterrent: in what instances, skeptics asked, is the use of nuclear weapons not a "supreme national emergency?"[34]

How and why did Britain come to depend so completely on Skybolt, and
why would only Polaris be an acceptable replacement? The most perplexing
element of the Skybolt story is how it had become synonymous with the
short-term future of Britain's deterrent capability, how a key element of Britain's role in international relations had come to be predicated to a remark-
able degree on the successful completion of an American missile defense
system.

Britain, Great Power, and Nuclear Weapons

"We have to pick the winners out of the stable," minister of defence Harold Watkinson told Parliament in early 1960, "We are not like the US who has a large stable and can pick the winners on their way down the track."[35] With Skybolt, instead of picking the winner, Britain picked a lame horse, or at least one prevented from running.[36] The winner turned out to be the submarine-launched Polaris system, which laid the basis for the Trident series seaborne deterrent still in service with the Royal Navy. With hindsight, it is easy to see that Polaris was the more promising of the two systems, but this should not obscure the central place that Skybolt occupied in British defense thinking for the better part of two years. In short, from early 1960, Skybolt became a central pillar of Britain's making of the *residual great power* role.

Despite the fact that at this early stage the missile was "little more than a pile of papers"—a pile that had already cost ten million dollars—the government deliberately emphasized the benefits of its procurement on a number of occasions.[37] Watkinson told Hugh Fraser, secretary of state for air, in April 1960 that he had "deliberately focused public attention on Britain's interest in acquiring Skybolt."[38] Macmillan argued in May 1960 for placing a provisional order for one hundred missiles to ensure that the Americans had no doubts about Britain's interest.[39] Skybolt retained this explicit government support right up until the Nassau meetings. As late as 10 December 1962, and in light of the clear US intention to cancel Skybolt, Macmillan maintained that the best course of action might be to "sit on" Skybolt for "a year to eighteen months" for political reasons.[40] Even at this late stage, Skybolt remained central to British strategy.[41]

This is not to suggest that there were no dissenters from the pro-Skybolt line. Some inside the government, including Derek Heathcoat-Amory, were reluctant to have Britain become too firmly committed to Skybolt because of the tendency of major weapons projects to encounter problems.[42] Should development come unstuck, the government could expect serious criticism of its whole nuclear policy. Others had more specific doubts. As the Government's chief scientific adviser, Sir Solly Zuckerman, later made clear, Britain had tied itself to a weapon that was barely off the drawing board.[43] Indeed, as early as March 1960, US chief of naval operations Arleigh Burke was soliciting the support of Royal Navy admiral Charles Lamb in persuading Britain of the merits of Polaris over Skybolt.[44] Britain's desire to obtain Skybolt, Burke argued, must surely be predicated on faulty information of its benefits relative to those of the submarine-based system.[45] Nonetheless, Polaris did not enter the picture until December 1962.

How had Skybolt gained such prominence in British nuclear thinking? The notion that the missile would prolong the life of the V-Bombers fails fully to account for the importance attached to the acquisition of the missile or for the gravity—however forced—of the December 1962 confrontation. There was nothing intrinsic to the missile itself that can explain British ministers' attachment to it; its significance, rather, was tied to the understandings in the UK and beyond about Britain's role, particularly with respect to defense and European policy, and how these understandings interacted with the roles of others—particularly the US and France. Specifically, Skybolt's significance lay in what it meant for Britain's retention of a credible nuclear deterrent within the context of severe fiscal constraint and what, in turn, nuclear status meant for Britain's role in the world.

First, and most basic, the importance attached to Skybolt demonstrates that there was little question that Britain should be anything other than a nuclear-armed power. The differences of opinion expressed by members of the government did not extend to serious consideration of Britain's possession of nuclear weapons per se. When British officials began to get wind of the seriousness of the possibility that the Americans might cancel Skybolt, all consideration turned to its effects in terms of Britain's nuclear deterrent rather than the existence of that deterrent.[46] The only caveat was the gap in the effectiveness of Britain's deterrent between the mid-1960s and 1969–70, when an alternative to Skybolt—be it Polaris, a solely British weapon, or a Franco-British system—could be brought on line.[47] The "gap," however, would be at most a temporary lapse in the quality of the deterrent, not a complete break from membership in the nuclear club. Britain's possession of nuclear weapons was a central, almost sacred, tenet of the role it attempted to make for itself in international affairs.

This was certainly a matter of prestige. Macmillan made it clear to the US delegation at Nassau that there was "a certain amount of keeping up with the Joneses involved" in the maintenance of Britain's nuclear deterrent.[48] However, notions of prestige and power brought to the fore by the possibility of Skybolt's cancellation were linked to Britain's role in a more complex manner than is suggested by Macmillan's comments. First, there was the historical dimension. The Manhattan Program that had developed the A-bomb began in Britain under the code-name Tube Alloys and was transferred to the US only under the threat of German invasion.[49] Consequently, policymakers were inclined to consider the Bomb very much a British invention, with the consequence that Britain should possess a nuclear capability. Moreover, the British government had also been informed of President Harry S. Truman's decision to drop atomic bombs on Hiroshima and Nagasaki,[50] an action that implied that Britain was a partner in the endeavor. In July 1962, speaking at Ann Arbor, Michigan, McNamara denounced small national deterrents as militarily useless—except in the case of Britain, on account of its role in the development of nuclear weapons.[51]

British policymakers' hostility toward giving up the deterrent cannot therefore be explained by reference to quixotic visions of *superpower* status.[52] It can be better understood with reference to the ideal typical role of *great power*. In that regard, the importance accorded to the acquisition of Skybolt was also a matter of international political practice. That is, one of the things *great powers* "do" is have the most advanced weapons available in a given era, both to back up their diplomacy and to keep in trust for the rest of the world.

Despite the growing numbers of weapons in the nuclear stockpiles of the *superpowers,* therefore, British policymakers clearly believed that the possession of a token strategic nuclear deterrent capability underpinned its international diplomacy. Macmillan made this argument to the Americans at Nassau: he cited Soviet leader Nikita Khrushchev's threats to Britain during the Suez Crisis as an example of a situation in which Britain must be able to rattle its own saber in reply if the event recurred in future.[53] On a less apocalyptic note, the two sides also discussed concrete instances in which British interests might be at stake and at least theoretical recourse to the use of its nuclear weapons would be necessary. The hypothetical scenario of an Iraqi attack on Kuwait was mentioned, bringing to the fore the divisions between the British and the Americans regarding the question of what constituted a "supreme national interest." To the British, this scenario counted;[54] the Americans, by contrast, interpreted the phrase to mean those situations in which Britain's territory itself was under direct threat. To them, the possibility of the use of nuclear weapons was simply a more thinkable proposition than it was for the British. It was also something of a burden that they could not understand others would wish to bear. To the British and French, however, although the links between their nuclear capabilities and actual use were tenuous, they did not wish to be without such weapons.

Britain's attachment to an advanced nuclear deterrent, therefore, was intimately connected to attempt to maintain military forces appropriate to a *residual great power.* The attempt to make this role did not go unchallenged at the domestic level, where the government faced an opposition that openly espoused disarmament.[55] When Secretary of State for Defence Peter Thorneycroft informed the House of Commons on 17 December of the Nassau talks over Skybolt, Labour member Joe Grimond asked whether the event did "not mark the absolute failure of the policy of the independent deterrent?"[56] Any problems with the deterrent, such as the cancellation of Blue Streak and the troubles with the US over Polaris, were thus grist for the opposition's mill, increasing calls for an end to "Britain's vainglorious attempt to maintain peace through the H-bomb," as Labour member of Parliament William Warbey opined in the House on 22 June 1960.[57] However, this policy was perceived as a point of weakness of the Labour Party, associated with the politics of opposition, not the realities of government: when Labour came to power under Harold Wilson, the party did not choose to surrender the deterrent.[58]

Britain's attachment to the possession of an advanced nuclear capability thus went beyond issues of party. This attachment severely limited the space for possible courses of action for the Macmillan government. Skybolt itself was compromised, but only a notionally independent and technologically advanced replacement would fit domestic expectations about Britain's role when it came to nuclear weapons. The onus was then placed on gaining an appropriate system from Britain's US allies. Before discussing the US views, however, it is important to highlight a number of paradoxes in how Britain went about making the role of *residual great power*.

Skybolt and Britain's Dependent Interdependence

At Nassau, Macmillan described what he called the "strange new game" of international politics in the Cold War era.[59] As he explained to the American delegation, "The world was not yet organized in a way that took cognizance of the disappearance of national independence."[60] He likened Britain to France and Germany in their attempts to come to grips with this new situation. "In this age of transition there were great nations like Britain, France and perhaps Germany, that felt they must have a means of defence which gave them the dignity and the authority of being participants."[61] Macmillan was trying to make a role in interaction with the United States below the status of the *superpowers* but above "normal" or "ordinary" states, which were not playing the nuclear weapons game.

British policymakers were also, however, fully aware of the limitations on Britain's ability to take part in this game, as evidenced by Macmillan's attempts to promote the notion of "interdependence" with the United States.[62] As he outlined in an early 1961 memorandum, the challenges the West faced necessitated "the maximum achievable unity of direction."[63] These words implied that the UK still had something to offer the US yet made clear the rather obvious point that "Britain—with all her experience—has neither the economic nor the military power to take the leading role."[64] The alternative was a relationship with the US that offered "influence," or a say with the Americans: "We shall play the Greeks to their Romans," Macmillan is reported to have said.[65] The possession of a small but advanced nuclear deterrent was not expected to change the nuclear balance, either within the West itself or vis-à-vis the Soviets, but rather to give Britain a place at any high-level discussions that would take place over these issues—so that they would be doing what *great powers* do. Although London's views would no longer be as decisive, they would at least be heard.

It was unsurprising that Britain should look to the US for assistance with its nuclear program in the late 1950s. Although Macmillan faced questions in the House of Commons such as whether he had consulted Khrushchev "about whether he could supply a better missile,"[66] there was no serious suggestion that Britain should do anything other than make its own warheads, perhaps in cooperation with the French, or buy them from the United States. Cooperation with the Americans brought the issue of Britain's independence to the forefront of political decision making during the Skybolt Crisis. To what extent was Britain truly independent in the use of the nuclear weapons, which formed such an important element of its role in international relations? Only six years earlier, the Suez affair had demonstrated that Britain could not mount a major conventional operation in the face of US opposition; if bombs began falling, could Britain at least launch a nuclear counterstrike?

It is thus testament to the importance placed on close relations with the US that the potential for Britain to be let down over Skybolt did not stop the nation from entering into a number of different arrangements aimed at increasing interdependence. Skybolt was to be a flagship in this regard: in allowing the British to cancel Blue Streak and later Blue Steel Mark II (the second generation of Britain's own standoff ballistic missile), the provision of Skybolt would result in significant savings since the US would cover the program's research and development costs.[67] As defence minister Harold Watkinson said of Skybolt in the House in June 1960, "We are in partnership with the Americans on this weapon."[68] In return, it was hoped, the US might deem it worthwhile to rely on the UK in certain areas of defense policy.[69] Britain's development of a virtual takeoff and landing airplane (eventually the Harrier) was intended to provide something toward Britain's end of the bargain.[70]

Both sides promoted interdependence. Given the international situation, a level of mutual need was a desirable attribute for such a relationship. In reality, however, it was almost impossible to paper over the fact that US defense spending outstripped that of the UK by some ten to one. The result was a number of disagreements over arms sales and procurement policy.[71] For the US, open competition was the preferred method of meeting allies' defense needs; for the UK, that procedure meant almost certain defeat in the search for contracts.[72] This phenomenon highlighted the tension at the heart of any proposed interdependence with the US: the UK could offer very little. Nevertheless, the UK would clearly offer whatever it could. The Holy Loch agreement was typical. British ministers felt that increased interdependence with the US was worth potentially significant domestic hostility. Alternative sites for the Polaris facilities were considered in the hope that the arguments could persuade the Americans that a densely populated area such as the Clyde, near Glasgow, was unsuitable.[73] But the US eventually secured the site. Evidently, tying the UK more closely to the US was deemed worth the political risk. As already noted, however, the US was in far less need of Britain than vice versa, and officials contemplating the Holy Loch arrangement worried that if Britain refused, the Americans would simply place their facilities in West Germany instead.[74]

"Interdependence," then, was the means to both "influence" and "status"—a way for Britain to gain leverage in the attempt to alter-cast the United States into a role complementary to Britain's *residual great power* role. Crucially, although interdependence had its problems, it was also seen as the solution to other more pressing issues. One such problem, paradoxically, was the charge of overdependence on the United States. The rhetoric that surrounded Skybolt, therefore, emphasized the cooperative elements of the deal and attempted to play down its dependent facets.[75] In particular, the government was sensitive to the charge that Britain's deterrent was not truly independent. Grimond pointedly asked Macmillan on 17 December to explain "in what sense it is an independent deterrent which depends entirely upon whether the Americans make it?" The prime minister defended cooperation with the US:

If the American Government decide to continue Skybolt and, according to their arrangement with us, to deliver it, it will be independent in the sense

that it will be our property. The warhead will be manufactured by us and will
be under our sole control.[76]

Together with the issue of a replacement, therefore, the question of independence consequently lay at the heart of the Nassau talks and agreement:
whether, in the final analysis, one of the queen's ministers would be in sole
control of the use of Britain's deterrent.[77] Ernest Bevin's words from October
1946 likely remained in the minds of the British delegation: "We have got to
have this thing over here whatever it costs. . . . We've got to have the bloody
Union Jack flying on the top of it."[78] As the meetings were ongoing, British
officials tried to persuade the electorate that whatever the outcome, the deterrent would remain truly independent.[79]

Yet despite assurances about the ultimate independence of the deterrent,
the lengthy and often heated negotiations on the terms of any communiqué
related to independence only obscured the reality that no operational plans
for independent use of Britain's deterrent existed at the time, nor were there
any serious intentions to draw up such plans.[80] This was made clear by the
prime minister's private secretary, Philip de Zulueta, shortly after Nassau.
Again, using nuclear weapons was nowhere near the forefront of British thinking. The government was much more interested in deeper cooperation with
the US and its NATO allies on targeting and the division of deterrent labor.[81]

Britain's independence in the nuclear field thus contained a number of
inherent paradoxes. The notion of Anglo-US interdependence warded off
criticism of dependence, while Britain acted in a conscious manner to re-
duce its own independence through increased transatlantic cooperation. As
Zuckerman later noted, one of the most striking aspects of Britain's nuclear
deterrent policy was that its discourse contained space for the seemingly
contradictory visions of the deterrent as, on the one hand, fully independent, while also on the other merely Britain's "contribution to the Western
nuclear deterrent."[82] Whether the V-Bombers were under ultimate national
control or not, therefore, was a matter of principle, not policy. Britain would
not use them independently, but use them to contribute to the combined
deterrent of the West.

Skybolt, the United States, and Britain's Role in the World

One of the most common interpretations of the Skybolt Crisis is that transatlantic relations almost broke down.[83] As Donette Murray has argued,

"Anglo-American relations were never so starkly and publicly in disarray as during the controversial Skybolt crisis."[84] The basis of this interpretation is that the US wanted Britain out of the nuclear club and tried to use the cancellation of Skybolt to achieve that goal. At least, that is what British policymakers feared.[85] McNamara's condemnation of small national deterrents, together with Acheson's ill-timed words, certainly seemed to give the impression that the US was out to accomplish just that.[86] Although McNamara later clarified that his comments did not apply to Britain, the implication of his words seemed clear: America did not support the role Britain was trying to make for itself when it came to the possession of nuclear weapons.[87]

However, the extent to which America supported Britain's role was obscured by divisions within Washington over Skybolt and how it related to US policy over the future of European defense. As a result, there was a lack of a clear role for British policymakers to take—no clear perspective that accurately represented the US position. To show how this situation arose and what effect it had, this section highlights the different viewpoints concerning these issues that were floating around in Washington in the years that preceded Nassau. It concurs broadly with the revisionist historiography on the events, associated most clearly with Marc Trachtenberg, which argues that Skybolt became caught up in the Kennedy administration's search for a more viable and concrete policy on the defense of Europe.[88] On this reading, Nassau represented less the end point of a crisis in US-UK relations than a new beginning for the Kennedy administration's attempts to move forward on European nuclear policy. The interactionist approach is particularly useful here because it draws attention to the wider context of the crisis, thereby identifying the space of possible actions for the Macmillan government in response to Skybolt's cancellation and hence the boundaries within which Britain could define its own role.

Given Acheson and McNamara's comments and the rumors of Skybolt's cancellation, it is unsurprising that when McNamara flew to London on 11 December to meet with his opposite number, Peter Thorneycroft, the British minister attempted to gain an explicit statement of US support for Britain's independent deterrent.[89] Thorneycroft was a canny political operator, little concerned with the technical aspects of Skybolt, on which the American had based his decision. He assured McNamara that he could no doubt find some technical expert to argue the merits of the system, but he preferred to talk about the political elements of the problem.[90] He realized that a statement of support for the British deterrent would be a powerful asset both with the electorate and in the forthcoming negotiations with the Americans over alternatives. McNamara, however, dodged the request, which was beyond his brief; he was likely aware that Nassau would decide the issue in any case.

If British policymakers read their American counterparts incorrectly and thereby misunderstood the significance of the Nassau decision, as Trachtenberg has suggested, it was in large part because influential individuals in Washington were known to quite openly disparage national deterrents, particularly Britain's. It was thus thought to have been dangerous to assume that Britain could get Polaris without strings whenever it desired. Undersecretary of State George Ball was notable for his strong views against Britain's deterrent, and he was joined by a group known as the "Europeanists" or "conceptualists" that included Undersecretary of State Christian Herter and that had strong links to Jean Monnet and the European project.[91] Members of this group believed that Britain's maintenance of an independent deterrent annoyed the French and consequently stood in the way of Britain joining the EEC and lending its considerable diplomatic and organizational capabilities to the development of Europe's supranational structure. Ball considered the Nassau decision a critical mistake by the Kennedy government that led directly to the problems faced by the EEC in the 1960s and Britain's failure to join in 1963.[92]

Europeanists believed that Skybolt's cancellation should be used to persuade Britain to give up its nuclear aspirations; the issue of Skybolt's procurement by Britain was thus something of a thorn in the side of the Europeanists in the State Department. But to what extent the Europeanist line was official government policy and hence how far the Kennedy White House was willing to go in pursuing it was not clear. It was also not clear, therefore, that British policymakers took the State Department line in seeking to define Britain's role.

They certainly would have been aware that Ball and the Europeanists' general influence on American policy toward European integration was strong. The climate that Kennedy inherited in January 1961 was in many ways shaped by the Europeanist agenda. As historian Pascaline Winand argues, "President Kennedy's appointment of George Ball as the third- and then second-ranking officer in the State Department is of crucial importance for understanding American policy toward European integration during his administration."[93] Three reports in particular showed how post-Eisenhower foreign policy was envisaged. The first, "The North Atlantic Nations: Tasks for the 1960's," known as the Bowie Report after its author,

Robert Bowie, addressed broad issues of transatlantic relations,[94] while the second, "Report on the Findings of a Task Force on Economic Policy," was written by Ball himself. In addition, in April 1961 Kennedy approved Dean Acheson's report on American views toward NATO and the future of the alliance.[95] The former secretary was also associated with the Europeanists and was particularly concerned with the part NATO could play in the process of unifying Europe and tying Germany closely to it. Together, these reports painted a picture of the increased political, economic, and military unification of Europe, and the UK's entry into the EEC was a centerpiece of that strategy.

The formation of the European Free Trade Area, or the Seven, under British leadership was acknowledged to be divisive, and the solution to that problem was for Britain to negotiate entry into the EEC.[96] But "rather than creating a Europe-wide free trade area" as the basis for an enlarged "Europe," Bowie favored a more radical approach under which the United Kingdom would "accept the philosophy of the Common Market and directly negotiate its adherence on terms which did not sacrifice the political institutions or objectives of the Six. The UK should be encouraged to adopt this course."[97] British membership in the EEC, then, not only would help to create a large potential trading partner for the US but would lend it valuable political guidance from a mature democracy—a democracy, moreover, that shared many of America's views with regard to international relations.

These reports formed a prominent part of the environment within which American policy was made in Kennedy's short incumbency in the White House.[98] Mixed signals from the US administration help explain why there was confusion regarding American views on Britain's role with regard to nuclear weapons and Europe.

Of particular importance here was the concept of the "Multi-Lateral Force" (MLF), which further muddied the waters as far as the British—and certain members of the US administration—were concerned. The idea of a European multilateral nuclear force was initially proposed in 1957 by NATO Supreme Allied Commander (Europe) (SACEUR) Lauris Norstad as the solution to increasingly pressing problem of organizing the defense of Europe in the changing context of the Cold War.[99] The perceived proximity of nuclear parity between the US and the Soviet Union, visibly demonstrated by the launch of Sputnik in 1957, led to a reappraisal of the doctrine of "massive retaliation" that had dominated postwar US strategic thinking.[100] A downgrading of the possibility of all-out nuclear war placed an increased emphasis on the capabilities of conventional allied forces in deterring and possibly repulsing Soviet activity in Europe. However, Britain and other Europeans perceived this move away from massive retaliation and toward "flexible response" as merely a weakening of the US commitment to defending Europe.[101] Would Washington really sacrifice a US city in response to an attack on Europe? This question was particularly pertinent to Britain, whose 1957 Defense White Paper[102] placed massive retaliation and the nuclear deterrent at the heart of its defense policy, in part in hopes of increased savings on conventional defense.[103] This approach ran directly counter to the US desire to upgrade nonnuclear forms of European defense, which Europeans themselves could assume, to achieve domestic savings. As a number of US State Department communications made clear, US officials really wanted "greater conventional [military] strength on the continent."[104]

With Europeans increasingly worried about a weakening of US resolve, a plan to share nuclear weapons was highly controversial and unlikely to find many friends. Norstad intended to give SACEUR control of a medium-range ballistic missile force and hence control of strategic nuclear weapons in Europe. Although Britain, Italy and Turkey accepted the first phase of the plan, the placement of Thor missiles in Europe, these weapons would soon become obsolete, and the second phase envisaged the deployment of land-based NATO Polaris missiles with the potential for joint control and the multination manning of crews. Only the Germans seem to have been at all persuaded regarding the plan's merits. Neither Britain nor France was favorably disposed toward it since, as Winand argues, "the MLF was undoubtedly directed against the spread, or maintenance, of national nuclear forces in Europe."[105] That meant the *force de frappe* and Britain's own deterrent.

Beyond expecting the British to "share their grog with the Turks,"[106] the MLF plan had a number of serious flaws from their point of view, which was certainly not an isolated one. The US plan to give "Europeans" control of strategic nuclear weapons through NATO included a veto for the SACEUR, currently an American and likely to remain so. Hence, the plan raised the specter both of a German finger on the nuclear trigger if this veto was relaxed and of a continued US monopoly on nuclear control. These features were unlikely to endear the plan to the British, since it was difficult to square with the role of *residual great power*. The negative European reaction to the plan is, therefore, unsurprising: although potential independence in the defense sphere sounded like a good idea in theory, it also brought more deep-seated fears to the surface. In fact, it could be argued—and some members of the US administration certainly thought—that the Europeans did not truly want independence and instead were hoping that the Americans would provide them with a strengthened defensive umbrella.

In short, MLF was not well received, particularly in Britain.[107] This was not, as has already been noted, because Britain wanted truly independent use of its nukes; British policymakers were certainly not averse to the development of European cooperation in the nuclear field. But cooperation had to be as nominal equals, and an ultimate US veto over the use of nuclear weapons, together with the disarmament of themselves and France, was clearly incompatible with the British role in the world as its leaders saw it. Moreover, British officials were also unhappy about inclusion in a plan that was designed to force Europeans to spend more on conventional defense: UK defense spending was significantly higher than its continental neighbors and was severely straining the country's economy. Finally, as the Nassau discussions made clear, the term *multilateral* had different nuances in Britain than in America.[108] For British policymakers, that meaning was clearly closer to *multinational*, allowing Britain to assign as much of its nuclear capability—or as little—as it wanted to a combined force. As envisaged by its supporters in Washington, conversely, the MLF consisted of a truly multinational NATO force under SACEUR command. Hence, while the MLF had had laudable aims from the outset in terms of giving Europeans a greater degree of say in their defense and hence a greater degree of dignity, from the British and European perspectives, it also contained a number of inherent problems.

Yet it is also not clear how far Kennedy supported the MLF in any case and especially whether the US was prepared to make sacrifices—perhaps even the special relationship—to achieve it.[109] As late as April 1962, in fact, the MLF was not official policy and "remained low on the list of Kennedy's and McNamara's priorities compared with a much more important agenda item: a new strategy for NATO."[110] This situation had not changed significantly by the time of the Skybolt episode. Until January 1963, the MLF remained much more of a "concept" than a firm proposal on which Kennedy was willing to move. In this light, Britain's inactivity on the issue is understandable.[111]

The gap between the Europeanists' prominence in discussions of US policy toward Europe and their influence can be explained by the fact that although they certainly represented a coherent and influential group, they were mirrored by a similar group in the White House that held more pragmatic views relating to European defense, and those views eventually came to dominate. Key individuals here were McGeorge Bundy,[112] whom President Kennedy appointed special assistant for national security, and Walt Rostow, Bundy's deputy before Rostow moved to the State Department. Rostow's replacement, Carl Kaysen, held similarly pragmatic beliefs about European policy. Consequently, "in general, the White House Staff, especially those on the [National Security Council], thus tended to adopt a more tempered, less dogmatic attitude towards the whole issue of European integration."[113] Other shades of gray also existed regarding Europe, Britain's participation in it, and hence its possession of nuclear weapons: internationalists and Atlanticists wanted to look beyond the narrow confines of Europe, especially since the creation of a strong and unified Europe might not turn out to be in America's national interest in the longer term.

Recent historical work has therefore argued that Kennedy's provision of Polaris at Nassau was a deliberate and decisive turn away from the influence of State Department men such as Ball rather than a mistake that sounded the death knell for the administration's Europeanist policies.[114] Far from the US attempting to alter-cast Britain out of its role as a nuclear power, Nassau signaled a shift in US policy precipitated by the White House. Trachtenberg argues in this vein that this is certainly how McNamara saw things: "As he pointed out soon after returning to Washington from the Bahamas, the Skybolt affair made it possible to 'cast off the old program and begin the new.'"[115] Trachtenberg thus claims that McNamara was the "senior member" quoted by political scientist Richard Neustadt in his report on the Skybolt affair, commissioned by President Kennedy, as saying that if the incident "hadn't happened it should have been invented to get us set on this new track of viable policy."[116] That "new and viable policy," then, included British and French nuclear deterrents and accepted the inevitable resentment they would cause with the Germans. As Neustadt notes, "'Nassau' resolved 'Skybolt.'"[117]

Yet although it is tempting to argue that Britain had succeeded in altercasting the US into support for its role, such would not seem to have been the case. In this reading, American plans for MLF and the future of European defense did indeed suffer a major blow at Nassau.[118] Britain and France's nuclear weapons would remain outside of any eventual arrangement on MLF, which might make it unworkable. But the decision to prolong Britain's nuclear deterrent capability by supplying it with Polaris and to make a similar offer to the French[119] was not made simply because Kennedy wanted to help a friend and fellow politician. To credit this shift in American policy to Britain would be to discount reasons related to America's own role as *alliance leader.* The Nassau decision was a conscious move to elevate the MLF to the position of a realistic policy proposal by accepting the existence of French and British nuclear forces.[120] As McNamara argued, MLF would not work: "There is no way in which we can persuade the Europeans to buy and pay for both a multilateral force and a full compliance with NATO conventional force goals."[121]

The victims of Nassau were not British "independence" and Britain's chances of persuading de Gaulle of the logic of British entry into the EEC but rather the Germans and George Ball and his fellow Europeanists. As Winand has written, "The key to the MLF was the German question."[122] As a concept, the MLF could serve to hold out the potential of future German control of nuclear weapons, albeit as part of a large conglomerate and not unilaterally, while saving US face in denying the Germans such weapons for what was a potentially indefinite time period. Moreover, the offer to the French of cooperation in building a Polaris fleet sent firm signals to the Germans that their annoyance at their deliberate exclusion from the nuclear club was a price Kennedy was willing to pay in return for a more sensible strategy for NATO and the West. With the Nassau decision, America chose to extend Britain's nuclear capability into the missile age. The nuclear element of Britain's role had been acknowledged and had gained the Kennedy seal of approval. So too, incidentally, had the French, although British officials had long since been convinced that nothing much could be done about de Gaulle's nuclear aspirations.

Skybolt, France, and Britain's Membership in "Europe"

Although typically portrayed as a bilateral affair between the US and the UK, the role that emerged for Britain in Skybolt was also strongly shaped by France as a consequence of two factors.[123] The first related to the French development of the *force de frappe,* the centerpiece of de Gaulle's attempts to make a *great power* role for France after the war.[124] Initially disparaging of France's efforts, the British and later the Americans realized that little could be done to prevent the construction of a French deterrent.[125] British policy therefore moved to attempting to integrate the French capability into the future arrangements for European defense cooperation—either through NATO or some more restricted forum—and France thereby came to have an impact on the status of Britain's forces within those arrangements.

The second factor was France's preeminent position in the fledgling EEC, which it was eager to protect.[126] Despite domestic opposition, the British government had backed proposals to seek membership in Europe on the grounds that doing so would bring both economic gains and political advantages.[127] Membership was considered critical since Britain's continuing economic problems contrasted sharply with steep growth among the members of the Six. This was exacerbated by the failure of the European Free Trade Area, Britain's construction to rival the EEC, which could not compete with the larger bloc.[128] Moreover, although the machinations of departmental politics in Washington made reading American views on Europe as a whole difficult for the British, there was a large degree of consensus that Britain should do nothing to jeopardize its entry negotiations. As a consequence, Britain had to factor a third party into attempts to convince the United States of the merits of providing an alternative to Skybolt and thereby openly supporting Britain's definition of its role.

To analyze the impact of France on Britain's role, it is useful to present and critique another interpretation of the events: the idea that the Nassau compromise caused de Gaulle's veto of Britain's first application to the EEC.[129] Had it not been for the blatant demonstration of "Anglo-Saxon" unity at Nassau, Britain's entry might not have been so dramatically brought to a halt. However, this notion casts a false light on the events of December 1962. In fact, it seems certain that de Gaulle did not support Britain's entry bid in principle and was either actively searching for an opportunity to veto it or was quite happy when Nassau provided him with a pretext for doing so.[130] Again, a refutation of this popular interpretation broadly concurs with the recent historiography of these events, in particular the readings of Trachtenberg and Winand.

De Gaulle's veto of Britain's bid for EEC entry was announced on 14 January 1963 at one of his characteristic televised press conferences.[131] Although he did not explicitly state that his aim was to halt negotiations, the meaning of his statement was far from hidden. His words represented a thinly veiled attack on the special relationship: one day, the general was sure, Britain would want to join the EEC "without conditions, without reservations, and in preference to any other arrangement."[132] This allusion to "other arrangements" was a two-pronged attack on the UK. In addition to the special relationship, it was also an implicit criticism of Britain's haggling during entry negotiations for recognition of its economic commitments to the commonwealth nations.[133] When these preferences no longer existed, implied de

Gaulle, "France would place no obstacle in front of British membership."[134] Until that day, however, the general would use France's commanding position to prevent Britain's entry, despite support for Britain's bid from the other members of the Six.

The interpretation that Nassau caused the veto suggests that the main reason was the French leader's fear that a Britain would behave as America's Trojan horse in Europe, wrecking his aims for the organization.[135] In this reading, the closeness of the Anglo-Saxon relationship demonstrated at the Bahamas meeting convinced de Gaulle that Britain was simply not ready to join Europe. Nassau had demonstrated to de Gaulle and his fellow Europeans that they would take a backseat to the special relationship even after Britain joined the EEC. Such a situation could never be acceptable to de Gaulle and his proud conception of France. Entry negotiations would have to be halted.

This picture is by no means inaccurate. The American hesitation to provide Polaris as a replacement for Skybolt was grounded in the fear that a deal might seriously damage the chances of British entry into Europe.[136] Opposition to the special relationship within the State Department, then, was predicated not on deep anti-Britishness but on the belief that Britain should be wholeheartedly encouraged to join the European project, even at the expense of special US-UK arrangements.[137] The possibility that Polaris would endanger negotiations was a conclusion reached by many, including Ball. In his memoirs, Ball recounts how another Europeanist, Bill Tyler, attempted to make quite clear to the president at Nassau that the agreement would outrage de Gaulle and push him to veto Britain's EEC bid.[138]

Yet while this interpretation highlights the importance of Britain's entry negotiations to the Skybolt Crisis and hence the importance of French views on Britain's role, it overstates the impact of the Skybolt episode on de Gaulle's veto. Nassau did not cause the French veto; rather, de Gaulle used Nassau as an excuse to veto Britain's membership, but he had likely intended to veto the application all along.[139] But more important, the belief that the Polaris deal caused de Gaulle's veto obscures the true significance of Skybolt in the history of the Western alliance—specifically, the decisive consolidation of US policy regarding French and British nuclear weapons that occurred at Nassau. Both the issues of close US-UK relations, reaffirmed by the Nassau agreement, and Britain's entry into Europe were more subtle than this rendition allows.

The argument that a visible signal of US-UK closeness, particularly in this sensitive sphere, was not ideal at such an advanced stage in the entry negotiations was not lost on either the British or the Americans. Macmillan made a concerted effort at Nassau to separate Britain's entry from the American obligation to supply an alternative delivery system for its nuclear warheads. As the official records of the meeting state, "As regards the Common Market negotiations [Macmillan] could frankly see no objection."[140] He reasoned that "the truth of the matter was that the French felt that they had made a very good deal with the Germans about agriculture and the real problem was whether they would be ready to abandon this. . . . [T]he outcome of the Common Market negotiations would not be affected by the decisions on the nuclear delivery systems."[141]

The American response to this argument is somewhat unclear. The Europeanists in the US delegation would have been unlikely to find these arguments convincing. They well understood that agriculture was an important element in the negotiations, and the issues were not as technocratic as Macmillan was implying; however much the British tried to treat it as a commercial bargain, EEC entry was a largely political issue. As political scientist Andrew Pierre has observed, "The French were later to make much of the fact that Britain negotiated for sixteen months with the Common Market, but reached a major defense agreement with the United States in forty-eight hours."[142] Those associated with the White House, conversely, were more concerned at the possibilities of continued cooperation with the United Kingdom and the potential for moving ahead on issues of alliance defense than with Macmillan's reasoning. Although Kennedy, McNamara, and Rusk, and others were no doubt also aware that this reasoning was probably more than a little optimistic, they, too, were inclined to hope that what Macmillan was saying was true.

Moreover, Macmillan's spirited appeal to the more emotive elements of the US-UK relationship had particular resonance. Kennedy recognized that Macmillan had little room for rhetorical maneuvering at home. That Macmillan had seen fit to resort to "massive retaliation" with Kennedy by bringing up the issue of Britain's worldwide commitments demonstrates the lengths to which he was willing to go to secure a Polaris deal rather than accept a substitute or a proposal to initiate a working group to look into further options. Kennedy sincerely preferred doing business with the Conservatives over facing a Labour administration that could not be relied upon to be as pro-American in its outlook.[143] More important, however, Kennedy also knew that to let down the British would not be popular in America, since a 15

December 1962 *Washington Post* article had criticized the State Department for its handling of the US's "most trusted ally."[144] As McNamara realized early on, under these circumstances, agreeing to supply Polaris to the British was inevitable. The only real issue was the terms. Once the phrase "supreme national emergency" had been concocted, the problem was essentially solved.

The short space of time between Nassau and de Gaulle's veto, however, obscures the possibility that the Polaris arrangement was intended to signal a new US policy in regard to nuclear forces in Europe in addition to a recognition of Britain's part therein. First, during the Cuban Missile Crisis, Kennedy had issued an explicit directive to change the American stance on France's nuclear capability.[145] This move appears to have been a genuine attempt to find a modus vivendi with de Gaulle and included an offer to provide the French with Polaris missiles on terms similar to those of the British. It is not inconceivable, for example, that de Gaulle thought seriously about the offer of American help in developing a French Polaris fleet, and he could have accepted. It has also been suggested—and the Americans clearly believed—that Macmillan had misunderstood an offer of Anglo-French nuclear cooperation at their meeting at Rambouillet.[146] The general, however, refused the Polaris offer, claiming that he was uninterested in a proposal that seemed to be merely a poorly disguised attempt to limit French nuclear independence.[147] In so doing, the general seems to have misunderstood the full extent and implications of this change in American policy, a misunderstanding Trachtenberg attributes to interference from Ball and the Europeanists during initial negotiations with de Gaulle on the issue before his veto.[148]

CONCLUSION

The brevity of the Skybolt Crisis has not resulted in any lack of scholarly attention. It is frequently cited as an example of the special relationship in action;[149] the cause of Britain's first failed EEC application;[150] the end of its independent deterrent;[151] and finally as another example of Britain's postwar "decline."[152] Beyond these interpretations, historians have debated whether the Skybolt Crisis was caused by "muddle" (a simple breakdown of communication between Britain and America[153] or two years of Britain and America working at cross-purposes)[154] or "mischief"[155] (the Americans seeking to put small independent deterrents like Britain's out of business). By focusing on the international context of the crisis and the perspectives of important others in the Skybolt interaction, however, the interpretation presented here differs from both of these earlier theses.

The crisis was created by the possibility that the Kennedy administration would use Skybolt's cancellation to force Britain out of nuclear deterrence, a fear that was tied to the expectation that Britain was a *residual great power*. Again, an identity-based explanation would get us this far, but it would not provide the conceptual vocabulary necessary to assess the interaction with important others and hence fully explain Britain's actions. Identity is a social construction: its effects are not, then, automatic but are based on the space opened up within British political discourse for thinkable and possible action, which flows from the context-dependent expectations arising out of a process of role-taking, role-making, and alter-casting.

Making Britain's *residual great power* role in the Skybolt incident required Macmillan to secure from the US a replacement on similar terms: Polaris with no strings. The Americans agreed to supply Polaris, however, not as a result of Macmillan's emotional plea to Kennedy but as a consequence of their lack of desire to force Britain to give up its nuclear weapons, much to the disappointment of Ball and his fellow Europeanists. While Washington had no wish to see Britain develop a truly independent nuclear policy with its small nuclear deterrent, Britain and France's possession of nuclear arsenals was deemed an acceptable starting point for future European defense policy—and the success of European defense policy appealed to the *alliance leader* more than it feared French and German hurt feelings. In contrast to a rationalist approach, then, we can understand the role-based origins of the solution the US found for the crisis. Britain's membership in the EEC would have to await de Gaulle's decision and could not be placed above the pressing political issue in London of Skybolt and US-UK relations.

CHAPTER FOUR

Britain's Second Application to the EEC, 1964–1967

CHARLES DE GAULLE'S VETO of Britain's first application to the European Economic Community (EEC) did not settle the issue of the UK's relations with Europe for long; indeed, the question of Western unity and Britain's place in its institutional architecture remains to this day a prominent theme in Britain's international relations.[1] The possibility of a second EEC application therefore reappeared on the political agenda soon after Charles de Gaulle's humiliating *non,* having never gone away at the planning level.[2] By October 1966, Britain's leaders were again ready to try to persuade the French president that the UK was a willing and suitable candidate for entry. This time, they could show bipartisan support as proof of intent. However, the international context was even less conducive than had been the case earlier in the decade. With America's descent into Vietnam, de Gaulle's challenge to the EEC and NATO, and financial instability in Britain, Britain's leaders faced a number of challenges in convincing de Gaulle that the time was ripe. After a year of prenegotiation diplomacy, in November 1967, the French president blocked the opening of negotiations, again slamming the European door in Britain's face.

This chapter assesses Britain's second application to the EEC between the Labour Party's election in October 1964 and the December 1967 veto. Why did the Labour Government choose to make the bid, and why did a change of heart occur at that time? The explanation again focuses on the emergence of a particular role for Britain that can be usefully characterized in *residual great power* terms. The second application thus resulted in a change in strategy by the Labour Party toward the maintenance of that role through EEC membership rather than through alternative arrangements, a strategy pursued by the Conservatives. What is crucial, however, is the specific meanings the *residual great power* role assumed during the interaction over Britain's EEC application and how those meanings affected the application as it unfolded. As in the first application, the meaning of Britain's approach was constructed in an interaction involving France, the United States, and the "Friendly Five"—the other members of the EEC. The key question was whether de Gaulle could be persuaded that Britain's entry could be squared with his attempts to make a *residual great power* role for France.

After providing an overview of the events and the puzzle, the chapter analyzes the role the UK took from important others. It also assesses what shape the ongoing interactions over British membership took as they progressed and what strategies the UK used with its various interlocutors—France, the United States, the Five, and others in the commonwealth and beyond. It subsequently assesses the role British leaders tried to make in response and the various alter-casts used in the interaction. It concludes with a short summary of the argument.

"WE MEAN BUSINESS"—HISTORICAL BACKGROUND AND PUZZLE

Harold Wilson's Labour Party came to power staunchly opposed to British membership in the EEC. Former leader Hugh Gaitskell's 1962 declaration remained the official party line: "British entry into a federal Europe would mean the end of Britain as an independent state . . . the end of a thousand years of history."[3] Wilson himself was more enamored of the commonwealth than the continent and was not inclined to press the matter.[4] This aversion to Europe translated into support for Britain's so-called East of Suez role—a string of military bases and associated commitments stretching from Aden to Singapore. East of Suez, in turn, underpinned Britain's "World Role," another of Wilson's favorite mantras: as he stated in November 1964, "We are world power, with world influence, or we are nothing."[5] Following this reasoning, Britain was not "merely" a European power, and "there was no prospect of a new negotiation for British adherence to the E.E.C.," Wilson told Danish prime minister Jens Krag in January 1965. Britain "expected to have . . . a continuing and probably increasing role east of Suez."[6]

However, as international historian Rhiannon Vickers has noted, "Labour had regained power at a time of considerable change, when questions were being asked about the role that Britain could, or should, play in the world."[7] As she goes on, "It was becoming increasingly apparent that Britain's relative economic decline . . . meant that it could no longer project itself as a major force in the world in the way that it had during the first half of the twentieth century."[8] The Wilson governments presided over a considerable restructuring of Britain's foreign relations, including the withdrawal from East of Suez, and within two years had effected a total about-face on the issue of Europe as well. The prime minister declared in the Commons on 10 November 1966 that Her Majesty's Government was looking into the question of a second membership attempt with the clear intention of acceding to the Treaty of Rome.[9]

Wilson's declaration was a historic occasion: the first time both parties had made entry to the EEC a point of policy. US president Lyndon Johnson called it a "courageous announcement" that would do much to "unify the West";[10] for Germany's UK ambassador, Herbert Blankenhorn, it was one of the "great historical events of European history."[11] Yet it was also tentative and couched in defensive language. A bid would depend on the negotiation of "certain safeguards" to protect Britain's essential interests, principally relating to the commonwealth.[12] Before any formal application might be lodged, moreover, a "probe" would be carried out of the governments of the Six to gauge opinion regarding the potential success, likely conditions, and timing of a possible application, while domestic opponents were assured that no final decision had been made.[13] Conducted in January 1966, the probe saw Wilson and Foreign Secretary George Brown travel to each of the community capitals. As expected, the Friendly Five—Italy, Belgium, the Netherlands, Luxembourg, and West Germany—were positively disposed toward the application; de Gaulle's France remained stubbornly noncommittal.

Having taken time to come around to the idea of accession, unlike some of his more pro-European colleagues, Wilson pursued membership with all the zeal of a convert. In early May 1967, despite clear warnings that de Gaulle would spare no energy to block the bid, Her Majesty's Government proceeded with a three-day debate in the Commons,[14] which gave overwhelming assent to a second application, by a 488–62 vote.[15] The political nation had spoken with one voice, and simple formal applications were submitted on 10 May.[16] The application was well received, in Europe and beyond, but no formal negotiations over entry took place in the face of French opposition. At a press conference on 16 May, de Gaulle poured cold water on Britain's application. "For our part there could not be and moreover, never has been, any question of a veto," the general insisted; "It is only a question of knowing whether a successful conclusion is possible in the framework and within the conditions of the Common Market as it is, without introducing destructive difficulties."[17] While claiming that no veto had been cast, de Gaulle's comments pointed strongly in that direction. With Wilson defiantly insisting that Britain would "not take no for an answer," on 27 November 1967 the general issued an emphatic and unmistakable *non*.[18]

Given de Gaulle's well-known hostility to *les Anglo-Saxons* it is puzzling that the new government chose to expend time and energy on a bid that always had a large likelihood of failure. Why did the Labour Party risk another foreign policy humiliation when it had other pressing international problems to confront, including persuading the West Germans to assume a greater share of the cost of the British Army on the Rhine, discussions about Britain's future East of Suez, and attempts to put Britain's economy on the right path?[19] In addressing these questions, the chapter first turns to the debate within Britain itself over membership in the EEC. It assesses the main issues raised by policymakers, MPs and commentators and identifies the most important other positions British leaders took during the interaction. Having done so, it turns to the United States, France, and the Five to explain Britain's actions in micro-interactionist constructivist terms.

EUROPE OR THE WORLD? BRITAIN'S ROLE AND THE SECOND APPLICATION

Labour's embrace of Europe was swift: less than eighteen months from election to the decision to consider membership, and a further six months to a statement of intent. This fast pace resulted from the emergence of a particular set of expectations regarding Britain's role in relation to Europe that opened up a political space in which a second application was deemed appropriate and even imperative. As in the previous case study, this role can be characterized by reference to the *great power* role: it was recognized, in Britain and beyond, that Britain's power base in international affairs—both in Europe and in the wider world—could only be secured by joining the European Economic Community. The US-UK special relationship, the East of Suez role, and the European Free Trade Association (EFTA) could not assure Britain a seat at the top table of international politics going forward. As historians have noted, Britain's second application did not therefore represent a choice of "Europe" over "the world" but a choice *for* the world *through* membership in a closer European union.[20]

Movement in this direction began soon after Labour took office, as the new leaders learned about the fragile state of the economy (a worrying balance-of-payments deficit of eight hundred million pounds) and the true extent of the country's foreign commitments (in line with Churchill's "three circles," Britain retained troops in Germany, a large military presence east of Suez, and a strategic nuclear deterrent).[21] Harsh domestic measures to curb imports would have to be taken as a first step in shoring up Britain's economy, while internal cuts would have to be balanced with savings overseas.[22] At the outset of a foreign and defense policy review that would last throughout Wilson's first two governments, an ordering of Britain's priorities was conducted that placed Europe at the very top. Although Wilson told Parliament shortly before Christmas 1965 that "whatever we may do in the field of cost-effectiveness, we cannot afford to relinquish our world role . . . sometimes called our 'east of Suez' role," this announcement belied a set of decisions reached at a November 1964 meeting that placed East of Suez last on a list of Britain's foreign policy priorities, behind Europe and the maintenance of a nuclear deterrent.[23] Rhetoric to the contrary, Europe was viewed as sacrosanct—fundamental to Britain's global position.

Recognition of the geostrategic importance of Europe did not directly translate to a second application, however. This prioritization of Europe initially meant maintaining Britain's troop strength in Germany and its contribution to NATO's defense of Western Europe. But many policymakers both inside and outside of Whitehall were thinking in the direction of EEC membership. The reason was a prominent sense, evident from internal documents of the period, of "drift" in Britain's foreign policy. Sir Con O'Neill, at that time deputy undersecretary in the Foreign Office and previously the British delegate to the EEC during the country's first bid, summed up these feelings in an April 1967 paper, "The Political Case for Going into Europe."[24] He noted that "ever since the war the people of this country have felt themselves to be adrift. . . . [T]he overall picture for ordinary people has been twenty-two years of steadily declining influence and power and opportunity."[25] O'Neill believed that the answer was EEC membership, "the one course which could reverse this feeling of being nationally, socially, industrially, personally adrift."[26]

Membership in Europe, then, appeared to be the way to address a sense of imminent decline in Britain's foreign relations, its "exit" from the world stage, the end of great power—Acheson's comment is not far in the background here. As O'Neill noted as early as the summer of 1964, we can decline again to what was for so long our proper place: but if we choose this course I feel we must be prepared for the decline to be rather rapid. In particular, I fear that unless we succeed in creating a satisfactory relationship with Europe we may have declined in a relatively short time into neutrality . . . a greater Sweden.[27]

By *satisfactory,* O'Neill meant membership or at least an end to the schism between the Six of the EEC and the Seven of EFTA, the alternative economic bloc created in May 1960 by those states not party to the EEC, led by Britain.[28] In either case, a growing number of leaders in London deemed a well-founded institutional relationship with Europe of paramount importance. Others shared the sentiment, even if they disagreed with the principle of a federal Europe. For George Brown, foreign secretary beginning in August 1966, there was "a case for going into Europe almost at all costs."[29] If Europe was the "League of the Defeated," he argued, "then we would qualify by defeat in Rhodesia and the larger sense of defeat which would come from a feeling that we really hadn't a role to play in the world."[30]

Thus, although the EEC was centered on the Common Market and hence represented a solution to the problem of economic growth (with British industry continuing to struggle against continental European and American competition, both politicians and business leaders considered the prospect of access to the Common Market to outweigh the potential for some industries to fall by the wayside),[31] membership in Europe was above all a political issue. Economic and political strength went hand-in-hand, of course, but the application's true goal was securing international political influence for Britain. As historian Helen Parr notes, "Behind the Foreign Office's support for a British future in Europe was an assumption of mastery: it was only via a *political* relationship with Europe that Britain could sustain an international role."[32] O'Neill stressed "certain negative arguments" in favor of entry: "How can we maintain our influence if we stand on our own?"[33] Such mastery could not, it was thought, be assured from outside the EEC.

Again, therefore, we see the emergence of a role for Britain that can be understood in terms of the notion of *great power,* if only in a residual form. This can be made clearer by assessing further the implications of the vague notion of "influence." The search for influence through Europe had three separate components. The first related to the US as the leader of the Western alliance. As briefs prepared for the foreign secretary ahead of the October 1966 Chequers EEC meeting noted, "Unless we are members of the Community, we are bound progressively to lose our influence with the United States and elsewhere."[34] Second was the goal of playing some part in the evolving superpower dynamic by influencing Soviet foreign policy thinking. As O'Neill warned, "The super powers are not going to listen to us if we speak alone. The United States and the Soviet Union will only listen to us if we speak" as Europe.[35] Having a voice, then, was not just the means of fostering a better East-West dynamic but an end in itself. As Wilson told Parliament in May 1967, "On the determined handling of [the East-West] problem by Europe, the United States of America and the Soviet Union may well depend. Can Britain, therefore, contemplate . . . being outside the Councils?"[36] Britain's problems in that regard were simply mathematical. As one member of Parliament put it, "We cannot possibly hold our own on our own . . . when America will have a population of 250 million, [and] Russia a population of at least as many."[37]

Third, solving the problems of the First and Second Worlds was also a means of addressing the problems of the Third. As Brown stressed in the November debate, if Europe did not come together, it "will be less and less able to play its full part in contributing to the development of those parts of the world where poverty, hunger, and lack of opportunity still constitute a major threat to our civilization."[38] European unification (through the EEC and not some association between the Six and the Seven) would therefore represent the "collective act of statesmanship [needed] to heal [the] Western rift in the fabric of our continent."[39] Britain's ability to play an independent role in relation to problems beyond the superpower conflict again was tied to the fate of East of Suez, the meaningfulness of which was being strongly brought into question in 1965,[40] and which would eventually be relinquished as part of Denis Healey's defense review. As an official committee report noted, "East of Suez there is already evidence that Britain alone cannot play a major role. India, for example, is not interested in nuclear assurances just from Britain. Britain, backed by the rest of Europe and in association with the United States would of course be of more interest to the countries in the area."[41] Membership in Europe in this context, then, was key: "If we had assumed the new political commitment of joining the European Community, we should be better placed than we are now from outside to persuade our European partners that our world role is in their and our joint interest."[42]

The implication was clear: an attempt by Britain to join Europe and help in the creation of a larger "Third Force" in world politics centered on Western Europe was appropriate. These implications were thus firmly related to

the notion of Britain as a *residual great power*. As the prime minister stressed
in the May debate,

> We in Britain are in loyal alliance with one of the two great world Powers, the
> United States; and we seek the closest and most friendly relationship, eco-
> nomic, commercial, and cultural, with the other great world Power, the So-
> viet Union. But . . . we do not accept the notion that all great issues should be
> left for settlement direct between these Powers because we in Europe are not
> sufficiently powerful economically—and, therefore, politically—to make our
> voices heard and our influence felt.[43]

As a number of historians have thus argued, a high degree of consensus existed regarding what Europe represented for Britain: not an alternative to
"the world" but as a *multiplier* of Britain's strength in international politics
that made claims to a "world role" more rather than less meaningful.[44] Former defence secretary Duncan Sandys made this clear in the May 1967 Commons debate: "In this age of super-States, Britain by herself is no longer in a
position to exercise any really effective influence in international affairs, and
it is as well to recognise that. Neither can Europe without us claim a seat at
the top table. But together, we could be one of the giants."[45] As Wilson told
members of Parliament, a united Europe, "strong economically, strong technologically, and—because it is strong and united—an independent Europe[,
would be] able to exert far more influence in world affairs than at any time in
our generation."[46] According to an official committee report,

> It can be held that, ever since the war, we have tried to play the part of a world
> power without a sufficient economic and military foundation; that, in fact,
> we have tried to live beyond our political means. Given this premise, a desire
> to join the EEC can be seen as either one of two things. It can be seen as a re-
> alisation on our part that we must abandon dreams of a world role, and that,
> after some three centuries of wandering, we must return to our original
> moorings, just as (say) Belgium and Holland have lost their colonies, concen-
> trated on Europe and derived benefits from this diminution of their area of
> effort. Alternatively, our desire to join the EEC can be seen as an effort to
> strengthen the Commonwealth by strengthening its leading member, or to
> have a better say in the formulation of United States policy, or to influence
> (and contain) Germany, or not to be denied playing a part in the eventual
> East-West settlement, or to increase our trade ourselves.[47]

These push factors were set against the difficulties with finding alternatives, so that cases against submitting an application became increasingly unpersuasive. Staying out of the EEC was one alternative. But arguments like those of Labour member of Parliament Michael Foot that "it is not the case that if we do not get into Europe we are robbed of our political influence. All diplomacy does not end if we are not able to get into Europe. This country will still be able to exercise its power in the affairs of the world,"[48] took on a hollow ring, countered by the belief that staying out of the EEC "would clearly confine the United Kingdom to a position of secondary influence in world affairs."[49] Stanley Henig was more forthright, saying, "I cannot fathom" Foot's argument "when he says that Britain alone can play a vital political role in the world."[50] To play its expected *great power* role, Britain would have to enter the EEC.

Fears about federalism too carried less weight than had previously been the case, as proponents stressed that Britain could use Europe to British advantage. "If we can get into this Community, we can lead it," O'Neill declared. "English is the natural common language for a European Community. . . . [T]his and our technological lead will ensure us the first place."[51] If the UK did not enter the EEC and "together with our new partners and allies, choose the things which we wish to do politically and economically in the world and try to do them—sometimes they will agree with us and sometimes they will not," the island nation would "stand aloof on our own," Henig argued.[52] Such statements were coupled with defenses of parliamentary sovereignty within the EEC and critiques of the notion of independent foreign policies in the postwar period. Entry "would involve the passing of United Kingdom legislation . . . an exercise, of course, of Parliamentary sovereignty."[53] As member of Parliament Eric Heffer noted sarcastically, "We are . . . told that if we join we will not be able to have an independent foreign policy. What is General de Gaulle doing? I had the vague feeling that his foreign policy was somewhat more independent than ours."[54] Even the US and USSR lacked genuinely independent foreign policies, claimed supporters of membership: "Independence in foreign policy is already a relative term. Not even the two super-powers can act to-day without regard to their commitments to friends and allies and to international organizations."[55]

Finally, the "Little Englandism" that underpinned arguments against entry were themselves politically unattractive in important ways. As a September 1966 Foreign Office memo stressed, turning Britain's back on Europe would "constitute a radical change in the thinking to which the British people have been accustomed and be a break with the rôle this country has tried to perform hitherto."[56] Perhaps more worryingly, the report's authors "are not sure that even the status of a prosperous 'little Britain' would be all that easy to achieve."[57] As a result, even those who rejected the call for membership at the same time had to reject the association with Little Englandism. As one member of Parliament argued, for example, "I reject the charge, sometimes made against those who hold my point of view, that we are 'Little Englanders.' We are not 'Little Englanders,' and we are not 'Little Europeans,' either. I am an international socialist."[58] As such, "I want to see a genuinely wider Europe play its constructive part in a permanently more peaceful world. I have still to be convinced that entry . . . would advance that cause."[59] Although entirely justified in its skepticism of Europe's socialism-enhancing capacity, much of the force of this rejection of membership was dissipated in the effort.

Opponents of EEC membership thus had few and dwindling rhetorical resources on which to draw given the convergence of traditional British internationalism and the possibility of European membership. This convergence rendered problematic other potential alternatives to the problem of Britain and Europe. The option to invigorate EFTA is a case in point: "It is too small. We are too big for it. Our partners in it are not interested in world politics or defence," O'Neill noted.[60] The commonwealth and the sterling zone, too, were rarely considered a basis of real influence going forward. As Nora Beloff wrote in the *Observer,* "The sterling zone, formerly treated as a sign of Britain's world role, is now regarded as a serious liability."[61] Finally, although notions of becoming the "fifty-first (or is it the fifty-second?) [US] state" were occasionally noted,[62] more formal relations with America above and beyond the special relationship were not viewed as a genuine option for securing Britain's long-term political future.

The result was that when Labour came around to supporting membership during 1966, it faced less opposition than significant support from the political nation. The Commons debate of May 1967 was almost unanimous in its backing for a second bid, spending far more time on the minutiae of agriculture, finance, and trade than on the principle of British membership. For this reason, the UK ambassador to France, Sir Patrick Reilly felt confident enough to express controversially how "for the great majority of the nation, this debate is now meaningless. By one of those extraordinary and mysterious processes which determine the destiny of great nations, the decision has been taken."[63] Harmar Nicholls noted similarly his "frustration in having to make a speech on an issue of this importance when one knows before one starts that one will be defeated in the vote."[64] While Wilson could still protest "let no one think . . . that there is no other course for Britain except entry, Britain is called to make a choice, and it is a choice between alternatives. . . . It is not a question of 'Europe or bust,'"[65] in reality, the scope for alternative policies had narrowed, pushing strongly in favor of an application. As Wilson acknowledged, "There is no question of Britain's power to survive and develop outside the Communities, though no one will be in any doubt about the determination that would be needed."[66] The tough choice was staying out; the justification for going in was complete.

IN THE "LOGIC OF HISTORY": THE UNITED STATES AND THE SECOND UK APPLICATION

As in the cases of Suez and Skybolt, the United States was the most important "other" during the interaction of Britain's second application to the EEC. Although Washington had little direct ability to secure British entry to the EEC—America did not hold the keys to Europe, France did, and France would not open the door—the second application would not have been made in the absence of sustained US pressure throughout 1966 for Britain to move toward Europe. This pressure contained no threats of retaliatory action, yet in many ways it was more powerful than overt compulsion because it represented a taken-for-granted understanding that Britain's future lay in Europe.

Support for a second bid for British membership was manifest at all levels of the US government. When reporting on his discussions on Britain and Europe in the US in November 1966, for example, Sir Richard Powell, permanent secretary of the Board of Trade, commented, "In none of these discussions were the desirability, and indeed the long-term inevitability, of British entry questioned on the American side."[67] Patrick Dean, UK ambassador to Washington, wrote to Brown in similar terms: "American support for the idea of an economically and politically unified Europe to include Britain," he noted, "had been repeated so often over the years that it is apt to sound like a conditioned reflex."[68] From the perspective of the US government, British entry was "in the logic of history."[69] "In time," a memorandum from the Acheson Group noted resignedly, "England will surely become a part of this Community. In the meantime, while we defend and strengthen NATO we must also give continuing US support to the European Community and the cause of a united Europe."[70]

This strong and unwavering support was communicated to Britain from the top of the administration to the bottom. The president expressed it on several occasions, both in public and in private correspondence. "I am immensely heartened by your courageous announcement about joining the EEC," Johnson wrote to Wilson in November 1966. "If you find on the way that there is anything we might do to smooth the path, I hope you will let me know."[71] Making a rare public speech on the subject of Europe, the president told an audience in New York in October 1966 that "the outlines of a new Europe are clearly discernible. It is a stronger, increasingly united but open Europe—with Great Britain a part of it—and with close ties to America."[72]

Other members and former members of the administration were equally explicit in emphasizing US support. George Ball, a longtime proponent of a European destiny for Britain, made the point on a number of occasions, both to the president and directly to Wilson and his colleagues. As Ball noted in discussions with British leaders in July 1966, "Both America and Britain were groping for some definition of their roles in the world."[73] Consequently, Ball "thought that the President would suggest to the Prime Minister that the British role should be one of leadership in Europe."[74] Ball himself had told the president to make such a suggestion. On 22 July 1966, during the crucial period of decision in the UK over a potential second application, Ball wrote a lengthy letter to LBJ on the topic of Britain and Europe.[75] With Wilson due in Washington the following week for talks with Johnson, Ball spelled out his support for Britain in Europe. There were, he suggested, two ways of dealing with Britain. The first, traditional, approach, was "to discuss . . . monetary measures, review additional ways . . . of bolstering the pound, press the British to put troops in Thailand and to maintain their expense expenditures, and offer to juggle our military sales arrangements to make this easier for them."[76] He continued,

> The alternative is to look beyond the immediate present and to talk with Wilson in some depth about the longer-range relations between our two nations based on a clear understanding of the respective roles which each country should play in the development of a rational world system. . . . Britain must recognize that she is no longer the center of a world system but that she can nevertheless play a critical role by applying her talents and resources to the leadership of Western Europe.[77]

Clear and determined statements also came from further down the administrative ladder and beyond the administration. Prominent journalist Walter Lippmann, for example, wrote several editorials on the necessity and progress of the application. In the aftermath of the "velvet veto," he questioned whether it was "not time to chuck the notion that it all depends on the whims of a cranky old man."[78] The simple fact, he went on, was "that the British decision to become a European power is one of the greatest historic events of this century. The historic process cannot be consummated suddenly."[79] Elsewhere, Lippmann deployed the stick rather than the carrot. In "This Time I Think Britain Will Get In," he argued although it "irks" people in Britain to be financially dependent on the US, "in these four years it has been borne on the British people that their role as a global power is over."[80] Entry into Europe was the answer.

American support for a second bid was thus an unspoken assumption. While headlines such as "U.S. View of Britain's Role in World Order: European Unity a Prime Necessity," which appeared in the *Times* on 27 July 1966, made the point starkly,[81] the day-to-day cooperation among various officials did just as much to bring the point home. There could, then, be no doubt that Labour's leaders were aware of US support for a second membership bid when they assumed office in October 1964. As a consequence, skeptics' and opponents' attempts to call into question American backing for British had little rhetorical force, as this exchange during the May 1967 Commons debate illustrates:

ERIC HEFFER: If we are to get out of the clutches of the United States and ultimately have an independent foreign policy . . . our position must be towards Europe and not towards anywhere else.

[ANNE KERR]: Why does my hon. Friend think that we will get out of the clutches of the United States . . . when the United States has been kicking and shoving us into joining the Community?

HEFFER: If my hon. Friend believes that the United States is kicking and shoving us to join the EEC, I suggest that she should not take the article in yesterday's *Sunday Telegraph* [by George Ball] as being necessarily the views of the Administration of the United States.

MRS. RENEE SHORT: Does my hon. Friend recollect that, in his presence at Strasbourg two weeks ago, I put this very point to Mr. Wayne Hayes, President Johnson's peripatetic Congressman, and asked him what he felt about the position if Britain went into the Common

Market, and that he made it clear that the American Administration
was 100 per cent behind our entry?[82]

American support for Britain's approach was difficult to question.

As important as the fact of American backing for a second British bid,
however, was the reasoning underpinning it, since it came to affect how Britain would go about trying to assure entry once the decision to apply had
been made. The rationale was straightforward: the EEC represented the creation of a polity able to match the US and the Soviet Union in economic and
politico-military terms. But while that might offer in the future a potential
economic competitor and independent voice in world affairs, it also offered
the best means for greater European contribution to Western unity. American officials thus argued repeatedly that European unity was in US interests.
As Johnson made clear in May 1966, "Every lesson of the past and every prospect for the future argue that the nations of Western Europe can only fulfill
their proper role in the world community if increasingly, they act together."[83]
Europe remained a problem for the United States. "So vast are the resources
of that continent, so important its policies to the rest of the world—so vital
its prosperity to the world economy—that Americans ignore the future of
Europe only at the expense of peace and prosperity on both continents."[84]
Twenty years after the end of the Second World War, European cohesion remained a top priority in Washington.

American views about Britain's EEC membership turned therefore on
questions of the Western alliance, a situation that had an important impact
on what membership in "Europe" meant for British policymakers and those
of other interested parties, notably the Six. Central in that regard was the
German question. For the US, the EEC was one of the main pillars of the attempt to tie West Germany to the West. As Johnson emphasized to Wilson in
May 1966,

> The heart of the matter is this: so long as France and Germany were working
> closely together to build an integrated Europe there was some assurance of
> stability in German policy and attitude. Now that France is no longer taking
> part in this joint effort . . . there is grave danger that the Germans will over
> time feel that they have been cast adrift . . . On our part, we cannot risk the
> danger of a rudderless Germany in the heart of Europe. On the other hand,
> any exaggerated bilateral relationship between the United States and Ger-
> many offers many disadvantages. . . . We have seen before an attempt to keep
> Germany in second class status. It failed then and it would fail again.[85]

Germany must be brought into the alliance as a full and equal partner, John-son concluded: "In the long pull, I am sure that the one best hope of stability and peace lies in the inclusion of Germany in a larger European unity, in which any latent nationalist drives can be submerged."[86] The potential for Europe emerging into a "third force" in world politics, then, was worth the risk. As Patrick Dean opined, "The Americans are prepared to accept and would even welcome the appearance of a 'loyal opposition' within the Alliance of which Britain is a part."[87] But Britain *had* to be a part, since its participation would give meaning to the political union that could restrain Germany. A weakened Europe "would be particularly dangerous if Germany became introverted and concerned with her own special problems. The Americans felt that it was essential to keep Germany involved in a larger framework."[88]

Far from a unified Europe representing a genuine and immediate threat to the coherence of the West, the problem in the mid-1960s—for the British, the Americans, and the other members of the Six, at least—was the opposite: alliance *dis*unity. Ball summed up the feeling by noting that "it appeared as if the forces of fragmentation were stronger than the forces of cohesion."[89] De Gaulle was not the only European thorn in the American side. Another problem, more closely related to American national security, was the issue of European inwardness and lack of ambition when it came to international affairs beyond Europe's borders. Several senior policymakers voiced concern, even contempt, for "Europe" during a May 1967 National Security Council meeting. Vice President Hubert Humphrey, for one, argued that "the Europeans are selfish. We should challenge them to participate in the world outside their borders. We must keep pounding at them on this problem."[90] National security adviser Walt Rostow argued similarly that "Europe is neglecting the world. It is in an isolationist cycle. We should get one of our Senators to make this point in a major speech."[91] Even Britain was not free from suspicion given the numerous indications that Britain was about to make drastic and far-reaching cuts to its defense budget and overseas commitments.

Britain's entry into Europe therefore was viewed as assurance that Europe would develop as an outward- rather than inward-looking entity. This idea had several major implications for Britain's role-making in relation to the application. First, the possibility of creating some sort of "Atlantic Community," with the EFTA countries more closely integrated economically and politically with North America, was a nonstarter in Washington despite Wilson and Brown's use of it in discussions with the French. As Powell reported to London, "There was no mention of possible alternatives to British entry, such as the idea of an Atlantic community. We gained the impression that the Americans are not themselves thinking at all seriously of U.S. association with regional economic groupings."[92] For O'Neill, "An Atlantic Free Trade Area is not an alternative. . . . It is not just that the Americans do not want it. . . . It is that we would be a small country in a group run by a super power, with all the consequences of that, both economical and political."[93] However, Britain retained this threat as a weapon in diplomacy with the French, but it was poor hand to play, and de Gaulle knew it. Britain's only institutional alternative to European membership was continued cooperation through EFTA, an unattractive prospect.

The second implication was that the Wilson government was forced to play down American support for its bid at every turn. American officials repeatedly suggested to their British counterparts that each side should refrain from advertising the "special relationship." US diplomatic posts were advised following Wilson's announcement that "they should treat UK decision in low, unemotional key so as to attract minimum diplomatic or public attention to US in UK-Community negotiations."[94] Given that questions were nonetheless likely, the instructions went on, "*If asked* about relation of UK bid to Kennedy Round, you should reply we see no reason to believe there is or should be any direct relation between need for urgent conclusion of Kennedy Round and longer term prospects for negotiations on British entry."[95] The American side even gave Britain allowances to oppose the US on certain issues. In June 1967 discussions with the new president of the European Commission, Jean Rey, US secretary of state Dean Rusk first asked whether "the U.S. should remain publicly silent on this matter. M. Rey responded with an emphatic 'yes.'"[96] He then suggested that "Mr. Wilson might at some point 'cock his snoot' at the U.S. for De Gaulle's consumption."[97]

Nonetheless, American and British perceptions of the UK's role closely aligned over the issue of the type of Europe that Britain was willing to join. In reply to Ball's insistence that Britain's role going forward should be as leader of Europe, Wilson "said that of course we accepted that this was one of our roles—but if this meant going into the EEC—[it] all depended on how [it was] done—[we] didn't want to be corralled into an inward-looking group."[98] He told Johnson in November 1966,

> Obviously this concept of an outward looking European Community, designed to play the constructive role in world affairs that each of us understandably is now finding difficult, is bound to raise once more the fundamen-

tal issue of our own relationship with the United States which stuck in de Gaulle's gullet last time. The prophets of gloom say that this remains as total an obstacle to our present approach as it proved for our predecessors. We shall see. My own belief is that the General has not changed one iota in his general view of the world or our own relationship with yourselves. [I thus reiterate] the firm determination of my colleagues and myself that there shall be no change in the fundamental relationship between our two countries and in our own basic loyalty to and belief in the Atlantic concept.[99]

Finally, American support for Britain's entry was subtly communicated to the Friendly Five to avoid annoying the French. Walter Stoessel, deputy secretary for European affairs, made it clear to Italian Socialist Party leader Mauro Ferri in December 1967 that the US favored British membership: "Britain has a natural role to play in Europe. Her entry into the Common Market would strengthen the Community politically and her technology would be a considerable asset."[100] The implications for the Friendly Five's roles as members of the Western alliance were clear.

American support for Britain's application was strong, therefore, but it was conditional on the UK acting in ways not too dissimilar from the Trojan horse of de Gaulle's fears. As Dean argued, "If we are unsuccessful on this occasion, the Americans are quite unwilling for us to contemplate that this would be the final parting of the ways."[101] In other words, not only was British entry "in the logic of history,"[102] it was in their opinion in the American national interest, and must be so. The Wilson government's proper response to a veto, therefore, would be to wait until the general had exited the political stage and try again. Britain's role, in their view, centered on leadership of a robust Europe capable of assisting the United States in governing the globe.

BRITAIN IS IN EUROPE: THE FIVE AND THE UK BID

The Five supported Britain's potential membership in the EEC throughout the second application, as they had during the first attempt earlier in the decade. For them, British entry was a natural step in the integration process, strengthening the EEC and providing it with greater economic and political clout on the world stage. Taking the role of the Five, and particularly the role of Germany, was thus a subtle yet important factor in leading Britain toward Europe and in shaping the role Britain made during the process and thus the form of the actual application. Yet at no point did any of the Five express a willingness to create a crisis by standing up to the French in their opposition to British entry. This was because, in short, they were cast by Britain's approach into the role of *good (Western) European:* Britain's membership was good for Europe in the long term and was appropriate, but not at the cost of destroying it in the short term in the face of de Gaulle's intransigence.

All of the Five therefore clearly stated their support for Britain during Wilson and Brown's January–February 1967 tour of community capitals. They first visited Italy—a symbolic choice as the birthplace of the EEC—where Prime Minister Aldo Moro concluded the first meeting by stating that "Europe was not Europe without Great Britain. Italian experience and advice would be placed fully at [Britain's] disposal."[103] Later, in Bonn, Chancellor Kurt Kiesinger told Wilson that West Germany "wanted Britain to join the EEC."[104] In Brussels, Prime Minister Paul Vanden Boeynants stressed that "the Belgian Government were in favour of Britain's accession and considered that for the future of Europe and especially for its political unity (the aim of which they all strove) the entry of Britain into the Community was indispensable."[105]

The Five thus saw no fundamental principled obstacle between Britain and EEC membership; a second application was entirely appropriate.[106] This was based on two considerations: what "Europe" meant in general, and what it meant for them in particular. Their answers to these questions in turn rested on the *good (Western) European* role. They were expected to support what was good for the European Community and the process of European integration as an end in itself. Therefore, the sincerity of Britain's approach—a point stressed at each stop on the tour, including Paris—together with the potential for other European countries such as Ireland and Denmark to join alongside Britain combined with a sense of responsibility to support these attempts. Moreover, Britain's political and economic power had the potential to assist in the construction of a Europe able to exert greater influence on international affairs. In this, the Five agreed with the French understanding of the meaning of Europe:

> Europe had an even wider role to play in the world . . . but she would not be able to play it unless she were powerful—and that meant economically powerful. The task of the European great powers—of France and of Britain—was not to be mere messenger boys between the two great Powers. They had a bigger role to play—and the other nations wished them to play it—than

merely waiting in the ante-rooms while the two great Powers settled everything by themselves. That is why France and Britain had to make effective
their enormous potential industrial strength by giving that strength a chance
to operate on a European and not a national scale, or series of national
scales.[107]

Vanden Boeynants developed the theme by reference to the idea of the "tri-
pod":

> Europe could only develop healthily if there were a balance between the
> three great European powers, Britain, France and Germany. Provided this bal-
> ance was maintained . . . the smaller powers like Belgium were prepared to
> accept a larger measure of influence in the Community for the Great Pow-
> ers. . . . Europe must include France . . . though one could not ignore the ten-
> dency on the part of France to wish to be the dominant partner. . . . Europe
> must include Germany. . . . [S]he could resist nationalism so long as visible
> progress towards building Europe was being made, otherwise there was a real
> risk that she would be affected by French nationalism. Finally, Europe must
> include Britain. It was inconceivable for Belgium to be associated with Ger-
> many in Europe while Britain remained outside.[108]

In each case, the issue turned both on Europe playing a larger global role and
Britain as a European great power together with France. British entry was
beneficial in both directions: it would help to balance French influence inside Europe and bolster European influence internationally. This was directly related to playing a larger part in solving East-West tensions, a priority
for all of the Five, especially the Germans, with Östpolitik ongoing.[109]

Wilson and Brown played on this theme during their tour of community
capitals. Asked directly by Moro why Britain was considering a second bid at
the present time, Wilson replied, "Briefly, we took the view that Britain and
the Commonwealth could only be strengthened if Britain joined Europe,
and that Europe would be strengthened too."[110] In particular, Wilson stressed
the technological contribution Britain could make to Europe. "If Britain
joined the Community," he told the Germans, "she would not weaken it but
strengthen it . . . by creating a larger market and widening technological
knowledge," especially in the area of civil and military aircraft, an area in
which the Germans also could contribute.[111] Just as Wilson had used technological progress to good effect in Britain—promising to modernize Britain in

the "White Heat" of technological innovation—technology served as the basis of Britain's contribution to the forging of Europe.[112]

The aim of this role-making as a European *great power* was to persuade the Five to use their influence within the EEC institutions to prevent a French veto. Such persuasion took place more or less explicitly during the tour. "Would it be possible for the Netherlands Government to apply any pressure?,"[113] Wilson and Brown inquired in the Hague. During the visit to Bonn, Wilson appealed to German leaders to do more than just support Britain's initiative; he asked them "to do all in their power to bring about Britain's entry into the EEC."[114] Germany's support, they made clear, "could be decisive."[115] However, Britain's requests were answered with muted assurances that its case would be presented to France in the best possible light but that pressure would not be brought to bear. Asked by an interviewer whether the German government supported Britain's desire to enter the EEC but "will not press this very strongly in Paris in order not to endanger the friendly relations between Paris and Bonn which have only recently been renewed," Kiesinger responded that the French view on the question of British accession was well known, so making Britain's case to the French was not the German task, although making apparent German support was appropriate. However, the German leader continued, "we have no pressure to exert on France. We would have no means to exercise such pressure nor would we wish to do so."[116] Asked whether Wilson had tried to persuade Kiesinger "to play the part of some kind of mediator," Kiesinger simply restated that "our English partners" expected Germany to support their point of view.[117]

Once again, this reluctance was related to the role of *good European,* which involved another set of expectations that overrode those in favor of promoting British membership: to preserve and avoid jeopardizing what had been achieved thus far in the European integration process. Britain's second application to the EEC was lodged shortly after the "Empty Chair Crisis" of July 1965–January 1966, during which de Gaulle had hamstrung European institutions by removing French chairpersons during the rotating presidency.[118] The crisis ended with the "Luxembourg Compromise," which gave the national governments an effective veto in matters of "supreme national interest," but it remained fresh in the memories of the leaders of the countries involved. For its part, the French government tried to shore up this understanding of the priorities of the Five by emphasizing the disruptive influence of Britain's accession. The French sought to alter-cast the Five into a particular understanding of the *good European* role that prioritized short-term cohesion over long-term expansion and thereby questioned the wisdom of British entry.

The Five were unconvinced by such French tactics. Wilson and Brown tried hard to persuade the Five that Britain had no intention of being a disruptive influence inside the community. "Logic and history taught us to recognize that, wherever there has been close economic union, it has led on eventually to political union of one form or another,"[119] Wilson told Kiesinger. "Just as the speed of a naval convoy was regulated by the slowest ship, so the progress of the European Economic Community would depend on its slowest member. We do not propose to be the slowest member."[120] When Vanden Boeynants sought assurances regarding Britain's views on the current EEC makeup, Brown stressed that the Treaty of Rome provided for institutional change on the accession of new member, meaning that accepting the treaty as it stood—which had been an open question—was no longer an issue for Britain.[121]

However, at this stage—January–February 1967—the British were still talking in terms of "safeguards" for British interests prior to entry. Doing so was not likely to convince the Five that French warnings were unwarranted. On this point, the influence of the Five, particularly the Dutch, on British role-making during the second application became apparent, since the Five suggested that Britain make a simple and straightforward application, with no mention of safeguards or special requirements of any sort. In reply to Vanden Boeynants, Brown replied that "there were different views . . . in Europe about the form which this political unity might take: it might for example be federal or national. On entering the Community we would expect to play our part in working out an answer to the problem."[122] Rather than make any suggestions that changes would be sought to the treaty base or EEC institutional architecture after Britain was admitted, "The conclusion reached [in discussion with the Dutch] was quite clear," a report on the tour stressed.[123] "The Dutch strongly advised us to start the ball rolling by making a very clear political declaration of intent, which would include a statement of acceptance of the Treaty of Rome." This approach, the memo went on, would "cut the ground underneath the French."[124] The application for entry should therefore be couched in as simple terms as possible.

The Five were also unconcerned about the possibility that, once inside the EEC, Britain would behave as a Trojan horse for American influence. The qualifier "Western" in the role that emerged for the Five over Britain's bid thus emphasizes the fact that there were considerations other than what

Britain could add to the European Community. Whereas France saw Britain's close relations with the United States as a fundamental obstacle to accession, the rest of the Six saw those ties as a potential asset. As the Dutch foreign secretary Joseph Luns told Wilson and Brown at the Hague, "Great Britain could and should play a very great role [in Europe]. This was not only because of the values which Great Britain could contribute to the expanded Community; the Netherlands Government saw in our accession the possibility of further harmonized development and close cooperation with America."[125] Britain was also sincere about furthering European economic independence from the United States since "politically, Britain had the same feeling towards the United States as the German Government had. We were just as attached to the Atlantic Alliance as the German Government, but we drew a distinction between the United States Government on the one hand and American business on the other."[126]

Moreover, turning the second application into a crisis was unnecessary for the Five because, like many in Britain, France, and the United States, the Five saw that British membership was inevitable. The first veto had not halted Britain's move toward Europe; there was little reason to think that a second French rejection would do otherwise. As German chancellor Ludwig Erhard noted while stressing Germany's support of Britain's bid, "The sooner Britain could be brought into the Common Market the better. The question was not now 'if' but 'when and how.'"[127] To the Five, the issue was de Gaulle himself. Not until the old warrior was off the scene would expending political capital on enlargement be worthwhile.

FRANCE, THE SECOND APPLICATION,
AND THE "RIGHT KIND OF EUROPE"[128]

The part played by France and de Gaulle in Britain's second application was in many ways ambiguous. On the one hand, "there is little doubt that Britain's application failed because of General de Gaulle's political and commercial opposition to British membership."[129] Despite their best efforts, "the British could not convince him to admit Britain."[130] France was in this sense fundamental, forcing British policymakers to present the bid in ways favorable to the French and particularly to behave in a manner that corresponded with de Gaulle's ideas about what it meant to be properly "European." Yet on the other hand, Britain's desire to join Europe was not dampened by taking the role of France; instead, the British responded to French actions with various alter-casting and role-making strategies designed merely to prevent a veto—and did so with some success. As Parr argues, "In 1967, the British won the long-term war. The Five, the British, the US and opinion in France stressed that Britain would accede to the European community eventually."[131]

The likelihood, even probability, of France preventing British accession was acknowledged at all levels of UK officialdom throughout the mid-1960s and was perceived by important others, particularly the United States, as conventional wisdom. As Michael Palliser, the prime minister's private secretary for foreign affairs, stated shortly before Wilson's declaration of interest in an EEC application, "I would say that my own conviction is that there is no prospect whatever of General de Gaulle letting us into the Common Market, as long as he is in control of events."[132] The fact was equally apparent in the US, as internal memoranda make clear. Assistant secretary of state for economic affairs Anthony Solomon and deputy secretary of state for European affairs Walter Stoessel noted to Ball while weighing a presidential push on Wilson toward membership, "even [i]f Wilson were to accept the President's advice, we think it highly unlikely that General De Gaulle would permit his entry into the Common Market."[133]

Again, French hostility to Britain was at base political, not economic or legal, despite the prevalence of technical questions regarding agricultural subsidies, Britain's financial health, and commonwealth interests in the British negotiating team's conversations over the course of 1967. As an internal memo of reflections on the January 1967 tour observed,

> Presumably the clearest factor to emerge from the very full evidence of the visits is the predominantly political nature of the problem which some of the Six see as obstacles to our entry. Thus Kiesinger was more concerned to discuss Strauss than Sterling, and de Gaulle had made plain that he is more concerned with the relative loss of control he would face in a wider Community, and our general attitude to the U.S., than with the real or imagined difficulties of running a reserve currency within the framework of a future Community's rules and institutions.[134]

French foreign minister Maurice Couve de Murville made the political nature of French objections clear in a January 1967 radio interview: "When things are important they are always political even when they are economic."[135] He continued, "The problem of British relations with the EEC . . . is a vast political problem which raises the whole question of what could be, in the political field, the orientation of a Europe whose unity is being sought."[136]

Basic to these political reasons then was the question of the meaning of "Europe" and the issue of French aggrandizement. "General de Gaulle's underlying motive is to assert the independent status of France in the world," the British cabinet's defense committee concluded, "This is not a means to an end; it is the end itself. It is the philosophy of the Le Roi soleil."[137] De Gaulle's overriding postwar aim was the restoration—arguably achieved by the mid-1960s—and then maintenance of France to *great power* status.[138] Only on that basis could he hope to achieve his other foreign policy aims:

> To assure security in Western Europe by removing any threat from the Reich: to collaborate with both the West and East, if necessary contracting alliances with one side or the other without ever placing France in a dependent position . . . to group together from the political, economic and strategic points of view the states bordering on the Alps and the Pyrenees to make this organization one of the three World Powers and even probably one day arbiter between the rival camps of the Russians and the Anglo-Saxons.[139]

Restoration of French great power meant, in turn, French leadership of a politically and economically integrated Europe of some form. As historian Alan Milward has persuasively argued, European integration represented not the transcendence of the nation-state but precisely the opposite, its rescue, and particularly the rescue of France.[140]

Beyond integration of economic spheres of domestic life, therefore, de Gaulle saw Europe as a "third force" in world politics, capable of acting alongside the superpowers and on equal terms. The notion of the third force, however, posed the question of whether Britain was a suitable partner in the venture, since the country's size meant that unlike the remainder of the Six—with the exception of Germany, which, for political and historical reasons, was unlikely to challenge French authority—could be nothing other than a partner. Elsewhere, the image was of "a cosy cottage with the General sitting in the grandfather's chair and being opposed to the idea of a game of musical chairs being played for his seat. The General had had enough trouble with Germany and the other members already in this respect and did not want Britain to join in the game as well."[141] And once Britain had joined the community, France would be unable to prevent Britain from shaping the EEC's future development.

Fundamental to the question of Britain's suitability, as in the first application, was its relationship with the United States, which was so important for de Gaulle because of the threat that he believed America presented to his vision of Europe. As the general explained to Brown in December 1966,

> France had two reasons for considering the American issue fundamental. One, that if France did not exist independently standing on her own two feet, one day she would be annexed. Two, that the extension of Europe eastwards was difficult to reconcile with the maintenance of special relations with the United States.[142]

As a result, it was clear that Britain was not a suitable member of the "club." As the Cabinet Committee on Europe suggested, de Gaulle's "intention is clearly a third force in Europe led by France in isolation from the United States. Britain is not to be a member, or at any rate not a founder member, of this Europe."[143] As Michael Foot argued in the May 1967 Commons debate, "The French will not agree to a proposition that we should go into Europe and sustain the kind of relationship the present Government has sustained with the United States."[144]

Again, this information was clear to policymakers both in London and Washington. US ambassador to London David Bruce told Wilson, "de Gaulle's anti-American feeling was basic to his whole philosophy. The General's suspicions of Britain derived from this attitude."[145] However, Bruce coupled this statement with a knee-jerk defense of strong US-UK ties: "It was a pipe dream for de Gaulle to believe that he could in the long run divide Britain from the United States."[146] But this diplomatic issue could only be fudged to a very limited degree. UK policymakers, therefore, had first to try to ascertain whether, as in 1963, the closeness of US-UK relations really was a red line for de Gaulle. A testy exchange during Georges Pompidou's July 1966 visit illustrates the problem of broaching the question head-on:

> [Wilson] At the end of the day, would we have to choose between the United States and Europe?
>
> Pompidou said he found this question difficult to understand. Britain was a European country and he failed to see why Britain, or indeed any other European nation, should feel that they were confronted with a choice between Europe and the United States.

The Prime Minister agreed that geographically Britain was a European power. But she had certain roles to fulfill outside Europe, including a limited and diminishing East of Suez role; we still had other obligations there. . . . [W]ould continuing this role make us "bad Europeans"?

[Wilson] What about relations with the United States?

[Wilson] Did the French really think that if we now continued in close association with the United States this would be inconsistent with an effective relationship with Europe?

M. Pompidou repeated that he still could not understand why relations with the United States were made such an issue. France too wished to have the friendliest relationship with the United States. But they also desired to prove their distinctive identity. Surely this must be true of Britain as well?

[Wilson] asked again in the French view, was the present state of relations with the United States incompatible with joining the EEC?[147]

Simply by putting the matter in such stark terms, the British signaled to the French that any distancing from the United States would not be genuine, making the British bid all the more likely to fail.

Britain nonetheless attempted to gain French support on the basis of a rhetorical emphasis on what the two countries shared when it came to their visions of Europe, not what divided them. First, Wilson and Brown stressed the extent to which Britain and France shared a reluctance to cede sovereignty to supranational institutions—exemplified by Britain's refusal to join in the creation of the EEC in the late 1950s and de Gaulle's attack on the community during the Empty Chair Crisis. Second, they stressed Britain's commitment to strengthening Europe's voice in world affairs and what Britain could add to this Europe, specifically in the area of technology. "The decisive argument had been political. By this he meant argument expressed in terms of the need to strengthen the voice of Europe in world affairs, of which Britain formed a part. But it would be a feeble voice as long as we and Europe did not put forth our full economic strength."[148]

De Gaulle was not persuaded, as British officials knew. According to one report, De Gaulle "is not yet convinced of the 'non-American' orientation of our general policy, despite the very clear way in which the Prime Minister explained [their] parallelism."[149] As the general explained in December 1966, "There were very many reasons why France and Britain were indispensable partners if they wanted to have the right kind of Europe"; however, the right kind of Europe "was something that was not American. If it was American, it would not be European."[150] By asking where Britain stood on this question, de Gaulle was forcing Wilson's government to make a choice, or at least betray its unwillingness to do so—an unwillingness that was clear from internal discussions. Aware that the Americans did not see an Atlantic arrangement as an alternative to British membership only strengthened de Gaulle's hand. In summing up his June 1967 discussions with Wilson, for example, the French president argued that Wilson's threatened "Atlantic grouping[,] which would constitute an even greater and more complete domination by the United States in technology, industry, finance, and politics than ever before . . . did not appeal to France."[151] Indeed, France "had accepted with resignation a policy of European integration . . . precisely in order to escape such domination."[152] However, given that Britain might want such American domination, "British entry [into the EEC] would not enable Europe to avoid such an Atlantic prospect. The purpose of French membership on the other hand was to prevent it."[153]

De Gaulle thus skillfully exploited the weakness of Britain's position. French officials consistently professed support for Britain's bid and denied the very possibility of a veto. "There was not either on [de Gaulle's] part personally or on that of France any objection in principle to the entry of Britain into the EEC," the general stated in his 16 May 1967 "velvet veto."[154] "On the contrary once she was ready to come in she would be welcome . . . it all depended on" Britain.[155] Given the fundamental differences of opinion, however, it was clear that France did not yet deem Britain ready: "without saying so explicitly," Patrick Reilly wrote in his summary of the meeting with de Gaulle, "he clearly implied that it all added up to an insurmountable series of obstacles."[156] De Gaulle sought to pressure Britain to drop the bid before negotiations began, since the French leader was aware that the use of a formal veto would might prove unpopular domestically and with the other members of the EEC. In April 1967, Brown told Wilson, "We must bear in mind that we have all along believed the General's objective to be to stop us *now* if he can—before we have made our application."[157] The general's alternative to entry was "association"—a connection between the EEC and the United Kingdom (and perhaps other EFTA members), short of full membership. For Britain, however, association was a nonstarter. At his 6 October

1967 meeting with Reilly, de Gaulle referred "regretfully to association as a sensible solution if only he would accept it."[158]

When threats did not work, Brown and Wilson turned to baser tactics: flattery and pleas for mercy. "The voice of France is listened to nowadays at it had not been 10 years ago when she was economically weak," Wilson told de Gaulle in June 1967, "drifting and in a real sense divided. The same was true of Europe today."[159] Playing to de Gaulle's ego in praising France's postwar recovery, however, was unlikely to convince the general that the strong UK-French partnership to lead Europe by which Wilson and Brown had set such store was worth the perceived risk. Her Majesty's Government's last throw of the dice was to reassure the general of its sincerity. Wilson wrote in a private telegram to de Gaulle—itself another trust-building move between Britain and France— that the decision to apply had been made with "confiden[ce] that it is the right one for Britain and for the future of Britain. I know that you too will consider it with the utmost care and in a spirit of friendship and goodwill."[160] De Gaulle considered it with the utmost care but on the basis of role-related expectations, not sentiment.

CONCLUSION

Britain's second failed attempt within a decade to join the EEC was not the foreign policy disaster the first had been. Unlike in 1963, there was no pronounced sense of shock when de Gaulle closed the door on British accession in December 1967. Everyone involved had realized that rejection was a strong possibility from the outset. It was, however, an important watershed in post-war British foreign policy—the moment at which both major political parties converged on a commitment to UK membership in the project of "ever closer union."[161] The chapter thus sides with the emerging historical consensus that Britain's second application was a "successful failure": its primary purpose was to ensure entry in the future, whenever that might be, not immediately, as is indicated by the fact that the veto did not spell the end of the Wilson government's efforts to gain membership.[162] The application maintained the pressure on the Community to allow Britain to enter at the soonest possible moment, and that pressure bore fruit in 1973, when the UK, along with Ireland and Denmark, signed the Treaty of Rome.

The chapter has argued that despite coming to power with a membership divided on the issue of EEC membership, the Labour government soon felt various pressures to make a new approach—from domestic groups within Britain as well as the United States, other EFTA states, and the Friendly Five. These pressures meant that it became more difficult to justify staying out than going in. This is not to argue that there was no alternative; rather, it is to show how even clear French opposition and the consequent likelihood of a veto could not dampen this pro-European spirit. Once again rejecting as oversimplified an explanation of Britain's turn to Europe based on the notion of identity or preferences, the chapter has demonstrated that it was made possible by the roles that emerged for Britain, France, the United States, and the Five prior to and during the accession bid. Waxing rhetorical in the Commons on 10 May 1967, George Brown argued that "we, a European country, still have a crucial and influential role to play in the world. And how we are to play it is really what we are considering today."[163] Britain, he continued, had an opportunity "to play our part in reasserting Europe's role in the world and with Europe, to reassert our own role."[164] Brown's folk wisdom masked deeper truths: Britain's membership bid was not a choice for Europe over "the world," it was a self-conscious attempt to strengthen Britain's "world role."[165] As Wilson told Johnson in July 1966,

> There were those in the United Kingdom and perhaps even a majority of the British Press, who would prefer us to give up our world role and to concentrate on securing entry into the European Economic Community, even if this meant accepting terms dictated by the French Government. . . . We were not prepared to endorse the concept of a merely inward-looking European role for Britain, with no Atlantic or Pacific part to play; it would be better to wait for the ordinary laws of mortality remove the French obstacle to entering the European Community on acceptable terms.[166]

As Parr notes, then, "Entry into the European Community was the only means by which Britain could preserve a global presence" beyond the 1960s.[167] The next chapter turns to a signal crisis in Britain's postwar foreign policy centered on this continued global presence.

CHAPTER FIVE

Britain's Reinvasion of the Falklands, 1982

BRITAIN'S MILITARY AND political readjustments of the late 1960s and early 1970s were based on the assumption that although the UK was not merely a "European" power, since it retained worldwide interests, it would not be required to defend those interests against a sophisticated enemy far from British shores except in conjunction with allies such as the United States. Consequently, Britain was not thought to need extensive power-projection capabilities for colonial-type missions; after all, Britain had few colonies left, and it remained in those colonies with their consent.[1] British defense policy, therefore, focused on the nuclear deterrent, conventional troop deployments in Europe, and antisubmarine warfare against Russia in the North Atlantic.[2] This thinking led to the abandonment of Britain's remaining aircraft carriers in the mid-1970s, the decision to cease using the naval base at Simonstown, South Africa, and a series of deep cuts in the armed forces, especially the Navy, during the first years of Margaret Thatcher's premiership.[3] Following the Argentine invasion of the Falkland Islands on 2 April 1982, however, Thatcher's Conservative government faced a situation of precisely this type—if, that is, it decided to try to retake the islands and was unable to do so by diplomatic means.[4]

The invasion of the Falklands would not only test the "Iron Lady's" mettle[5] but would represent a key test of Britain's sense of self in the 1980s. Would Britain accept the role cast on it by Argentina of a *colonial power,* which should not—and indeed could not—react with force to restore its sovereignty over the islands? Britain did not accept this role, instead sending a naval task force to the South Atlantic and removing Argentine forces from the islands. It did so because it was able, in interaction with important others—primarily, and again rather predictably by now, the United States—to make a *residual great power* role instead: in this context, that role meant standing up for the primary rules and principles of international society in reversing Argentina's invasion, by force if necessary. Doing so was no easy task: in an international environment hostile to any hint of colonialism and the reckless use of force, this role did not go unchallenged. Throughout the conflict, Argentina charged Britain with outdated and aggressive conduct; British policymakers were thus preoccupied with presenting the action as rightful and necessary, a precarious diplomatic and military task that would likely have failed without American support.

Following a historical overview of the main events, this chapter begins the analysis of Britain's actions during the Falklands War by examining the initial role assignments that emerged after the Argentine invasion. Britain had little international support on the substance of the conflict and thus had a difficult task in defending itself against being alter-cast as the "colonial" aggressor. The chapter then discusses the role Britain took from others in Europe and the commonwealth. The fourth and fifth sections subsequently address the role Britain tried to make in response—once again termed *residual great power*—and hence the opening up of a space for resolute military action. The discussion focuses on the international principles that Britain argued it was acting to protect and the identity-based arguments that underpinned Britain's firm response to the Argentine invasion. The chapter then turns to the most important other in the Falklands episode: the US, the only actor capable of fundamentally affecting the outcome of the dispute. Because Washington remained neutral during the first phase of the conflict, Britain was not prevented from attempting to make a problematic *residual great power* role. A brief section draws together these themes and concludes the chapter, and with it the empirical sections of the book.

THE FALKLANDS WAR—HISTORICAL BACKGROUND AND PUZZLE

The Falkland Islands/Las Malvinas lie some four hundred miles northeast of the southern tip of Argentina and approximately eight thousand miles from the UK. In 1982, the islands were populated by fewer than two thousand people, of predominantly British extraction and by all accounts unanimous in their desire to remain under the British Crown.[6] British claims to sovereignty derive from the islanders' right to self-determination and Britain's unbroken administration since 1833.[7] Argentina also lays claim to sovereignty over the islands, primarily on the basis of inheritance from the Spanish South American Empire, from which Argentina became independent in 1816.[8] Whereas before 1982 the islands had barely registered on the radar of British politics, the perceived injustice of Britain's possession of the islands and Argentina's unresolved claim stood at the center of Argentina's national histories and foundational myths.[9] In the anticolonial postwar atmosphere, the Argentine claim resurfaced, and in 1965, UN Resolution 2065 was passed, urging the two parties to seek a negotiated settlement.[10]

Negotiations began shortly thereafter and lasted until early 1982, when, exasperated by the lack of progress and the impending 150th anniversary of Britain's seizure of the islands, the Argentine ruling junta began to prepare for an invasion.[11] During the negotiations, London had put forward numerous plans in the belief that, the sovereignty issue aside, the Falklands' future prosperity would indeed be secured only by close and amicable relations with the Argentine mainland, whatever form they might take. However, initiatives such as a proposed "leaseback" agreement only raised suspicions among the islanders and their lobby in London that Britain was looking to "sell them out."[12] Such is the intractable nature of sovereignty disputes, by early 1982, the British negotiators were left with no other option than to continue to talk for the sake of talking, with little to offer the Argentines, who would settle for nothing less than a full transfer of sovereignty.[13]

The Argentine invasion of 2 April 1982 has typically been explained as the action of a fascist dictatorship seeking foreign victories to hide domestic failures.[14] But it was also a genuine attempt to change the situation in Argentina's favor based on the belief that the international community would remain silent and that Britain would not attempt reinvasion.[15] However, British admiral Sir Henry Leach informed Thatcher soon after the invasion that contrary to received wisdom, the Royal Navy could launch a task force capable of reinvasion, prompting the prime minister to order him to do just that.[16] The first ships designated to the force set sail on 3 April; after reaching the islands, the British force implemented a total exclusion zone.[17] While the British forces were augmented with a view to reinvasion, naval and air forces clashed, resulting in the loss of numerous Argentine aircraft and the destruction of an Argentine ship, the *Belgrano,* on 2 May and of the British destroyer HMS *Sheffield* the following day.[18] On 26 April, British forces recaptured the island of South Georgia, also claimed by Argentina and captured prior to the main Falklands operation. On 21 May, British troops landed on East Falkland. Fighting continued until Argentine forces surrendered on 14 June.[19]

The Argentine invasion caused consternation and bewilderment in the international community in almost equal measure. The US was "simply astounded at the prospect of conflict." President Ronald Reagan could not fathom how war was possible over that "little ice-cold bunch of land down there."[20] After the initial shock wore off and with the British task force on its way, diplomatic initiatives designed to reach a negotiated solution began. International efforts took place in two distinct phases. During April, while the British force sailed south and conflict was preventable, US secretary of state Alexander Haig undertook a round of shuttle diplomacy between Buenos Aires and London.[21] The UN Security Council had already passed Resolution 502, which demanded immediate Argentine withdrawal from the islands.[22] Britain also secured support from the EEC in the form of a trade embargo. The Haig mission failed to arrive at a solution acceptable to both sides; judgments differ as to how close it came with its plan of mutual withdrawal of forces and a neutral interim authority.[23] The failure marked the beginning of a new episode in the conflict, as America openly "tilted" toward Britain. This period was marked by worsening conflict and the eventual defeat of Argentina, together with more urgent diplomatic initiatives, most notably through the UN secretary-general, Javier Pérez de Cuellar.[24] He too, however, failed to gain agreement on a simpler plan, while concurrent military activity progressively reduced the range of options acceptable to the belligerents.

The puzzles of the Falklands War are straightforward: Why did Argentina's invasion lead Thatcher's government to launch and carry out a risky reinvasion plan? And risky it certainly was: British military success was far from assured.[25] The window of opportunity for an assault against the islands was narrow, with the South Atlantic winter fast approaching, and although Argentina's armed forces were inferior to Britain's, they were certainly not negligible: the Argentine Air Force, armed with French-made Super Étendard jets and Exocet missiles, was a particular threat.[26] The islands' distance from the UK also rendered military operations a serious logistical challenge. Why, then, did Britain and Argentina fail to come to terms without the use of force? Secondary puzzles include the question of why the United States supported Britain's actions in the Falklands. How did this case differ from the Suez episode?

GREAT POWER OR COLONIAL POWER?
INITIAL ROLE ASSIGNMENTS

Two roles emerged to structure the interaction between Britain and Argentina following the Argentine invasion of the Falklands/Malvinas, those of *aggressor* and *victim*. The ability to cast the other into the role of the aggressor, in the knowledge that doing so would rally international support to their cause, meant that from the outset, Britain and Argentina each tried hard to portray itself as the victim. For many, Argentina's invasion of the islands and the disregard the move showed to the principle of nonuse of force to settle international disputes automatically cast Buenos Aires into the role of aggressor, with London assuming the role of the aggrieved party. But Britain's military response generated significant hostility, with the consequence that this alter-casting process continued throughout the conflict. Argentina sought to cast Britain into the role of a *colonial power;* British policymakers tried to make a role that was explicitly not colonialist in nature but was a *residual great power* role.

Argentine leaders sought to justify their actions by casting their country into the role of the victim of colonial aggression. This strategy had two aspects. First, it highlighted the injustice of Argentina's position and argued that Britain's military response cast it into the role of aggressor. This task required playing down the argument that Argentina had broken international law and emphasizing the strength of its claim to the islands. Since Las Malvinas were deemed sovereign Argentine territory, the use of force to take control could not be construed as aggression.[27] In short, if Argentina rightfully had sovereignty over the islands and their dependencies, retaking them was an acceptable sovereign action. While this argument did not quite make Argentina the victim, it was also not the aggressor. Argentina's case was further strengthened by reference to the precedent of India's annexation of Goa from the Portuguese in 1967[28] and by the largely bloodless nature of Argentina's operations on the Falklands and South Georgia, which the Argentines cited as evidence of their nonaggressive intentions.[29] Finally, Argentina argued that the islanders' rights and property would be respected and that it would be more than generous to the island's people if they swiftly came to terms with the new status quo.[30] By presenting the invasion as a peaceful fait accompli, Argentina sought to deny Britain any reason to challenge it through military means.

The second aspect to the Argentine strategy was actively to cast Britain into the role of aggressor. As ambassador to the UN Eduardo Roca argued in a letter to the president of the Security Council, "The means employed by the British Government and their unilateral acts have created a situation of serious tension whose continuation could jeopardize the maintenance of international peace and security."[31] Buenos Aires was helped in its strategy by the overtly colonial nature of Britain's possession of the Falkland Islands, the automatically anticolonial attitude of the majority of states in the world, and by Britain's history as the imperial power par excellence. Foreign Minister Carlos Mendez epitomized the latter impression when he told Haig during the secretary of state's visit to Buenos Aires on 15 April that although he agreed that international law did not permit Argentine actions, he also thought that "no one can challenge Great Britain on her title of world champion on the use of force in the conquest of her territories."[32] For Argentina, pointing out the historical inconsistencies that accompanied pictures of a British armada setting sail for the South Atlantic was sufficient to cast Britain into the role of colonial aggressor.

This argument had some purchase in the international community.[33] A majority of UN members sympathized with the anticolonial underpinnings of Argentina's position even if they understood Britain's predicament. As Pérez de Cuellar later wrote, even his undersecretary, Rafeeuddin Ahmed, who was in charge of the negotiating task force, "being a Pakistani . . . could not help but be hostile to colonialism in any form, and the Falklands were unquestionably a colonial possession."[34] British leaders were aware of this. UK ambassador to the United Nations Anthony Parsons had immediately stressed to the Foreign Office the tenuousness of Britain's support in New York: "It became only too clear that as I have consistently reported, we have virtually no support on the substance of the problem. We must bear this in mind for the future in the UN context."[35]

Not even everyone in Britain was convinced the issue was not colonial. As member of Parliament Andrew Faulds argued in the Commons debate on 20 May, "We should frankly admit that for 20 years we have been trying to withdraw from this outpost of empire, if we could decently cede sovereignty. Every British ambassador over that period will confirm that view."[36] Faulds consequently opposed the deployment of the task force. "For an ex-imperial power to embark on a course of negotiations by pounding shot and shell in countries of the Third world is not an advisable policy," he argued.[37] Some commentators have followed suit in viewing the war as a colonial one. In his study of the domestic political context of the war, for example, historian George Dillon refers to the conflict as "a microcosm of imperial retreat and colonial enterprise in decline,"[38] noting that "British decision-makers . . . were often trapped by a defence culture imbued with nostalgia for the global age of British power."[39] What reasons other than colonial designs could account for the determination to restore British administration?

But the argument that Britain was the aggressor and that the issue was one of colonial possession had little purchase in the British debate over the appropriate response to the invasion. British officials and policymakers, conversely, attempted to reinforce what seemed to them the initial role assignments and tried to strengthen those revised assignments among the international community. Thatcher began this process immediately in her speech that opened the emergency Commons debate the day after the invasion. "I am sure the whole House will join me," she said, "in condemning this totally unprovoked aggression by the Government of Argentina against British territory."[40] "It has," she went on, "not a shred of justification and not a scrap of legality."[41] Sir Anthony Parsons had done likewise at the UN two days previously. "We are not the aggressors, as my Argentine colleague has again and again suggested we are," he appealed to the president of the UN Security Council on 1 April. "What possible or conceivable reason could we have for aggressive intent?"[42] The British line, therefore, was that it was the victim of aggressive action by Argentina and consequently deserved the international community's support. To reiterate the point, the identification of Argentina as the aggressor was a prominent feature of British discourse surrounding the conflict.[43]

The definition of Argentina's actions as "the invasion of British sovereign territory by a foreign power,"[44] Nora Femenia has argued, enabled their "characterization as unprovoked, unexpected, naked, foul and brutal aggression."[45] This approach, in turn, had important implications. In particular, it shifted the blame firmly away from the governments, amid demonstrations of domestic dissatisfaction at its failure to resolve the situation. At the same time it challenged the British people to put it right.[46] It therefore also underpinned arguments in favor of a swift military response. Resorting to the exhortation, "We are not the aggressors" served as a rallying call to those in and around the British policymaking establishment that Britain was in the right in sending a task force, despite the inevitable desire of many to avoid military confrontation. This became imperative as the conflict worsened, and specifically following the sinking of an Argentine ship, the *Belgrano,* on 2 May. As Patrick Cormack urged in an exchange in the Commons two days later, amid calls for a peaceful settlement, probably through the UN, "Will [Foreign Secretary Francis Pym] lose no chance to point out that the responsibility for the tragic deaths in the South Atlantic lies fairly and squarely with President [Leopoldo] Galtieri and the junta?"[47] In other words, Britain's response was justified because the other side had "started it."[48]

Britain held other high cards when it came to casting Argentina as the aggressor. In particular, the Argentine regime and domestic situation was one that aroused little sympathy. As Sir Bernard Braine, a member of Parliament, stressed during the emergency debate, "We are dealing here not with a democratic country that has some claim to the Falkland Islands—with which the matter could be thrashed out in a civilised way—but with a Fascist, corrupt and cruel regime."[49] Braine was referring to the Argentine junta's "dirty war" against Peronistas and other political opponents, leading to the disappearance of thousands in the years before the invasion.[50] Member of Parliament Arthur Palmer's assertion in the Commons that "the regime in Argentina is . . . an evil regime"[51] was widely repeated during debates in Britain. In the first debate on 3 April, for example, Labour Party leader Michael Foot reminded MPs that "thousands of innocent people fighting for their political rights in Argentina are in prison and have been tortured and debased. We cannot forget that fact when our friends and fellow citizens in the Falkland Islands are suffering."[52] As Freedman and Stonehouse-Gamba have noted, even the many ex-colonial states that populated the UN General Assembly "were not [Argentina's] natural allies. It had not given much support to anti-colonial campaigns of others nor shown much sympathy for those issues which mattered most to this group."[53] The nature of the Argentine regime thus favored Britain's interpretation of the events.[54]

Nevertheless, Argentina's emphasis on the wrongs of the British seizure of the islands in 1833 jarred too readily with the colonial experience of a large number of the international community to be ignored simply as a consequence of the unsavory character of the regime in Buenos Aires. As historian Hugh Bicheno has caustically noted, "There are few regimes so disgusting that the 'international community' will bring effective pressure to bear on them. . . . In practice a regime may do whatever it likes so long as it pays the bills and does not attack the interests of another strong enough to punish it."[55] In particular, hemispheric solidarity brought Argentina automatic support from a number of countries. For the most part this was declaratory, as the South American context simply could not offer displays of support comparable to what Britain might receive from its neighborhood. As Thatcher chided in the Commons on 14 April,

What have the Argentines been able to produce to balance this solidarity in support of our cause? Some Latin American countries have, of course, repeated their support for the Argentine claim to sovereignty. We always knew they would. But only one of them has supported the invasion, and nearly all have made clear their distaste and disapproval that Argentina should have resorted to aggression. . . . Almost the only country whose position has been shifting towards Argentina is the Soviet Union. We can only guess at the cynical calculations which lie behind this move.[56]

But South American support was not negligible, as the conflict offered opportunities to countries such as Peru, Venezuela, and Brazil "to make their mark on regional politics and extend their influence in Washington,"[57] despite the self-created isolation of the Argentines. The staunchest supporter of Buenos Aires turned out to be Panama, which attempted, beyond vigorous proclamations of support for Argentina and anger at Britain made by its diplomats, to block the passage of Resolution 502 by putting forward a procedural motion that would have delayed the vote, thereby making passage in its then current form all the more unlikely.[58]

It is of course to be expected that each side would try to cast each other in a negative and bellicose light and gain support from members of the international community. What make this alter-casting process of interest are the rhetorical strategies they used to justify their actions and condemn those of the other and what these strategies tell us about the salient expectations attached to them—and particularly of Britain. These wider expectations emerged from the intense interactions of the Falklands War that provide the material with which to explain Britain's response.

TAKING THE RESIDUAL GREAT POWER ROLE: EUROPEAN AND COMMONWEALTH PERSPECTIVES

The colonial overtones of Britain's possession of the Falkland Islands narrowed considerably the number of acceptable responses to Argentina's actions for the Thatcher government. Overt British jingoism and warmongering would be interpreted as the revival of an imperial and militaristic heritage, ill suited to the postimperial environment of international politics at the beginning of the 1980s, and would lead to international condemnation and pressure to reverse course. The "more the Falklands could be presented as a matter of colonialism," the war's official historian, Lawrence Freedman has noted, "which is how it had previously been developed in the General Assembly, the more awkward Britain's position would become."[59]

Although sections of the British press were strongly jingoistic, British policy-makers and officials steered clear of any language and diplomatic maneuvers that might be interpreted as giving extra credence to this interpretation.[60] Opposition leader Michael Foot set the tone during the 3 April debate: "There is no question in the Falkland Islands of any colonial dependence or anything of the sort."[61] Such statements implied that Britain could go about making a different role in the interaction with Argentina over the Falkland Islands, a role that did not equate a military response with colonialism. This can be again understood in terms of a *residual great power* role.

To reiterate, from a micro-interactionist constructivist perspective—as opposed to one based on structuralist understandings of what roles are and how they work—the intention is not to outline a priori what great powers in general would be expected to do in a situation such as the Falklands crisis. Doing so would leave unexplored precisely what the approach seeks to grasp: how British foreign policymakers came to understand what actions were expected of them in response to the invasion. The task, rather, is to interpret what expectations emerged for Britain through the taking of the roles of important others and on that basis what role Britain could make in terms of appropriate actions and what alter-casting attempts were present. In other words, the expectations attached to Britain and consequently the creation of a space of possible action for British policymakers do the explaining, not a transhistorical *great power* role. Naming the role throughout here serves as a hook on which to hang the expectations, to keep them at the forefront of the reader's mind. The *residual great power* role during the Falklands Crisis both included a military response to the invasion and excluded associations with imperial ambitions.

Contrary to identity- or preference-based explanations of foreign policy, a micro-interactionist constructivist approach stresses that this role emerged in interaction with important others. Britain's taking of the role of the US over the Falklands was central. Also crucial was the European perspective. Britain took the role of its partners in the European Community and its rejection of the colonial connotations of its action was bolstered by the moral and economic support the EEC offered in the dispute's opening phase.[62] An arms embargo was immediately put into place, while a ban on imports came into effect on 16 April. Given the difficulties of finding common ground among the ten members, these efforts were significant. Indeed, as Geoffrey Edwards has noted, "The Community and its member states have rarely moved with such speed as they did in the Falklands case."[63]

The imposition of an EEC trade embargo was more than symbolic, suggesting that European support was genuine. Because Europe was Argentina's largest market, the embargo had significant potential to damage the Argentine economy.[64] As Pym crowed in the Commons on 14 April, "To see about one quarter of [Argentina's] export trade wiped out at a stroke was a body blow to its already rather shaky economy."[65] This development was also significant since it went against the expressed interests of some member states, most notably the Republic of Ireland, which more than any other state was sensitive to the colonial overtones of British military action, and Italy, which had cultural links to Argentina and trade interests in Argentine leather and beef. Liberal leader David Steel stressed in the House of Commons on 13 May,

> The importance of external opinion should not be underrated. European opinion, not only European Governments but the European Parliament, which has twice passed resolutions on this . . . is in full support of resolution 502 and in full condemnation of the Argentine position. It is important that European governments support us, particularly on the economic front. When one considers that 40 per cent. of the Argentine population are of Italian descent, one realizes the enormous significance of the support that the Italian Government has given us, as have others. The Government are right to stress the solidarity of European opinion.[66]

Even Thatcher, no great supporter of Europe, managed a note of thanks in the House when stressing the importance of European efforts.[67]

Among the Europeans, the French were particularly staunch in their support for Britain, in large measure as a consequence of the implications of Britain's response to the invasion for France's remaining overseas territories and possessions.[68] The supply of French-made Exocet missiles to Argentina and allied countries was halted, while the British received technical information on French Mirage jets in service with the Argentine Air Force as well as some of the jets themselves for training purposes.[69] France also persuaded Senegal to allow British aircraft to land in Dakar, releasing some of the mounting pressure on the Wideawake Airfield at Ascension Island.[70] British minister of defence John Nott later noted, "In so many ways Mitterrand and the French were our greatest allies"[71] during the conflict, but that fact was recognized at the time. Foot noted "how strongly the President of France spoke out" in Britain's favor on 3 April, urging that "every other country in the world speak out in a similar way."[72] Even after France and other European nations voted for a UN resolution calling for an immediate cease-fire shortly before Argentina's surrender on the Falklands, appreciation of French support remained strong. Asked by member of Parliament John Townend whether the government had been "surprised and disappointed at the failure of the French Government to join Britain and the United States in vetoing the ceasefire resolution,"[73] Pym responded simply that British leaders had been "grateful throughout for the general support which France has given us."[74] Others seconded his statement.[75]

Finally, Britain took the role of *residual great power* from prominent members of the commonwealth, chief among them Australia and New Zealand. The latter banned not only imports from Argentina, a move also taken by Canada, Australia, and later Norway, but also exports, earning strong praise from Thatcher. "The New Zealand people have been absolutely magnificent in their support of this country," she stated on 20 May. Moreover, Robert Muldoon, New Zealand's prime minister, had "only yesterday, reminded me 'Don't forget. In New Zealand, we are still a member of the same family.'"[76] The impression, then, was that a significant proportion of opinion beyond Europe felt that Britain had a right to reinvade the Falklands and that colonialism was not at issue. As Edward Gardner reported to Parliament on 22 April, "Those of us . . . who have just returned from the spring meeting of the I[nter] P[arliamentary] U[nion] in Lagos found that delegates from all parts of the Commonwealth recognised the justice of our cause, and expressed firm and unequivocal support for what Her Majesty's Government are now doing to deal with the crisis."[77] The point was reiterated at each debate held during the conflict. "The Commonwealth remains steadfast and resolute in its backing for our stand," Pym stated on 13 May.[78]

It is unlikely, however, that even European and commonwealth support alone would have been sufficient to stave off charges of colonialism on Britain's part. The flip side to taking the role of *residual great power,* therefore, was the need to actively make that role, and doing so meant behaving in such a way that respected norms and rules of international society—again, typical of *great powers.*

"WITH GREAT POWER . . .": MAKING THE
RESIDUAL GREAT POWER ROLE

For the British, in the *residual great power* role, the main issue at stake over the Falklands was not the sovereignty of a small collection of islands in the South Atlantic or even the future of the islands' population, although these phenomena certainly represented the form the crisis took. The main issue was the violation of the principles of international conduct committed by Argentina through its invasion and the risk that this action would set a precedent in international affairs.[79] These seemingly lofty principles were self-determination, the sanctity of international law, and perhaps most important, the nonuse of force to settle disputes. Although the invasion of the Falkland Islands provided the substance of Britain's grievance with Argentina, Britain sought to uphold these principles by sending a task force to the South Atlantic.

The attempt to make a *residual great power* role manifested itself in the central place given to the defense of international law and order in British discourse surrounding the Falklands War. Typical was Michael English's declaration in the House of Commons on 7 April: "The most important thing is that what we are defending is the rule of law in the world."[80] So too was Foreign Secretary Pym's assertion that Britain should "see to it that Argentina's illegal and intolerable defiance of the international community and of the rule of law is not allowed to stand."[81] Foot extended the rule of law to include the United Nations charter. "It is that charter," he stressed, "and the United Nations as an institution, which are under threat."[82]

This legal argument underpinned a more general concern with the fabric of international order, loosely but not entirely equated with international law. As Pym reiterated on 4 May, "The re-establishment of international order on proper rules will bring an enormous amount of relief to an enormous number of countries and millions of individuals."[83] Put simply, if Argentina "got away with" the invasion of the Falkland Islands, what was to stop others around the world taking their disputes into their own hands? The number of similar territorial conflicts was too large to contemplate, above and beyond the most obvious examples of Taiwan, Gibraltar, and Sakhalin Island. Pym thus thundered,

> There are many such territories across the world which are vulnerable to aggression from powerful neighbours. The preservation of peace depends on the exercise of responsibility and restraint. It depends on the strong not taking the law into their own hands and imposing their rule on the weak. It depends on the international community supporting the principle of self-determination and punishing those who wilfully and forcibly violate that principle.[84]

Argentina itself had only recently rejected an independent arbitration decision by the Papacy over the country's dispute with Chile over the Beagle Channel Islands.[85] First submitted to the British Crown for a decision, the case was swiftly passed over to the Vatican, which found in favor of Chile. Argentina dismissed the result as nonconclusive as a consequence of British meddling. If Britain refused to stand up for the status quo in the Falklands, then many observers anticipated similar and possibly worse future infringements.

If Britain conceived of itself as a defender of international order, however, it is unsurprising that accusations of plain colonialism leveled against it appeared so strong to a good many members of the international community. The same principles Britain sought to defend were those that upheld an international status quo that many outside the most developed states considered in effect colonial. That fact was not lost on the Argentines: as Mendez reported to the Argentine cabinet on 8 April after his recent trip to Washington, "The major powers wished to preserve the international status quo and were unhappy with the precedent created by Argentina in the South Atlantic."[86] These principles rendered changes in the current territorial division, like those Argentina wanted to effect with regard to the Falkland Islands and its dependencies, difficult if not impossible. In many ways, therefore, the abstract roles of *colonial* and *residual great power* were two sides of the same coin.

Indeed, the thesis that Britain was motivated by international principles has found numerous opponents, who argue instead that these principled arguments were cynical ploys to cover other, less wholesome, motives. These other motives are not hard to identify: potential oil revenues, a sense of shame or a dose of national jingoism, a warmongering prime minister seeking to save her job, and of course colonialism.[87] However, a microinteractionist constructivist approach does not speculate about the existence of "real" motivations or efficient causes. Rather, it focuses on the emergence of role-based expectations and spaces of political action. It is thus crucial that British policymakers attempted to make a *residual great power role* by justifying Britain's response to the Argentine invasion of the Falkland Islands in terms of certain international principles of appropriate behavior and by acting accordingly.

In spite of the knowledge that the UN General Assembly, with its large number of postcolonial members, would be hostile to its case, British policymakers were aware that a complete lack of UN support would be more damaging than a potential anticolonial backlash. Throughout the conflict, the prime focus of domestic opposition to the response of the Thatcher government was the need for greater UN involvement.[88] It was thus a significant diplomatic coup that enabled Britain's ambassador to the United Nations, Sir Anthony Parsons, to gain the passage of Security Council Resolution 502 calling for an immediate cessation of hostilities, the withdrawal of Argentine troops, and the commencement of diplomatic efforts to solve the dispute.[89] Buenos Aires came up with its own interpretation of the resolution, which did not include the withdrawal of Argentine forces.[90] But Resolution 502 was a key element in Britain's attempt to make the role of *residual great power* in the aftermath of the Argentine invasion. It allowed Thatcher and her war cabinet to move forward militarily with a view to bringing about the situation called for by the resolution: a return to the island's preinvasion status. The resolution, together with Britain's strong position in the UN Security Council relative to Argentina and the commencement of US-sponsored negotiations, also moved the diplomatic action away from New York during the first phase of the conflict. This development suited Britain, helping to mute voices of international concern regarding the colonial overtones of the sending of the task force and thereby the possibility of combat, until Britain's forces had reached the islands—a journey of approximately three weeks.

Resolution 502 gave substance to Britain's assertion that it was not behaving in a colonial manner in preparing for potential reinvasion. Making a *residual great power* role based on upholding international law and order, however, also required Britain to abide by the other principles and norms that went along with a *great power* role—that is, proportionality of response and a commitment to finding peaceful settlements of disputes. With a large armada sailing to the South Atlantic, this idea represented a problem for the government. While Resolution 502 was a success from the British perspective in that it called for an immediate withdrawal of Argentine forces from the Falklands, it also called for the two belligerents to "seek a diplomatic solution to their differences and to respect fully the purposes and principles of the Charter of the United Nations."[91] Britain thus entered negotiations, first led by Haig and subsequently led by Pérez de Cuellar.

The extent to which Britain entered these negotiations in good faith is difficult to discern. There is reason to believe an agreement could have been reached as long as it included an Argentine withdrawal. Members of Parliament pressed the government on the need to court international opinion by negotiating seriously. Norman St. John-Stevas argued on 29 April, for example, that "there must be no suspicion in the minds of the leaders of other countries that we are not sincerely and committedly working for peace."[92] British leaders also repeatedly stated that diplomatic efforts were genuine. As Thatcher stated on 18 May,

> We have done everything that we can to try to secure a peaceful settlement. The Argentines have shown their intransigence by flouting every single part of the United Nations mandatory resolution. Not only did they flout the resolution, they have gone in the contrary direction by piling extra men and equipment into the islands.[93]

The next day, after Argentina's leaders had rejected the British proposals and the British government had withdrawn the offer, Thatcher reiterated that the proposals "represented a truly responsible effort to find a peaceful solution which both preserved the fundamental principles of our position and offered the opportunity to stop further loss of life in the South Atlantic."[94]

At the same time, British leaders professed their belief that the defense of the United Nations charter and principles of international law and order could be based on the use of force, thus justifying the task force. As Lord Privy Seal Humphrey Atkins argued on 2 April, Britain associated itself "immediately with a request from the President of the Security Council that both Britain and Argentina should exercise restraint and refrain from the use or threat of force, and continue the search for a diplomatic solution."[95] That said, "We are taking appropriate military and diplomatic measures to sustain our right under international law and in accordance with the provisions of the United Nations charter."[96] Thatcher argued similarly two weeks later, "We seek, and shall continue to seek, a diplomatic solution. [But d]iplomatic efforts are more likely to succeed if they are backed by military strength."[97] As possibility of war loomed larger, these vague statements were translated into clearer legal arguments, with the right of self-defense under Article 51 of the charter the linchpin of the British case. Argued Thatcher on 27 April,

> under the United Nations charter, until that resolution is complied with Great Britain has the right to self-defence under article 51. We have taken, and continue to take, the view that, unless we bring military presence to bear, the Argentines are unlikely to withdraw from the Falklands.[98]

More than a right, restoration of the Islanders' rights was considered a duty for many in Britain. For Pym, "If we do not stand par excellence—which we do—for international law and order, and if other countries with the same interest in parliamentary democracy do not join us in this endeavor, the outlook for the world is bleak."[99] For Rhodes James, "A strong, unambiguous and determined Britain is the best guarantor of the maintenance of peace and security in the world."[100] Britain was a great power, and great powers supported the United Nations and international law and order. Given the UN's inability to act on its own behalf, Owen stressed,

> the charter envisages the right of an independent nation to use all peaceful means to defend its interests. It is purely and rightly within the context of the United Nations charter that the British peacekeeping force has been despatched.[101]

Resolution 502 thus had important implications as the conflict progressed and particularly as the prospect of military confrontation changed from distant possibility to present reality. London's desire to justify the sending of a task force as a response to the invasion using arguments based on principle strengthened the instincts and wishes of many, at home and abroad, in favor of moderation. As member of Parliament Betty Boothroyd professed, while it was clear that UK had the ability and will to use military force, "If we believe in the rule of law, we must develop our actions in concert with the United Nations charter, to which we have been committed for many years."[102] Beyond negotiations, this idea meant—as had been the case for the Argentines—engaging in military actions aimed at restricting casualties. After informing the House of British forces' successful recapture of South Georgia, for example, Thatcher emphasized that "British forces throughout the operation used the minimum force necessary to achieve a successful outcome. No British casualties have been notified and it is reported only one Argentine sustained serious injuries."[103] Even if military action occurred in the Falklands, therefore, it would have to be proportionate to the aggression suffered. Failure to abide by these principles would certainly amplify colonial images and charges of hypocrisy. As Foot argued, Article 51 not only allowed self-defense but had other requirements, including reporting to the Security Council and to the United Nations on measures being taken. "Article 51 does not give this or any other country operating under it an unlimited right to act as it wishes," he warned.[104]

The sinking of the *Belgrano* on 2 May with the loss of 321 Argentine lives was therefore a notable turning point in the conflict, when the horror of modern warfare was made plain to every observer.[105] From that point until the end of the hostilities, international support for Britain weakened— despite the loss of a British ship the day after the *Belgrano* attack—and concern about the possible consequences of sustained military confrontation grew correspondingly.[106] An almost immediate consequence was the redoubling of diplomatic efforts aimed at bringing about a peaceful end to the dispute. Within hours of the ship's destruction, a peace plan sponsored by Peruvian president Belaunde Terry was put on the table.[107] Indeed, so soon after the incident—and so short-lived—was this initiative that the British government later faced charges that it had launched the attack on the Argentine ship in the deliberate hope of simultaneously torpedoing the initiative.[108] The Peruvian plan was quickly replaced by Pérez de Cuellar's offer to mediate, which continued throughout May and at one stage again came close to securing a cease-fire. However, both initiatives came to naught as the negotiating posture of both sides hardened.[109]

The need to be perceived as acting in a manner appropriate to the *great power* role became salient once again during the final phase of the war, after the total defeat of the Argentine forces had become a foregone conclusion. The US was particularly eager for Britain to remain "magnanimous" in victory; Washington supported Britain's attempt to stand up for the values and principles of the rule of law and nonuse of force but did not want the British to seem to be enjoying it.[110] From the sinking of the *Belgrano* until the end of military action on 14 June, therefore, Britain faced the task of avoiding charges of aggression and of taking jingoistic pleasure in military action, attempting instead to reiterate the principles underlying its response. However, Britain's military planners and task force commanders had to weigh these principles against the prevailing conditions in the South Atlantic. As was repeated on numerous occasions throughout May, it was not possible for the Royal Navy to "bob around down there" forever: every day that passed presented operational obstacles and made a potential invasion of the islands more hazardous, with the window of opportunity for a possible operation— 18–22 May—only likely to shrink further.[111] A space had opened up, however, in which Thatcher could launch a reinvasion, which she duly did.

AFFIRMING BRITAIN'S IDENTITY

Thatcher's decision to approve the reoccupation of the Falklands was made possible, then, by the emergence of a role for Britain consisting of a spirited rejection of the imperial role into which Argentina tried to cast Britain and the construction of a *residual great power* role in its stead. An important question remains, however: Why was Britain the type of actor that seemingly had to make a role for itself based on the defense of international principles and the demonstration of resolution in the face of aggression? In other words, why did British leaders choose to make a residual great power role? The notion of "identity"—or from a micro-interactionist perspective, the "self"— and the importance of role-playing as a vehicle for identity affirmation in international politics becomes apparent here. The arguments Britain's leaders put forward for making the *residual great power* role were frequently identity-based—about "who" Britain is and therefore who it should be. As a result, these arguments involved the use of prominent images and themes that attempt to capture the identity-forming aspects of reputation, honor, and collective esteem that made decisive counteraction appear necessary to the Thatcher government.

As the prime minister later made clear, Britain's honor was at stake in the Falklands: "We were defending the honour of our nation."[112] In this sense, Britain's defense of the rule of law and of right international conduct was related to more abstract notions such as the ability of Britain as a state to "hold its head high" in the world. Britain had to recover the islands, according to one member of the task force, "so that our children can walk about in the world with their heads high."[113] Failure, conversely, would bring shame on the nation, already humiliated from the Argentine invasion. "Britain has been humiliated," member of Parliament Sir Nigel Fisher stated plainly.[114] "The third naval power in the world, the second in NATO, has suffered a humiliating defeat," repeated Julian Amery, another member.[115] The implication was clear: Britain's self-esteem could best, perhaps only, be repaired by retaking the islands.

The desire for international esteem resonated with a still-prevalent feeling that Britain had recently lost its way internationally. Although typically exaggerated, Alan Clark's diary entries for the initial phases of the conflict are indicative. "It's all over," he exclaimed on 2 April, "We're a Third World Country, no good for anything."[116] During the emergency debate on 3 April, Foot asked, "What has happened to British diplomacy?"[117] Indeed, Bicheno has argued that prior to the Falklands War, British diplomats were commonly asked, "What has happened to your country?"[118] After the Falklands conflict, this question was no longer asked. But in the immediate aftermath of the invasion and until the task force reached the islands, many observers felt that Britain still had time to show the weakness that had characterized its recent history. As journalists Max Hastings and Simon Jenkins later noted, "The entire history of British foreign policy since Suez suggested that, after a period of prolonged dithering, a diplomatic settlement on the Falklands would be reached."[119] Or as member of Parliament Eric Ogden charged in the Commons, "I smell the smoke of appeasement. I smell a sell-out."[120]

The idea that Britain should therefore negotiate with the Argentines following what represented a clear breach of international law held little attraction for the Thatcher government for reasons that went beyond its own immediate survival. Negotiating would send a clear signal to the international community that Britain was no longer prepared to fight in such situations and would thus deprive it of any leverage in circumstances when Britain's immediate interests were not at stake. When Admiral Leach "learned of the imminent Argentine invasion [he] bypassed the chain of command to tell his Prime Minister that if a counter-invasion were not undertaken and carried through to a successful conclusion, then Britain would be a different country, one whose word would count for little."[121] Opined Winston Churchill in the Commons, "The failure to achieve these objectives would have repercussions beyond the fate of the Falkland Islanders and the Falkland Islands themselves. . . . Britain's standing and credibility in the world, in the eyes of both her adversaries with her allies, will be judged by the resolution and determination with which we meet this challenge."[122]

Attempting to reverse this course by sending a strong naval task force brought to the fore two particularly salient historical metaphors. The first was Suez, which proved something of a "how not to do it guide for Thatcher."[123] But as Healey told the House on 7 April, although "some people have sought to see a precedent for the dispatch of this force in what happened at Suez a quarter of a century ago," the analogy was inappropriate.

> The argument in Suez was about property rights—that in the Falkland Islands is about human rights. At Suez a British Government violated the United Nations charter. In the Falkland Islands crisis the Argentine Government have violated the United Nations charter and the British position has won overwhelming endorsement from the Security Council. Suez offers no precedent here.[124]

Thus although less salient, a more important image was that of Munich: the charge of appeasing dictators. Foreign Secretary Pym told the Commons in no uncertain terms that "Britain does not appease dictators."[125] Thatcher repeated the sentiment the following day.[126] By making this analogy, they offered another form of rationale beyond the necessity of supporting international law and the status quo under these specific circumstances: "What was the alternative?" Thatcher later argued, "That a common or garden dictator should rule over the Queen's subjects and prevail by fraud and violence? Not while I was Prime Minister."[127] Not responding strongly would have been, in this interpretation, tantamount to appeasement: Anthony Kershaw argued in the House,

> If we do not defend the Falkland Islands, some may believe that we will not defend other territories and interests. Would we be led, step by step, down a road of appeasement, which some of us have seen before? Would we defend ourselves in NATO? Would we even defend ourselves on this island? If such questions were asked and were not answered clearly, sooner or later the choice would be offered to us again and again until finally our option would be world war or defeat and humiliation.[128]

Beyond both of these historical analogies lay a less coherent but perhaps more powerfully held belief in the body politic that since Suez, Britain had indeed lost something and had been unable to regain it. Clark believed "that this is the last chance, the very last chance, for us to redeem out history over the past twenty five years, of which we may be ashamed and from which we may have averted our gaze."[129] This idea found most resonance in charges that the government, particularly the Foreign Office, had brought shame on Britain by attempting to negotiate a transfer of sovereignty to Argentina. This shame found its most powerful image in the photograph of the British garrison at Stanley lying facedown in a line after having surrendered to the Argentine invaders. For the sake of British honor, therefore, Argentina's invasion required an assertive response. This went beyond the question of Thatcher's job or the ability of the Conservative government to remain in power, although most observers agree that Thatcher would have resigned had she not made the "painful choice" to attempt recapture; the choice of Britain's response involved the issue of the country's future viability.[130] As Haig noted, "Mrs. Thatcher's objective, after all, was to demonstrate that Britain was still Britain."[131]

Britain's leaders consequently were expected at least to attempt to recover the islands, since it was clear from the outset that doing so would be impossible by diplomatic means alone. Otherwise, Britain would have to get used to a very different and reduced level of engagement in international affairs that was not in keeping with Britain's sense of self. As Clark suggested, the least Britain deserved was that "if we are going to go . . . let us go out in a blaze—then we can all sit back and comfortably become a nation of pimps and ponces, a sort of Macao to the European continent."[132] Even here, however, the implication that Britain must be something in the world is clear, even if it is merely an offshore hedonist paradise.

Throughout the conflict, therefore, British policymakers attempted to walk a tightrope between steadfast refusal to show weakness in the face of aggression, including an acceptance of the military consequences of that stance, and the necessities of making the role of a *residual great power*. Britain's leaders did so by displaying a deep ownership of the tenets of the international community and by justifying a military response in terms of moral principles and legal arguments. However, while both regional and international support was welcome and could be bolstered by carefully considered actions, the position of the United States remained of utmost importance.

A "DIFFICULT SITUATION FOR THE UNITED STATES": WASHINGTON AND BRITAIN'S ROLE

Britain's leaders expected American support for their cause from the outset. Thatcher and President Reagan had struck up a strong friendship based on shared political philosophy, and their time in office represented a high point in the US-UK special relationship.[133] Yet many in Washington were concerned with the adverse effects on US policy in Latin America that could result from siding with Britain. Although American friendship with the junta in Buenos Aires was not based on historical or cultural links like those that supposedly provided the bedrock of the special relationship, the souring of relations with Argentina—or, worse still, its "loss" to the Soviet Union—was worrisome.[134] Conflict in the South Atlantic appeared to open the door to Soviet interference precisely at a time when the Reagan administration in Washington was hoping to appear tough on communism, particularly in Latin America. It was, consequently, "a very difficult situation for the United States," as President Reagan stressed on 6 April, "because we're friends with both of the countries engaged in this dispute."[135]

Aware of the responsibility resting its shoulders but unwilling openly to

take sides, therefore, the US government decided to provide mediation assistance in hopes of reaching a negotiated settlement. Soon after the task
force had sailed, Haig began a mission of shuttle diplomacy—undoubtedly
inspired by the efforts of his predecessor, Henry Kissinger, in the Middle East
nine years earlier.[136] The Haig mediation seemed to offer the opportunity to
solve the dispute without damaging the US relations with either party and
perhaps even providing a little prestige in the bargain: as Reagan said to Haig
at the start of his mission, "Imagine when—if—you do settle this, Al. We'll
be the envy of the world."[137]

However, from the outset, Haig had no doubts regarding the difficulty of
the task he had taken on; not only were the distances to be covered far greater
than those Kissinger had traversed, but there was no dense web of issue areas
with which to create intricate trade-offs on the path to a solution.[138] Moreover, throughout the episode, the zero-sum nature of the dispute militated
against compromise and hence an avoidance of conflict. Little wonder then
that Haig feared—correctly—that this would be his Waterloo.[139] Yet in the
opinion of the US, a diplomatic settlement offered the best solution that
would not damage the country's perceived interests.

Mediation was also backed by a number of key figures in Washington
who supported the maintenance of strong links with South America and
thus hesitated to offer overt support for the United Kingdom. This Latin
American dimension to US foreign policy was represented during the Falklands War by the so-called Latinos, headed by Jeanne Kirkpatrick, ambassador to the United Nations, and Thomas Enders, undersecretary of state for
Latin American affairs. Although they were aware of Britain's value to the
US, they argued against the "Europeanists"—Undersecretary of State for European Affairs Lawrence Eagleburger and Secretary of Defense Caspar Weinberger among them—that America's best interests would be served by neutrality.[140] An awareness of the influence of this group had helped convince
the Argentine junta that the goodwill it had built up with Washington would
translate into American neutrality, even in the face of a breach of international law such as the invasion.[141] Indeed, Britain's defence minister, John
Nott, later argued that had Reagan been a white Anglo-Saxon Protestant
rather than from the West Coast, American support for Britain would have
been secured from the outset.[142] The perception that Kirkpatrick in particular was anti-British was not helped by a number of diplomatic faux pas. On
the day of the invasion, for example, she attended a dinner in her honor at
the residence of Esteban Takacs, the Argentine ambassador to the US.[143]

More bizarrely, on 4 June, after she (and Britain) vetoed a UN Security Council resolution calling for an immediate cease-fire, she proclaimed that if she could vote again, she would abstain.[144]

Knowledge of the Latinos' influence in Washington likely helped convince the junta that the US would acquiesce to military action in Las Malvinas. When this idea proved mistaken, Argentina's leaders decided to play on the American fear of Soviet involvement in South America, both denying their intention to go over to "the other side" but making it very clear that the option remained on the table. As Haig later noted in his memoirs, "During the negotiations, Galtieri had told me repeatedly that, in case of hostilities, he would be forced to accept the assistance, including munitions, which had been offered by the Cubans and the Soviets."[145] Indeed, "At one point, Galtieri confided that the Russians had insinuated that they might be prepared to have one of their submarines sink the British carrier *Invincible* with Prince Andrew aboard and let Argentina take the credit for their action."[146] Whether or not this statement was true, Argentina's leaders calculated that the US might be more inclined toward neutrality if Washington believed that serious Cold War consequences might result from supporting Britain.

Britain's attempts to alter-cast Argentina as the aggressor were therefore complicated by the pressing need to avoid the charge of having thrust Buenos Aires into the hands of Moscow. This tack was pursued via two seemingly mutually exclusive strategies. On the one hand, Britain sought to convince the US that its military action in the South Atlantic would not turn the Argentines over to the Soviet Union. On the other hand, Britain argued strongly that Argentina and the USSR were already in bed with one another. British officials played up or down American fears as the situation required. Britain's ambassador to the US, Nicholas Henderson, noted in his diary for 10 April, "My main aim is to expose the unholy alliance between the Soviets and the Argentines. The playing of the anti-Communist card is the best way to win any game here."[147] British action would not, consequently, thrust the Argentines into the arms of the Bear since they were already there, leaving a strong response as the only course of action.[148]

Despite the outward neutrality initially shown by the Americans, the US in fact leaned toward the United Kingdom. American support was most evident in defense cooperation and the provision of military equipment and other supplies needed for the complex logistical effort of putting a task force to sea that was capable of retaking the islands. Secretary of Defense Caspar Weinberger was aware of Haig's mediation effort but continued the traditional cooperation between the US and the UK in the defense sphere. "Some of us (and I was one)," he noted in his memoirs, "felt that if the British were going to start a counter-attack to retake the Islands, we should, without any question, help them to the utmost of our ability."[149] Shortly after the task force was sent, he "passed the word to the Department that all existing UK requests for military equipment, and requests for equipment or other types of support, short of actual participation in their military action, should be granted immediately."[150] Although many people in Britain were intensely annoyed at Washington's officially neutral stance, others were aware of the level of covert help being offered.[151] As Freedman makes clear, "The British defence Staff at Washington reported back to [Admiral Sir Terence] Lewin that: 'the co-operation we are getting from the Americans is truly marvelous.'"[152]

The implications, again, were twofold. Not only did such cooperation facilitate Britain's military efforts in practical terms, but it also proved that Britain's aims themselves were appropriate. America's support was clearest, therefore, in the defense sphere, but was also evident in the April negotiation effort—although this interpretation would not have sat easily at the time with British members of Parliament, who felt that the US should have been fully behind them from the beginning.[153] The Haig mission may well not have been a cynical way of avoiding taking sides and more a genuine initiative by the secretary of state to find a solution that was in the best interests of all sides. "While my sympathy was with the British," Haig noted, "I believed that the most practical expression of that sympathy would be impartial United States mediation in the dispute."[154] Indeed, he argued in his memoirs that he did not approach the shuttle as attempting to "urge a compromise of principle" on the British prime minister: "My purposes were the opposite. I wished to assure her that she had the support of the United States in the right course of action."[155] By tempering the worst consequences of a White House unsure about how to deal with the conflict, the Haig shuttle served a useful purpose for the British in convincing international opinion that Britain genuinely favored a peaceful solution to the dispute.[156] Moreover, Haig's efforts allowed the British to continue military preparations in case force was needed and thereby to maintain pressure on Argentina to comply with Resolution 502 and withdraw its forces, restoring the situation ex ante.

When it became evident by the end of April that a diplomatic solution was not forthcoming, the US openly tilted toward Britain.[157] Military exports to Argentina were suspended, Export-Import Bank credits and guarantees were canceled, and Commodity Credit Corporation loans were frozen.[158] Military assistance, until this point largely secret, was no longer to be kept quiet. Support for the interpretation that American support for Britain's rejection of the *colonial power* role and subsequent attempt to make a *residual great power* role comes from the British government's muted response to the tilt. Thatcher told the Commons simply, "We now have the total support of the United States, which we would expect, and which I think we always expected to have."[159]

The tilt has traditionally been explained as the result of growing pressure from American public opinion, channeled in large part through Congress, to show support for the British cause.[160] The tilt has also been seen as the result of the intransigence demonstrated by the Argentine junta in its negotiations with Haig.[161] As Louise Richardson has detailed, the comparison with Suez was stark: whereas in 1956, top-level agreement masked deep disagreement and eventual breakdown at the operational levels of the US-UK alliance, in 1982, operational cooperation underpinned initial separation at the intergovernmental level, paving the way for the subsequent tilt.[162] In either case, America's turn toward the UK in late April signaled a willingness to agree with the major tenets of Britain's role-making efforts with regard to the Falklands. Although throughout the remainder of the conflict the US remained heavily engaged in the dispute and capable of fundamentally affecting Britain's role construction, its support granted Britain space to make a role for itself that included an overt display of military force in support of seemingly colonial possessions without affirming the colonial connotations of that course of action.

CONCLUSION

The Falklands operation was the largest mounted by Britain since 1945, and although it is often dismissed as an historical aberration, it has just as frequently been cited as a signal turning point in Britain's post-1945 foreign policy. To member of Parliament Kenneth Carlisle, it was "a fine moment for our country," and he urged the prime minister to declare that "wherever British power can reach, nobody should embark on aggression."[163] To Bicheno, "as one who was abroad to experience it[,] I can testify that international perception of Britain as a self-defeated nation was changed almost overnight by the Falklands War."[164] To geopolitician Klaus Dodds, "Victory in the 1982

Falklands War finally erased Dean Acheson's hurtful jibe . . . that 'Britain had lost an Empire but not yet found a role.'"[165] And to historian John Keegan, "The Falklands War marked the point at which Britain's late twentieth century renaissance as an international power may be dated."[166]

This chapter has sought not to assess the significance of the Falklands War as an event but rather to grasp the expectations emerging about Britain in world affairs in the Falklands episode as part of a broader historical analysis of Britain's changing engagement with international politics since 1945. In that regard, the conflict highlights the problem of trying to define Britain's role in the world once and for all. Policymakers were not, by and large, hankering after imperial days lost. They recognized that Britain in 1982 was far from being a *superpower* and that the empire was a thing of the past. But they also remained convinced that Britain retained significantly greater interests and capabilities than a regional power or "another Belgium." Reflecting on the war, Thatcher used the term "Middle Power" to describe Britain,[167] while others have preferred "world power grade two."[168] Each grapples with the question of what Britain's role in the world is or should be while remaining within the Bevinite consensus that Britain is a major power. The Falklands conflict thus disproved journalist Jon Connell's argument, made shortly after the invasion, that, "realistically, the fate of the Falklands in the face of any serious aggressor has been settled since Britain decided to abandon its global responsibility and concentrate her defense spending on Nato and home commitments."[169]

The success of Operation Corporate should not, however, lead to the conclusion that Britain was again a *great power* following its military victory over Argentina. Only three days before the invasion, the *Times* was dampening islander expectations about the possibility that an armada would come to their rescue by stating plainly, "Britain is no longer a world power."[170] Indeed, had Britain really still had great power credentials in early 1982, Argentina would not have invaded.[171] But I have warned throughout of explanations based on essences rather than expectations, relations, and practices. As such, the question of what Britain was should be put to one side; instead, analytical focus should be placed on a set of understandings about Britain and its place in the world as a state deeply committed to central principles of international order, with a desire and capacity to enforce them—qualities associated with the *great powers*. Thus Britain's role in international relations as it emerged from the Falklands conflict of 1982 can most fruitfully analyzed with reference to the role of *residual great power*.

What, finally, does this argument imply for Britain's actions over the ongoing dispute over the islands?[172] Argentina's claim has recently been made a political issue by President Cristina Fernandez de Kirchner, set against the backdrop of oil and mineral development off the islands and the thirtieth anniversary of the war. Hypotheticals and prediction can, of course, be dangerous; the exact scenario of 1982 will not be repeated. Today, Argentina is a democracy, and the fact that war took place affects the meanings of any actions Argentina and Britain might take. Nevertheless, this analysis—and the argument of the book as a whole—tentatively suggests two claims.

The first is that since the Bevinite consensus remains intact, similar expectations and associations are likely to continue to structure British-Argentine interactions regarding the islands. Short of war, British leaders would be expected to defend islanders' rights, meaning that sovereignty remains nonnegotiable; should Argentina use force—unlikely as that might today seem—British leaders would come under extreme pressure to attempt another reinvasion.[173] The second, more enlightening implication, however, is that whether those expectations translate into negotiation or confrontation would depend less on what party was in power or the personality or determination of the leaders themselves than on the perspective and position of other key states as they might emerge in the specific interaction. Again, Britain's decision and ability to retake the islands in 1982 depended on the construction of a *residual great power* role, principally with the United States but also with Britain's commonwealth and European allies. Future British actions will depend in large measure on how this process plays out. Focusing solely on Britain would, then, be a mistake.

Conclusion

IN LIGHT OF THE foregoing investigations, it is now clear that former US secretary of state Dean Acheson's assertion that Britain "had lost an empire and not yet found a role" was not a statement of fact to be proven or refuted. Rather, it was the expression of Acheson's opinion about the appropriateness of British foreign policy in the early 1960s given certain expectations regarding Britain in international affairs.[1] Acheson was talking as much to his own country as to London: by castigating British leaders for being unequal to their "historic role," he was urging American policymakers to pressure Britain to maintain its Cold War efforts.[2] The force of his words, therefore, was based on a widespread fear that Britain no longer had the will or the capacity to carry out tasks both the British and others expected of it.

Although Acheson might not have realized it, his choice of phrase resonated with an important feature of international politics: state action, like the action of individuals in everyday life, is fundamentally role-based. That is, policymakers come to know what is expected and appropriate for their state on the basis of social expectations communicated in and through interaction. In this book, I have developed an approach to state action based on this insight, which is both entirely familiar and frequently neglected in political science. This concluding chapter reviews the main empirical points that emerged before elaborating on the theoretical implications of my argument. I have left for a separate epilogue the question of what my findings mean for UK foreign policy in the twenty-first century.

REVIEW OF MAIN EMPIRICAL FINDINGS

The case studies traced the emergence and development of a set of expectations attached to Britain in world politics in four signal episodes in its postwar international history. In each I termed the operative role *residual great power*. I chose the same name for heuristic purposes: to stress the continuities in the expectations that emerged and to highlight some general similarities to the *great power* role as typically understood in IR theory. Crucially, however, I also retained the focus on what this role meant in terms of expected behavior in the case at hand, which is elemental to a micro-interactionist perspective.

The status of Suez as the moment at which Britain's decline from true great power status became apparent is by now a historiographical commonplace, and I have unsurprisingly reaffirmed it here. However, I have also demonstrated that this commonplace does relatively little in terms of explaining Britain's actions. Understood in micro-interactionist terms, the *great power* role was in fact very much central. This was not because Britain was still a *great power* and therefore had to respond with force but was because the decisions made by Anthony Eden and his close advisers would have been impossible without the mutual construction of the *residual great power* role with the French and the permissive actions of the US—until, that is, the crisis reached its crescendo.

Similarly, underpinning Harold Macmillan's desire to gain an alternative to Skybolt after its late-1962 cancellation was the expectation that only a technological equivalent or superior technology—that is, Polaris—quickly secured from the Americans would be politically viable.[3] Moreover, the terms of any agreement reached had to secure the independence of Britain's nuclear deterrent, even when there were serious problems in planning for its use in any case.[4] Once again, Britain's decision making both affirmed a British sense of self and attempted to secure Britain's nuclear status—but these goals were made possible only by the emergence of a *residual great power* role and the negotiation of the meaning of that role with important others, especially the United States. Britain secured Skybolt, then, because the Kennedy administration used the crisis to signal a new policy related to European nuclear defense that made a clear distinction between nuclear-armed allied states—Britain and France—and those deemed less worthy of nuclear capability in the near term.

The Skybolt Crisis also opened up the question of Britain's relationship to the European integration project, which was examined in chapter 5 in the context of Britain's second EEC application. This analysis confirmed the conclusions of historians Saki Dockrill, Alan Milward, and others that Britain's application represented not a movement toward Europe and away from "the world" but a strategy of national aggrandizement through European integration. It focused specifically on the importance of American influence on the timing of Prime Minister Harold Wilson's conversion to the possibility of a second application, persuading Britain to seek application during the early part of 1966. The chapter also detailed how the expectations of the Friendly Five altered British negotiating tactics in subtle but important ways. Britain's strategy of seeking safeguards for and stressing the alternatives to Europe shifted to one of making a clean application that French president Charles de Gaulle could not use to demonstrate Britain's retention of an extra-European—meaning pro-American—dimension to its foreign policy.

The final case study addressed Britain's reinvasion of the Falklands/ Malvinas following Argentina's capture of the islands in April 1982. Explanations based on preferences and identity were once again found to overplay British elite opinion and to underplay the expectations about Britain's appropriate behavior that emerged from the interaction itself. Argentine leaders attempted to cast Britain as a *colonial power* to prevent Britain from launching a reinvasion attempt by gaining sympathy from the rest of the world, particularly in the Americas. However, another role emerged for Britain to play: that of *residual great* power, with the right and ability to defend international norms and principles, which Argentina had violated with its resort to military force in the dispute. This role was constructed, once again, with the United States—which assisted Britain, at first secretly and then openly—and Britain's partners in Europe and the commonwealth.

A central finding of this book is that since 1945, there has been no gestalt switch in relation to British foreign policy. Despite the loss of empire and the decision to join Europe, a prominent set of expectations have emerged time and again in Britain's international interactions. These expectations can be understood in terms of the *residual great power* role. What that role has meant in concrete instances has been driven to a significant extent by others, notably the US and Britain's European partners, particularly France. These are, nevertheless, large claims difficult to substantiate over only four cases. More specifically, to what extent has Britain's role in the world shifted since the Falklands War, and, perhaps even more important, after the Cold War?

BRITISH FOREIGN POLICY AFTER THE COLD WAR

None of the foregoing is meant to suggest that nothing has changed in Britain's international relations since 1945. Much has indeed changed. The UK has downgraded from the most prominent international actor politically before the Second World War to only one prominent voice among many in a world dominated first by two superpowers, then just one. Yet the principal foreign policy expectations attached to Britain have remained stable over the period. This was clearly the case with the post–Cold War Conservative governments, first of Thatcher (1979–90) and later John Major (1990–97), marked by initial opposition to and only slow acceptance of German unification, the securing of opt-outs from the Maastricht Treaty, and the firm resistance to full humanitarian intervention in the former Yugoslavia.[5] But it was also the case for New Labour, in contrast to what appears an emerging conventional wisdom.

The consensus, at least among popular commentators, is that New Labour changed Britain's role in the world. This view is bound up with the conviction that Tony Blair personally had a particular impact on the conduct of Britain's external relations under his tenure. For example, defense expert Michael Clarke states, "Tony Blair made a big difference to British foreign policy during his decade in Downing Street."[6] Before 1997, he argues, the Major government had implemented a small-C conservative foreign policy, reacting to international events with little sense of how such events might be shaped for Britain's benefit. Not so Blair and New Labour, which jumped on the liberal internationalist bandwagon and shaped international relations by gaining privileged access to Washington and pushing it toward an interventionist agenda. Important, much of this change was attributed to the personality and inimitable style of Blair—a completely believable idea for anyone who reads his memoir.[7]

Not everyone has been convinced by the bluff and bluster of New Labour's rhetoric, however. Commenting on the then ongoing Strategic Defence Review (SDR), Corelli Barnett observed in 1997 that the New Labour project amounted

> to what General de Gaulle would have called un *projet ambitieux*. It signifies that even today a new British government is repeating the mistake perpetrated by all its predecessors, Labour and Conservative, since the Second World War. And that mistake has been first of all to choose the kind of grand world roles that they rather fancied Britain playing; then deciding what size, shape and deployment of armed forces would be needed to sustain these roles . . . and calling it a defence budget.[8]

This statement echoes the sentiments of those who suggest that beyond the rhetoric, New Labour's foreign policy did not confront but actually perpetu-

ated certain deep-seated British traditions.[9] In justifying making claims that
Britain's role in the world remained unchanged by New Labour, I concur
with these judgments. Stripped back to its fundamentals, Britain's role remained the same under New Labour as it was under many previous governments. Britain's relations with Europe remained frosty, while those with the
United States remained strong.

As Foreign Secretary David Miliband argued in 2009, certain notions are
thus today axiomatic to the expectations about Britain's proper behavior in
world politics: that Britain is strategically placed between Europe and America,
and that location underpins an internationalist orientation. Anything less represents the end of the UK's international role: "The choice for the UK is . . . simply stated: we can lead a strong European foreign policy or—lost in hubris, nostalgia or xenophobia—watch our influence in the world wane."[10] The notion,
he went on, "that the UK can maintain its influence in Beijing or Washington
or Delhi or Moscow if we marginalise ourselves in Europe is frankly fanciful."[11]

Again, this is not to say that there were no elements of novelty in Labour's
1997–2010 foreign policy. Perhaps most markedly, Labour displayed a very
different foreign policy style than its predecessors. The international prominence of Blair was also in marked contrast to Major, and the extent to which
Blair articulated and in some sense embodied the liberal interventionist spirit
of the age was marked. Blair was unusually strong in his convictions, especially regarding his willingness to use armed force in support of his goals,
with a self-assurance bordering on the hubristic. As he professed in 2003, in
again typical terms, "Our very strengths, our history, equip us to play a role as
a unifier around a consensus for achieving both our goals and those of the
wider world."[12] However, the expectations attached to Britain in world politics in 2010 remained very much the same as those the party inherited in May
1997. Thus, whatever other changes the "New Labour effect" and indeed the
"Blair effect" brought to British politics in these years, it cannot be concluded
that one of these was a fundamental change to Britain's role in the world.

As noted, however, I leave the empirical implications of the book for the
epilogue. The remainder of this conclusion deals with theoretical implications, in particular the future of constructivist theorizing in IR.

REVIEW OF THEORETICAL CONTRIBUTION

In this book I have confronted the status of "identity" as the watchword of
constructivist international theory, suggesting that there is more going on

in the social construction of international politics than it allows for. A "social identity," I have stressed, is better conceived as a "role," since healthy individuals in society in fact have one identity; identity, or the self, is related to action but can only be understood as a product of processes related to the emergence, construction, and casting of roles that are thoroughly relational. I consequently developed a role-based approach to the analysis of state action in international politics that retains the valuable insights gained by constructivist research thus far.

Developing this approach involved taking issue with the Holstian agenda within FPA and Wendt's systemic constructivist theory. Holsti's focus on the "role-conceptions" of foreign policymakers, as Wendt correctly points out, overemphasizes the agentic, role-taking side of the equation at the expense of the structural, role-constituting side, "which strips the concept of role of much of its interest."[13] Wendt's theory is an inappropriate alternative, however. He invokes the role concept to demonstrate how the culture of the international system creates the identities of states, refuting Waltz's assertion that the structure of the international system is given by the material distribution of capabilities. But while his work has been hugely influential, his limited number of roles—*enemy, rival,* and *friend*—are too abstract, ahistorical, and removed from the actual practices of international political life.

The book developed instead a *micro-interactionist constructivist* approach more suited to understanding the social bases of a particular state's actions in world politics. Here, roles are sets of expectations attached to the behavior of states, and these roles are always being renegotiated with important others in the international system, whether states or nonstate actors. The label "interactionist" thus refers to the way in which roles emerge, develop, and change through interaction with others. Three key concepts are borrowed from symbolic interactionism to illustrate how this process works, in deliberately stylized ideal-typical form: role-taking, somewhat confusingly, corresponds not to playing a predetermined role but to assuming the perspective of the other from which to assess the appropriateness of one's role definition and corresponding behavior. Role-making, meanwhile, captures that part of state action aimed at defining a particular role for itself and demonstrating that the behavior in which it is currently engaged is appropriate to that role. The final concept injects a degree of dynamism into this quite fixed and consensual picture, suggesting that elements of argumentation, persuasion, and coercion are present in interaction. Alter-casting is thus an augmentative concept that characterizes role-making strategies that have the specific aim of gaining approval for a particular role definition.

ALTERNATIVE THEORETICAL ACCOUNTS

A convinced IR realist might respond to this argument by saying that it represents an interesting description of British foreign policymaking since 1945 but makes few genuinely explanatory claims. Further, such a realist might suggest that Britain's foreign policy is quite easily explained by arguing either (1) that Britain has moved from *great power* to *middle power* status and has increasingly sought to balance against potential threats or (2) that Britain's role has not changed over the period.[14] In this sense, although London disbanded the British Empire and moved into a closer set of relationships with its European partners, Britain has nonetheless retained the role of *great power* to the extent that it can be considered a status quo power, and it has behaved accordingly.

Explanation 1 is not without points of correlation with Britain's transition over the past six decades. Declining in power and influence, Britain has consistently chosen to align itself with the United States, first in the face of the Soviet threat and since 1989 in the face of continuing uncertainty about the future of international politics. In realist terms, this behavior would be referred to as "bandwagoning."[15] Moreover, a number of events that seem to discredit this interpretation can also be explained away relatively easily. Suez could—and indeed often is—considered a transition point that marked the death throes of Britain's great power pretensions. It was duly short-lived and clearly more a case of recalcitrant client behavior than an attempt to reshape Britain's international relations. The second explanation, meanwhile, adds another degree of depth to this realist-inspired interpretation by suggesting that a status quo power can be assumed to have a fundamental interest in the maintenance of international order. Britain would thus be expected to closely associate itself with the dominant norms and rules of the international system and with the dominant players therein. This explanation also has strong correlations with certain aspects of Britain's recent history—most noticeably Margaret Thatcher's decision to send a task force to the South Atlantic to recover the Falkland Islands.

Evaluation of the relative merits of these accounts turns, not surprisingly, on metatheoretical issues. The interpretation I offer has added value because it can incorporate elements of both of these approaches without the requirement of asserting a priori and in abstract terms the actual role Britain played. The analysis thus runs from what the notion of *great power* or *status quo power* meant, if these labels were invoked at all, to the object of study—

Britain itself—rather than the other way around. It is thus possible to note at appropriate times the intensely status quo orientation of Britain's behavior, as in the case of the Falklands, without being troubled by instances such as the Kosovo Crisis, when Britain's behavior amounted to a desire fundamentally to alter the status quo—in that instance, by drawing into question the meaning of state sovereignty. Moreover, Britain's balancing behavior not only can be noted and essentially described but can in fact be explained as the result of numerous conscious decisions that have consistently placed the special relationship central to Britain's role in international politics, even when that relationship has hit rough waters, such as over Suez and Vietnam.

CONSTRUCTIVISM AND INTERNATIONAL POLITICAL SOCIOLOGY: BEYOND THE ANARCHY PROBLEMATIC

As I noted in the introduction, this book forms part of a wider drive within the discipline to continue the constructivist research program and take it beyond norms, identity, and culture in resocializing IR's traditionally predominant image of world politics as an anarchical realm: the view that in a world without an overarching government—a sovereign for the sovereigns—there is no society or social order. As Hayward Alker has noted, the consequences deemed to follow from this assumption not only are historically inaccurate for many periods but involve faulty causal reasoning.[16] He believes that this view should be abandoned as an uncritically accepted starting point for theoretical and empirical research in IR.[17] And it is not only constructivists that have come to this conclusion—rationalists, too, have begun to dispense with the anarchy problematic.[18] As Nicholas Onuf has stated, "International relations was never a matter of anarchy, any more than domestic societies could have been."[19] The international sphere is filled with rules, norms, manners, a history, culture, practices, and—crucially—roles. It is conditioned not by an all-encompassing ordering principle of anarchy but by multiple hierarchical and heteronomous forms of authority relationships among and between states and nonstate actors.[20]

This book has therefore continued a current trend of opening up—perhaps *reopening* is a more appropriate word—IR theory to insights from the discipline of sociology.[21] At a simple level, there is more to do when it comes to understanding the roles nations play in world politics, and further explorations in sociology and social psychology would pay rich rewards. This book has not stressed the performative aspects of roles and role-playing, for example. In search of a degree of parsimony, I chose instead to focus on the substantive content of role-making and role-taking in particular interactions in international politics rather than on the mechanisms underpinning what Erving Goffman famously referred to as the "presentation of the self."[22] The approach here, however, has natural affinities to other works that stress, for example, the importance of the "framing" of issues in both domestic politics and international affairs and consequently the politics inherent in any such limitations of possible courses of action. An investigation into how this occurs might provide further theoretical depth to an understanding of the creation and re-creation of the roles nations play on the international stage.[23]

But it would be misleading to think that moving beyond the anarchy problematic in IR means simply "bringing in" aspects from the work of sociologists. Resocializing the discipline presents a more far-reaching challenge. It tasks constructivists and nonconstructivists alike with working out their relationship to political sociology as a broad intellectual tradition with a disciplinary history and trajectory of its own. The turn to political sociology thus offers a route back to the sociological canon—from Marx, Weber, and Durkheim—and to more contemporary theorists such as Michel Foucault, Pierre Bourdieu, and Bruno Latour. The work of sociologists and social theorists has also provided much food for thought in recent works.[24] The task, however, is to resist a minimal incorporation of those ideas into the narrow debates of disciplinary IR, which remains in thrall to the anarchy problematic and the wider liberal tradition that produced it.

This is a particular challenge for constructivist IR theorists. Aside from the exceptions noted earlier, rationalists broadly speaking accept the anarchy problematic and are not concerned with moving beyond it. The historiographical turn in IR has shown that classical realism is a normative theory of statecraft matched with a particular philosophy of history and does not fall within the same tradition as political sociology.[25] For IR constructivists, conversely, the rejection of the anarchy problematic and the move toward political sociology mean a move back to the roots, particularly the work of both Friedrich Kratochwil and Nicholas Onuf, who drew heavily on the work of Durkheim and Foucault, respectively.[26] These works are not just about norms and rules in international politics; they also address practices and relations as well as conventions, order, rule, and so on. In addition, they reject the stark division between domestic and international politics that was made possible by the anarchy problematic.

As a number of scholars have pointed out, leaving anarchy behind opens up a number of questions about the nature of the international and international theory when it is impossible to posit the existence of the international as an unconditional a priori. These questions include theoretical and historical matters of the nature of the state, liberal modernity, capitalism, and their predominant expressions. My achievements in this book have in that regard been more limited. I have offered a theoretically informed and historically supported argument that seeks to have practical utility for British policymakers in search of more prudent foreign policy. To that end, I have rejected the notion of some timeless entity known as "Britain" and assessed instead the concatenations of relational expectations and practices that have constituted Britain in the world since 1945.

Epilogue: Britain and World Power in the Twenty-First Century

The continuity in the roles that have emerged for Britain since 1945 might lead the reader to misunderstand my argument as reaffirming the determinacy of structure in international politics. It seems to suggest that there is a set of expectations "out there" constitutive of the UK's role in world politics, rendering it unlikely that UK foreign policy will change in the near future. What, then, does my argument imply for Britain's international relations in the twenty-first century? What is the likelihood of meaningful change? How would we recognize change if it occurred?

I believe that genuine change is unlikely in the short to medium term, but such a structural reading of my argument must be resisted. The expectations that shape state action in world politics emerge within unique interactions. Every interaction by definition brings different expectations to bear on those involved, however subtle those differences may be. How role-based expectations translate into foreign policy is a result of the specific relations or configurations between the state in question and other actors and the political strategies policymakers choose to navigate these configurations. Crucially, therefore, at the same time as particular political options within the British debate were deemed more live than others, they were not the only options on the table: Anthony Eden did not have to order British troops to invade Egypt any more than Tony Blair had to invade Iraq. Men (and women) make their own history.

More concretely, my argument suggests that change in Britain's foreign relations will most likely come about in one of two ways. First, UK leaders have the ability to develop innovative political strategies to do things differently in the face of similar sets of emergent expectations. In 2002, for example, space undoubtedly exists for the UK to resist US pressure and refuse to

send British troops to Iraq, just as former prime minister Harold Wilson resisted sending troops to Vietnam in the 1960s. The US would certainly have
exerted sustained pressure on such a leader not to defect from the special relationship, but Blair could have resisted. The domestic debate was strongly
polarized, with Blair facing significant opposition in the Commons and on
the streets.[1] A space could have been carved out for opposition, perhaps using Blair's metaphor of Britain as the "bridge" between Europe and America
as the operative rhetorical resource.[2] Rather than stepping firmly onto the
American side of the bridge, Britain might have offered vocal support without troops and thus positioned itself as the bridge. Scholars have a responsibility to remind policymakers when such opportunities have arisen.

Second, my argument emphasizes how foreign policy decision making is
often driven by dynamics outside of the state in question, shifting our focus
away from Britain and toward changes and developments in key other countries and the shifts in political strategies underpinned by these developments. To take the example of the US and Iraq once again, UK opposition to
the war in large measure constituted a reaction to the Bush administration,
its unilateralist foreign policy, and its conservative domestic agenda and
character. The idea of a *"Love Actually* moment"—a scene from the 2003
movie by that name in which a UK prime minister played by Hugh Grant
stands up to his bullying American counterpart—captures well this dynamic. It is possible, therefore, that a future neoconservative revival in
Washington could result in the emergence of live options in British political
decision making in favor of actions that go against the US-UK special relationship. In more general terms, it is imperative to extend our focus beyond
London when looking for possible sources of change in UK foreign policy
and for moments when spaces for innovative policymaking open up.

Two contemporary developments—the UK's potential exit from the European Union and Scotland's potential exit from the United Kingdom—help
demonstrate why. Both of them portend far-reaching change in Britain's role
in the world and carry an importance that justifies what might otherwise be
considered a dangerous excursion into contemporary politics.

The recent Conservative Party promise to hold a referendum on the UK's
EU membership should the party win the 2017 general election is puzzling
from the perspective of my argument: Why would David Cameron risk ced-
ing control of fulfilling Britain's role in relation to Europe—"awkward
partnership"—by exiting the European Union?[3] In line with what micro-
interactionist constructivism would expect, key others including the United

States have already engaged in alter-casting behaviors designed to persuade the Conservatives of the folly of this course of action.[4] Other parties have opposed the Tory decision, citing loss of standing with the US as an important reason to remain in the EU.[5] A prediction based on my argument would suggest that at most, the Tories will offer a referendum and argue in the strongest terms in favor of UK membership. The reason, once again, is the crescendo of international voices urging Britain to remain within the European project and how these voices narrow the space for alternatives within the British debate on Europe.

Yet it is no bad thing that the Cameron government is contemplating a move that might significantly change the bases of Britain's international relations, because the government's action proves that my approach is not deterministic. The referendum promise shows that the international political logic I outline exists alongside other pressures. Domestic voices in the UK urge the government to resist perceived subservience to antidemocratic "Brussels," again highlighting the importance of developments beyond Britain for the roles that emerge for it to play in world politics: here, the EU's continued movement toward a technocratic superstate, exercising quasi-sovereign control over increasing numbers of its members, particularly Greece and Cyprus.[6] The Conservative promise of a referendum, then, shows that Britain's leaders retain the capacity to open spaces for alternative political decisions, as we should hope they do for democratic reasons.

The second development concerns Scotland's position as a constituent part of the United Kingdom—indeed, the outcome of a referendum on independence scheduled to take place in late 2014 could render this book more a work of international history than originally intended.[7] In this case, change comes from the substate rather than international level. Role-based dynamics are at play in the debate over the future of Scotland and "Rump United Kingdom" (rUK). Although the referendum raises much discussion regarding Scotland's identity or sense of self, the specific way in which that identity can be affirmed internationally leads to the invocation of roles, specifically that of *small (European) power*. The Scottish electorate faces a choice between two roles: as part of the familiar role of Britain as *residual great power* and the less familiar and hence less ontologically secure role of *small power*.[8] Should the vote result in independence, at the same time, rUK will face the question of whether Scotland's departure changes the expectations attached to it on the world stage. Will *rUK* still be cast into and try to make a *residual great power* role?

I hope that the argument I have made in this book has gone some way toward convincing commentators and perhaps policymakers themselves that Britain's leaders since 1945 have not been harking back to a lost imperial age and therefore do not simply need to be convinced that Britain "is no longer a superpower" to do better at foreign policymaking. That point is true but quite trivial since the main drivers of British foreign policy cannot be understood as beliefs inside UK policymakers' heads. Instead, Britain's practices in world politics matter, and they are a function of the roles it plays. These are not mere ideas but expectations that are a thoroughly contextual and relational outgrowth of its international interactions. Although this argument reaffirms the inertial quality of British foreign policy, it also alerts us to possibilities for change. Real and meaningful change in UK foreign policy will require the taking of different paths, however fraught with political costs they may be, rather than shifts in Britain's material position in world politics. If this change brings about more prudent foreign policy, all the better. But making the decisions remains the task of the policymakers, not the academic realm. This book cannot even illuminate the path ahead; all it can do is assert that a path is there for those brave enough to look.

Notes

Abbreviations

AIR—Files of the Minister of State for Air
CAB—Files of the Cabinet Office
FCO—Files of the Foreign and Commonwealth Office
FRUS—Foreign Relations of the United States, available at http://history.state.gov/
historicaldocuments, accessed 16 August 2012.
FO—Files of the Foreign Office
Hansard—Hansard Commons Parliamentary Debates
PREM—Files of the Prime Minister's Office

Preface and Acknowledgments

1. See McNay 2001; Acheson 1963; Macmillan 1973.
2. Steele 2007.
3. Legro 2005.
4. Oros 2008.
5. Jackson 2007.
6. Zarakol 2010.

Introduction

1. Although the terms *Britain* and *the UK* are broadly synonymous in the literature on the foreign policy of the United Kingdom, *the UK* has become the more common term over the period. While they can in general be considered interchangeable, therefore, I have tried to echo this shift in my usage of the labels in the empirical chapters.

2. The question of what social constructivism is and how the book contributes to it forms one of the central themes in what follows, given that the meaning of constructivism and the goals of constructivist research remain contested within the discipline and among self-professed constructivists. See Fierke 2010.

3. An important exception being Alexandra Gheciu. See Gheciu 2005.

4. On Britain's military capabilities, see the Institute of Strategic Studies's annual review of international military postures, "The Military Balance," http://www.iiss.org/, accessed 27 August 2012.

5. See Kampfner 2003; Coates and Krieger 2004; Williams 2005. For an assessment of the Libya operation, see the Royal United Services Institute's interim report at http://www.rusi.org/downloads/assets/RUSIInterimLibyaReport.pdf, accessed 2 September 2012.

6. The phrase was coined by former foreign secretary Douglas Hurd during a speech at the Royal Institute for International Affairs at Chatham House on 27 January 1993, but it now represents one of the most oft-cited comments about British foreign policy. On Hurd's tenure as foreign secretary, see Hurd 2003.

7. See, e.g., Bartlett 1972; Frankel 1975; Northedge 1974.

8. This is one of the principal themes of Nunnerley 1972. The literature on the "special relationship" is large and growing. See Watt 1984; Louis and Bull 1986; Reynolds 1986; Bartlett 1992; Dumbrell 2001; Freedman 2006; Wallace and Phillips 2009.

9. On Britain's evolving relationship with the European project, see George 1998; Milward 2002; Hugo Young 1998; Wall 2008, 2012.

10. Adamthwaite 1985, 223. For a typical critique, see, e.g., Shlaim 1975.

11. Barker 1983; Croft 1994; Michael Dockrill and Young 1989; Reynolds 1991.

12. On Bevin's influence at the Foreign Office, the classic account remains Bullock 2002. See also Ovendale 1984; Pelling 1984; Zametica 1990; Vickers 2011.

13. Peter J. Taylor 1991, 87.

14. Ibid., 87–88.

15. Ibid., 88.

16. Adamthwaite 1985.

17. Ibid.

18. Croft 1994, 33.

19. Ibid., 13; emphasis added. Here British foreign policymakers were in agreement with Fox (1944), categorizing Britain as a superpower.

20. Kent 1993, ix.

21. For an extensive analysis of changing conceptions within the Foreign Office, see Croft 1994.

22. Waltz 1979.

23. See Winand 1993; Mahan 2002; Mangold 2006; Ellison 2007.

24. As, of course, Waltz (1979) pointed out. For a counterargument, see Elman 1996. The French case is again instructive here. Does it matter that diplomatic relations between France and the US have frequently been cool, since France in fact remained part of the NATO alliance and hence can be said to have "bandwagoned" with the US, as structural realists would predict? Here, de Gaulle's removal of France from NATO's integrated command structure in 1966 is crucial. Is it important or epiphenomenal? Here, I argue the case for the former.

25. Morgenthau 1993. On the internationalization of values, see Carr 1946.

26. Moravcsik 1997.

27. Focusing on think tanks, Parmar (2004) adopts a Gramscian perspective. See also Curtis 2003, 2004.

28. This equation is not unproblematic, as Jackson (2011, chapter 7), among others, has discussed. In brief, since constructivism is not a theory of international politics but a sensibility about how the world hangs together, there is no a priori philosophical justification for equating constructivism with interpretive/ historical/constitutive methods. For an innovative use of mixed methods, see Rousseau 2006.

29. Zakaria 2008. See also the debate among Christopher Layne (2012), Joseph Nye (2012), and William Wohlforth (2012) over the issue of American decline.

30. For different viewpoints on the "American decline" debate, see Prestowitz 2010; Ikenberry 2011; Kupchan 2012; Luce 2012; Walter Russell Mead 2012.

31. See esp. Barnett 1972, 1986, 1995. For a balanced assessment, see Peter Clarke and Trebilock 1997.

32. Britain's ambivalence toward Europe is well known and will be analyzed at length. Britain is formally committed to reform of the UN Security Council, including the provision of permanent seats to India, Brazil, Japan, Germany, and an African delegation. See the Conservative-Liberal Democrat Coalition "Programme for Government," May 2010, at www.conservatives.com/~/media/ Files/ . . . /coalition-programme.ashx?dl=true, accessed 2 September 2012. However, actions seem to suggest that reform is not as pressing as these statements claim. Security Council reform was absent from Conservative foreign minister William Hague's major campaign speech on foreign policy. See www.conserva tives.com/News/Speeches/ . . . /William_Hague_The_Future_of_British_Foreign_ Policy/aspx, accessed 2 September 2012. Britain's negative reaction—along with that of the other P5 members—to recent requests for greater openness in Security Council decision making confirms this impression. See "Small Countries Call for More Transparency at the United Nations," http://www.bbc.co.uk/news/world-us-canada-18123768, accessed 2 September 2012.

33. For a discussion, see McCourt 2011.

34. See Dessler 1989; Wendt 1999 (following Giddens 1984). For a thorough analysis from the perspective of critical realism, see also Wight 1999, 2006.

35. Tucker 1978, 595. This is not to imply the Marxian view that the context in which man makes his own history is one of class struggle.

36. On the importance of ideas in IR and political science, see Hall 1989; Goldstein and Keohane 1993; Blyth 2002; Craig Parsons 2002; Williams 2004. With the point now made, scholars have more recently moved to attempts to combine the two. See Georg Sørensen 2008. For specific attempts, see Pouliot 2008; Acuff 2012.

37. I thank Friedrich Kratochwil for drawing my attention to the fundamental importance of this point and its relationship to the more general issue of what makes the study of politics unique within the human sciences. See Kratochwil 1989, 2006b.

38. See Jackson 2007, following Shotter 1993.

39. The use of *paradigm* here is figurative. For a good discussion of the use of terms such as *paradigm* and *research program* to describe IR theoretical practice, see Jackson and Nexon 2009. For an example of a rationalist approach, see Glaser 2010, 33.

40. See Kratochwil 1982; Finnemore 1996; Weldes 1999.

41. The relationship between norms and identity has typically been glossed over. For an exception, see Gurowitz 2006. This relationship will be taken up in chapter 2.

42. Finnemore 1996, 2.

43. I thank an anonymous reviewer for stressing the importance of this point.

44. See Hynek and Teti 2010; Alexander J. Barder and Levine 2012.

45. Adler 1997; Hopf 1998; Ruggie 1998b.

46. Keohane 1988.

47. The dominance of positivist and rationalist approaches in American IR is well known, with King, Keohane and Verba 1994 remaining the standard primer in the field. See Maliniak et al. 2011. Criticisms of this position are, of course, common. This is particularly the case beyond the US, where postpositivism is arguably the norm. See Waever 1998. For a broader vision of metatheoretical positions in IR, see Jackson 2011.

48. Klotz 1995; Finnemore 1996; Reus-Smit 1999; Weldes 1999.

49. Jackson and Nexon 1999; Pouliot 2008; Adler and Pouliot 2011.

50. See Coles 2000. On the notion of ontological security, see Mitzen 2004; Steele 2008.

51. Hopf 2002, 1.

52. Ibid.

53. Wendt 1999, 230.

54. Hopf 2002, 11. This choice is deliberate on Hopf's part, as he does not want to engage in what he calls "theoretical preloading." His model rather begins with the basic assumption that identities help individuals understand and order the social world. However, while I am sympathetic to the desire to leave as much to empirical work as possible, the neglect of roles on this basis is questionable since Hopf's invocation of identity does not lack sophisticated theoretical development.

55. Klotz and Lynch 2007, 133.

56. Bukovansky 1997, 211.

57. Legro 2009.

58. Ibid., 41.

59. See, e.g., Sen 2006. For a good discussion of contemporary usage, see Fearon 1999.

60. See Brubaker and Cooper 2000.

61. On the notion of conceptual stretching, see Sartori 1970.

62. Practices also figure highly in attempts to move beyond the ideational/material and agent/structure dichotomies, a movement within which this book also falls. See also Neumann 2002; Adler and Pouliot 2011. "Configurations" and "re-

lations" form a natural and necessary complement to the return of practical log-ics in social analysis. Such is the case because to understand action from this per-spective, analysis should proceed on the basis of fine-grained historical accounts of the emergence of specific configurations of social phenomena. For two differ-ent theoretical elaborations, see Nexon 2009b; Jackson 2007.

63. The centrality of the notion of identity in IR is part of a wider prominence of identity in all spheres of life, linked to secular modernity and neoliberalism as a political and economic form. See Giddens 1991.

64. Wendt 1992.

65. Kratochwil 2006b.

66. Rosenau 1990, 212.

67. On the process of socialization, with particular reference to the "self," see Hewitt 1997.

68. See, e.g., Kennedy 1988; Pastor 1999; Mearsheimer 2001.

69. See Waltz 1979; Morgenthau 1993; Bull 2002.

70. See Waltz 1979.

71. Kindleberger 1973; Gilpin 1981; Keohane 1984.

72. For English School theorists and classical realists, "great power" is a cate-gory of practice within recent international politics and consequently receives little sociological analysis. Interestingly, however, proponents of both views would likely agree with much of the approach developed in chapter 2. Neoreal-ists, by contrast, draw on Talcott Parsons's sociological understanding of roles, which is overly spare and now thoroughly outdated in sociology.

73. The central work here is Holsti 1970. Interest in roles in FPA has subse-quently waxed and waned. Interest is currently quite strong. See esp. Harnisch, Franck, and Maull 2011. See also Thies 2010a, 2010b, 2010c.

74. Holsti 1970, 245–46.

75. Ibid., 239.

76. Magid 1980; Wish 1980; Walker 1987; Shih 1988; Le Prestre 1997; Krotz 2002. One possible approach to characterizing what roles are and how they work in world politics is consequently to follow Holsti's approach, which is to view them as the conceptions of policymakers themselves—that is, their conscious con-structions about the roles their states should play. This type of approach under-pins the work of Lisbeth Aggestam in her discussions of the role conceptions of German, French, and British decision makers toward the European Union's Common Foreign and Security Policy (CFSP). The role conception of a "bridge" with the US, for example, is seen as an important factor in explaining British policymakers' attitudes toward greater coordination of foreign policy at the Eu-ropean level. Britain feels uncomfortable with European defense arrangements that privilege purely European capabilities yet remains sensitive to calls from Washington for increased burden-sharing in the defense sphere. See Aggestam 1999, 16. Such pressures are made more comprehensible when the tensions of this role conception are foregrounded. See also Aggestam and Hyde-Price 2000.

77. Wendt 1999, 227.

78. Indeed, Holsti acknowledges the importance of these outside influences by making the *role prescriptions/role conceptions* distinction. The reasoning behind Holsti's choice to focus on the latter is relatively clear, however, and is not without strength: role conceptions are accorded priority in view of the fact that, in Holsti's words, "Generally the expectations of other governments, legal norms expressed through custom, general usage, or treaties, and available sanctions to enforce these are ill-defined, flexible, or weak compared to those that exist in an integrated society and particularly within formal organisations" (1970, 243) The normative structure of the international system, unlike domestic society, is not seen as sufficiently strong to enable stable role prescriptions to develop and be maintained that would override this fact—certainly not to the extent to which researchers can design their empirical investigations around them. As a result, Holsti argues that leaders' role conceptions have the most force in defining state roles (239).

79. Wendt 1999, 251.

80. Ibid.

81. Wendt makes the arguable claim that Waltz's theory is materialist (see ibid. 249, 252) since Waltz's international structure is made up of the distribution of capabilities, where ideas are absent. This viewpoint could be countered by noting that capabilities for Waltz also include nonmaterial elements, such as political stability. See Waltz 1979, 131.

82. Wendt 1999, 251.

83. Ibid., 217.

84. See Guzzini and Leander 2006.

85. See chapter 2 for the rationale for labeling the approach in this way.

86. I draw primarily on George Herbert Mead 1934. Mead's influence within American sociology was strongly influenced by his student, Herbert Blumer, founder of the influential Department of Sociology at the University of California, Berkeley. See Blumer 1966, 1986. For a discussion, see McPhail and Rexroat 1979.

87. See Trachtenberg 1999; Jackson 2007; Hopf 2012.

88. See also Gordon 1969; Peter J. Taylor 1991.

89. For a rejection of the notion that Britain is no longer a great power, see Morris 2011.

Chapter One

1. Durkheim 1982, 53.

2. I follow throughout the more common designation in IR of *constructivism* rather than *constructionism* preferred by some (e.g., Jackson 2007). However, the emphasis with the term *constructionism* on the process of construction, as opposed to action in an already constructed world, is useful to keep in mind.

3. Harnisch 2011 has noted the potential of Mead's work and of symbolic interactionism more generally for IR. Wendt 1999 also uses Mead extensively. The approach developed here, however, displays crucial differences from Wendt's ap-

proach: He uses symbolic interactionism to show conceptually how agents and structures in international relations are "co-constituted." My approach takes this as an assumption and stays closer to Mead's intention of understanding the social sources of action itself and not the creation of either agents or structures as such.

4. See, e.g., Waltz 1979; Wendt 1999.

5. The literature on norms and identity is already voluminous. Important contributions include Kratochwil 1989; Klotz 1995; Hymans 2006; Katzenstein 1996; Lapid and Kratochwil 1996; Ringmar 1996; Bloom 1990; Hall 1999; Neumann 1999; Reus-Smit 1999; Wendt 1999; Bukovansky 2002; Hopf 2002; Bially Mattern 2005; Youde 2008.

6. The distinction between "method" and "methodology" is important. See esp. Jackson 2011. See also Pouliot 2007.

7. Also noted by Katzenstein 1996, 67. For an innovative use of "binary role theory" using game-theoretic techniques, see Walker 2013.

8. Pouliot (2011) uses the same term in his development of a theory of practice of security communities, which should be unsurprising given the historical and sociological underpinnings of our respective approaches.

9. This also forms part of a wider trend in the discipline to move beyond the traditional understanding of causality. See Jackson 2007; Kurki 2008.

10. See Banton 1965; Heiss 1981.

11. Wendt 1999, 329.

12. Joas 1993, 226.

13. See esp. Talcott Parsons 1951.

14. Ibid., 25.

15. Ibid., 27–28.

16. See Homans 1964.

17. See Emirbayer 1997; Jackson and Nexon 1999. The term *interaction* itself is tainted with associations of substantialism as it does not distance itself sufficiently from a vision of two or more self-sufficient agents. However, I retain the label here because of its familiarity within the sociological literature while making clear that no associations with substantialism are intended.

18. Waltz 1979. For a discussion, see Keohane 1986.

19. Wendt 1999. See also Guzzini and Leander 2006.

20. As Goddard and Nexon (2005) have noted.

21. For a restatement of the scope of his neorealist theory, see Waltz 1996.

22. Goddard and Nexon 2005, 26.

23. Despite sustaining two decades of attack, structural realism remains an active research agenda. See, e.g., Choi 2012. Issues of power balancing have also reemerged recently on account of the "rise of China." For a good discussion, see Nexon 2009a.

24. Wendt 1999, 259–79.

25. Wendt (1999, 313–69) uses Mead specifically to show that change is possible since agents and structures are co-constituted.

26. Ibid., 279–97.

27. Ibid., 297–308.

28. Adler and Barnett 1998.

29. Wendt 1992.

30. The most forceful critique of Parsons remains Gouldner 1971. For a good overview of the numerous other critical engagements with Parsons, see Hamilton 1992. On Parsons's conception of humanity, see Wrong 1961. On the deficiencies of his understanding of culture, see Swidler 1986.

31. For a powerful critique of Waltzian neorealism, see Ashley 1984. See also Goddard and Nexon 2005. On Wendt, see Kratochwil 2000.

32. Again, both Waltz and Wendt would acknowledge this charge but reject as missing their larger point about explaining broader historical trends. Nonetheless, the point is important if our aim is to explain foreign policy.

33. Hollis and Smith 1991, 155.

34. This is not entirely surprising given the overlap between psychological and constructivist approaches in IR. See Shannon and Kowert 2011.

35. Holsti 1970, 245–46. For an overview of foreign policy role theory, see Thies 2010b.

36. Wendt 1999, 227–29.

37. See, respectively, Goldstein and Keohane 1993; Little and Smith 1988; Leites 1956.

38. Lukes 1982, 16. See also Collins 1981.

39. The phrase *micro-interactionist tradition* was coined by Randall Collins (1985).

40. Mullins (1973) termed symbolic interactionism itself "the loyal opposition" for its position vis-à-vis Parsons-dominated mainstream American sociology.

41. See Blumer 1966, 2004.

42. Goffman 1974, 1990.

43. Garfinkel 1967, 2002, 2006.

44. Schutz 1967; Schutz and Luckmann 1973, 1989.

45. See Husserl 1982, 1988.

46. See esp. Heidegger 1962. For a pragmatic reading of Heidegger that brings out these sensibilities, see Dreyfus 1991.

47. Both Goffman and Blumer place roles central to their distinct approaches to social interaction. The potential of a Goffmanian approach is discussed in the conclusion. Garfinkel's common categorization as a symbolic interactionist is somewhat misguided, however, since he disagreed strongly with grounding interaction in role-taking. For a discussion, see Garfinkel 2002; Anne Warfield-Rawls, introduction to Garfinkel 2006.

48. The potential of symbolic interactionism has not gone unrecognized within IR; both Wendt and Ted Hopf, among others, have drawn on it, and it forms an important part of their constructivist theorizing of international relations. The role-based approach developed here differs from theirs in a number of key ways. Both Wendt and Hopf use symbolic interactionism as a justification for the argument that interests and identities are formed during interaction. My approach draws more explicitly and consistently on the writing of Mead and his

symbolic interactionist followers. Unlike Hopf, therefore, it is explicitly role-rather than identity-based; relative to Wendt, it is less abstract and more social and context-specific.

49. On symbolic interactionism, see Stryker and Statham 1985; Plummer 1996; Hewitt 1997; Charon 1998. George Herbert Mead's 1934 *Mind, Self, and Society* has been particularly influential. It is frequently noted, however, that Mead's influence should not lead to a neglect of important others such as William James. For a good summary, see Plummer 1996. Blumer played a large part in establishing symbolic interactionism as a distinct school of thought within US sociology, and it remains very much alive today, with professional associations and academic journals devoted to this mode of analysis, including the Society for the Study of Symbolic Interaction; its journal, *Symbolic Interaction;* and the journal *Studies in Symbolic Interaction.* The approach has persisted in spite of the periodic pronouncements of its actual or imminent demise. See Fine 1993.

50. Blumer 1986, 2. Blumer's role as a gatekeeper of the true meaning of symbolic interactionism has always been somewhat controversial, and symbolic interactionism is today a more diversified set of "schools" that share certain essential features rather than a consistent agenda. See Plummer 1996.

51. See, e.g., Finnemore 1996; Lynch 1999; Jackson 2007.

52. Hewitt 1997, 28–74.

53. Jon Levi Martin 2011, 305.

54. George Herbert Mead 1934, 151–63.

55. On the need for clarity on this point, see Coutu 1951.

56. Ralph H. Turner 1956.

57. The notions of "play" and "game" are crucial for Mead, as his development of the notion of role-taking followed empirical observation of childhood development. The role is here viewed as a first step in human socialization, as children begin simple role-playing at an early age.

58. George Herbert Mead 1934, 152–63. This notion strongly corresponds to the idea of social norms. See Tugendhat 1986.

59. George Herbert Mead 1934, 154.

60. On the importance of logics of habit in international relations, see Hopf 2010, which he foreshadowed in Hopf 2002.

61. John Baldwin 1986, 99.

62. George Herbert Mead 1934, 151.

63. Unfortunately, stick figure design has not kept up with norms of gender equality. The figure should therefore be considered gender-neutral.

64. Pragmatists and by extension symbolic interactions are frequently criticized for their optimistic views about human interaction and progress, usually a veiled attack on the innate "Americanness" of the tradition itself—tied to a social context significantly more free than Continental Europe. While I accept the inherently American nature of this tradition, there would seem to be no good reason to reject it on that basis, especially since it need not be viewed as zero-sum vis-à-vis other sociological traditions. See Collins 1985.

65. Hewitt 1997, 29.

66. Wendt 1992.

67. The term *stock of social knowledge* is from Schutz 1967, 80-81. It is more commonly associated with Berger and Luckmann 1966. For a useful discussion, see Hopf 2002, 4-7.

68. On "significant symbols," see George Herbert Mead 1934, 71-72, 181

69. Ryle 1968 as cited in Geertz 1973, 6.

70. Wittgenstein 1953, 151, 153, 179.

71. Hewitt 1997, 38.

72. Charon 1998, 37.

73. Heidegger 1962, 98.

74. See Friedrichs and Kratochwil 2009.

75. See George Herbert Mead 1934; Callero 1986.

76. George Herbert Mead 1934, 173-78, 192-200.

77. Ibid., 175.

78. Cited in Collins 1994, 256.

79. The contrast between "explanation" and "interpretation" will be addressed further when the argument turns to method and methodology.

80. Similar, although not identical: I do not value "elegance" in and of itself, for example. See Waltz 1979. See also Waltz, "Assaying Theories," in Waltz 2008. For a discussion, see Waever 2009. Much of the following also draws on Jackson 2011, which lays out in greater depth many of the issues touched on here.

81. The 1:1 map in question was ordered by a Chinese emperor, according to the short story by Jorge Luis Borges tellingly titled "On Exactitude in Science." "In that Empire, the craft of Cartography attained such Perfection that the Map of a Single province covered the space of an entire City, and the Map of the Empire itself an entire Province. In the course of Time, these Extensive maps were found somehow wanting, and so the College of Cartographers evolved a Map of the Empire that was of the same Scale as the Empire and that coincided with it point for point. Less attentive to the Study of Cartography, succeeding Generations came to judge a map of such Magnitude cumbersome, and, not without Irreverence, they abandoned it to the Rigours of sun and Rain. In the western Deserts, tattered Fragments of the Map are still to be found, Sheltering an occasional Beast or beggar; in the whole Nation, no other relic is left of the Discipline of Geography" (Borges 1998, 325). I am indebted to Friedrich Kratochwil for this illustration.

82. Without, of course, abstracting too much, as has driven much criticism of Waltz's extremely spare vision of international politics.

83. Framing in particular has been drawn upon to good effect in IR and would certainly seem to be a key part of social life and hence likely role-playing. For alternative uses, see Maoz 1990; Boetcher 2004.

84. Hewitt 1997, 63-65.

85. Ralph H. Turner 1956.

86. Hewitt 1997, 64.

87. Le Prestre 1997, 5.

88. See Bull 2002, 194-222.

89. Weinstein and Deutschberger 1963. This name has been retained here even though it should be clear that no use is made of the concept of the "ego." Indeed, a Mead-inspired symbolic interactionist account has no space within it for an initiating "ego," as the invocation of the concept attempts to place agency outside of interaction.

90. Krebs and Jackson 2007, 37.

91. Wendt 1992, 419–22.

92. Paraphrasing Legro 1996.

93. Buzan and Little 2000, 18–22.

94. Bartelson 1998. In the interim, however, it would seem wise to continue to use the best tools at our disposal to foster the wisest possible statecraft. We should, in other words, continue to study foreign policymaking.

95. Hobson 2000 has elaborated at length on the consequences of IR theorists' neglect of theories of the state.

96. This argument would not then hold for "failed states."

97. Bartelson 1998.

98. Ibid., 298–305

99. Ibid., 305–12.

100. Ibid., 312–17.

101. Ibid., 319.

102. See Jackson 2004, 281.

103. Bartelson 1998, 321.

104. Ibid.

105. Anderson 1983.

106. Bartelson 1998, 319.

107. The etymology of *politics* I owe to Friedrich Kratochwil.

108. Jackson 2004, 281.

109. Hopf 2002, 11.

110. Kratochwil 2006b, 19.

111. Blumer 2004, 79.

112. Hollis and Smith 1991, 155.

113. Ibid., 165.

114. Wendt 1999, 329.

115. Milner 1997; Rathbun 2004; Narizny 2007.

116. George Herbert Mead 1934, 154–56.

117. Ibid., 154–55.

118. Ibid., 155.

119. Hollis and Smith 1991, 163.

120. See, e.g., Collins 1981; Chang 2004; Athens 2005.

121. See Morrow 1994; Walsh 2007.

122. See Fearon 1994; Leeds 1999.

123. Two-player games, for example, underplay the number of actors whose roles are, in fact, taken in international interaction—hence the increased interest in n-player games, where $n > 2$.

124. See Legro 1996. For a good discussion, see Fearon and Wendt 2000.

125. I thank Patrick Jackson for encouraging me to think carefully through this important point.

126. Wendt 1999, 370.

127. See Wight 2006; Jackson 2011.

128. Jackson 2011, 25, citing Sartori 1970, 1033.

129. See March and Olsen 1989; March 2004. The use of the term *ideational* is somewhat confusing, as it has become attached to approaches that focus on "ideas" viewed as subjective beliefs inside the heads of actors. For a critique of this approach, see Weldes et al. 1997; Jackson 2007, 21–24. Social roles are not "ideational" in this sense but also are not "material."

130. March and Olsen 1989.

131. See Ward 2002; Allingham 2006.

132. Hopf 2002, 13.

133. Ibid., 10–12.

134. Ibid., 12–16.

135. Adler and Pouliot 2011.

136. Pouliot 2011.

137. Hopf 2002, 11.

138. Ibid.

139. Quoted in Bevir and Rhodes 2002, 137.

140. The literature here is large and has moved beyond norms themselves. See Brown 1994; Wendt 1999; Doty 2000; Hopf 2000; Keohane 2000; Crawford 2009.

141. This follows the distinction between regulative and constitutive rules emerging from speech act theory while divorcing it strongly from this context. See Searle 1969. It was present in Rawls 1955. For a discussion, see Onuf 1989.

142. See, respectively, Biersteker and Weber 1996 on the notion of state sovereignty—the predominant norm governing acceptance as a member of international society—as a social construct; Kratochwil 1989 and Onuf 1989 on the notion of rules in international affairs; and Tannenwald 2005 and Price 1995 on the nuclear and chemical weapons taboos.

143. For a good discussion, see Hopf 2002, 278–95. See also Adler 1997; Ruggie 1998b; Alexander J. Barder and Levine 2012.

144. Wendt 1999.

145. These rules are set out most clearly in King, Keohane, and Verba 1994.

146. Jon Levi Martin 2011, 335.

147. Ibid., 106. See also Jackson 2011.

148. John Levi Martin 2011, 321.

149. Hempel 1942.

150. See Aristotle 1979. See also Hankinson 1995.

151. Hankinson 1995, 121.

152. Ibid.

153. Ibid.

154. Ibid.

155. Ibid., 122.

156. See Kurki 2006, 215.

157. See, for example, Kurki 2006; Patomäki and Wight 2000. See also Wendt 2003, which uses a teleological argument in support of the inevitability of world state.

158. On the latter, see Bevir 2008.

159. See e.g., Edkins 1996.

160. See Hollis and Smith 1991.

161. Ibid., esp. 196–216.

162. Ibid.

163. Nagel 1986.

164. Hollis and Smith 1991.

165. Wendt 1998, 102.

166. Ibid., 85.

167. For a sociology of science perspective on scientific practice, see Knorr Cetina 1999. In relation to IR, see Bueger and Gadinger 2007.

168. Jon Levi Martin 2011, 333.

169. Ibid.

170. Ibid., 298.

171. Ibid., 327.

172. Hempel 1942. For a discussion, see Jackson 2011.

173. Jon Levi Martin 2011, 314.

174. Ibid., 310.

175. Ibid., 320.

176. See Kratochwil 2008.

177. See Weber's methodological writings, collected in Max Weber 1949. Given the weaknesses identified in the translation of Weber 1949, I draw extensively here on Kedar 2007; Jackson 2011.

178. Jackson 2011, 46.

179. The value commitments of the researcher (here, in terms of strengthening the constructivist research agenda and rethinking British foreign policy) are not only openly stated but included in the process of concept formation and hence considered a proper part of scientific activity. Ibid., 142.

180. Kedar 2007, 341.

181. Jackson 2011, 149.

182. Ibid., 144.

183. Jon Levi Martin 2011, 308.

184. There is a large and growing literature within political science and IR on the adequate relationship between these disciplines and history. This explication of a historical interpretative approach touches on many of the issues raised by this literature, but a full expansion on these issues is beyond the scope of this book. See, e.g., Smith 1999; Isacoff 2002; Puchala 2003; Pierson 2004; Vaughan-Williams 2005.

185. Callero 1985.

186. Indeed, history is often used as IR's "call girl." See Thorne 1983, 123, cited in Vaughan-Williams 2005, 116.

187. The debate over causal laws in history is too large to be summarized here. For the original statement, see Hempel 1942. See also Charles Taylor 1994.

188. See Abbott 1992, 2001.

189. Abbott 1992, 53.

190. Ibid.

191. Kratochwil 2006b, 22.

192. See esp. Bevir and Rhodes 2003.

193. Blumer 1986, 32.

194. Jon Levi Martin 2011, 106.

Chapter Two

1. See Kunz 1991; Lucas 1991.

2. Lucas 1996; Cooper 1978.

3. Not, however, Anthony Eden or his foreign secretary, Selwyn Lloyd. See, respectively, Eden 1960; Lloyd 1978.

4. The best general histories of the Suez Crisis are Kyle 1991; Love 1969; Neff 1981. I have relied primarily on these works, as well as works on specific aspects of the crisis, in developing this historical background. See also Robertson 1965; Thomas 1970; Cooper 1978.

5. As Eden notes in his memoirs (1960, 478), the UK received around half of its oil imports from the Middle East, and at the time of the nationalization, Britain had only six weeks of reserves should supplies be disrupted.

6. On East of Suez, see Darby 1973; Pickering 1998; Saki Dockrill 2002.

7. On the formation of the pact, see Kyle 1991, 56–60.

8. For a French account of Suez, see Beaufre 1969.

9. Neff 1981, 276.

10. Eden 1960, 54–55.

11. On the US role in the Suez crisis, see esp. Freiberger 2007. On Eisenhower's influence, see Nichols 2011.

12. Neff 1981, 253–72; Kyle 1991, 123–34.

13. On the Tripartite Declaration, see Slonim 1987.

14. Kyle 1991, 192–99.

15. For a good discussion of the British, French, and American opinions, see Thomas 1970, 53–66.

16. The Egyptians also took this position. See Fawzi 1956; Heikal 1987.

17. Neff 1981, 304–22.

18. Kyle 1991, 272–81.

19. Lucas 1996, 75.

20. "'No War' Rally in London," *Times*, 17 September 1956, 4.

21. Lucas 1996, 75–76. See also Nutting 1967, 91–93.

22. Neff 1981, 336.

23. Nichols 2011, 199–204.

24. "Britain and France Veto U.S. Move in Security Council," *Times,* 31 October 1956, 8.

25. The vote was sixty-five in favor, five against (Love 1969, 564).

26. "Russian Warning to Britain and France," *Times,* 6 November 1956, 10.

27. On the economic aspects of the crisis, see esp. Kunz 1991.

28. For the best overview of the background context of the crisis, see Kyle 1991.

29. Nutting 1967, 31.

30. Shaw 1996, 23.

31. Ibid.

32. Although Britain and France acknowledged that the labor to build the canal, forced in many cases, had been Egyptian. See Kyle 1991, 12–14.

33. *Hansard,* vol. 557, col. 1602, 2 August 1956.

34. Ibid., col. 1714, 2 August 1956.

35. PREM 11/1099—117/244. The use of the phrase *international waterway* meant that the canal was not the same as, say, an oil company, as was noted on a number of occasions. This was, however, an inappropriate example given the image it most likely conjured up in many people's minds: the nationalization of the Anglo-American Oil Company by Iran in 1953 and the subsequent CIA/MI6-backed overthrow of Mohammed Mossadegh.

36. *Hansard,* vol. 558, col. 5, 12 September 1956.

37. Neff 1981, 278.

38. *FRUS,* 1955–57, vol. 16, doc. 5, "Message from Eden to Eisenhower."

39. Ibid.

40. Neff 1981, 276.

41. PREM 11/1098, "Confidential Annex to Conclusions of Meeting Held in the Prime Minister's Room, House of Commons, 27 July, 11.10am."

42. Ibid.

43. See, e.g., "Mr. Selwyn Lloyd on Threat to Life of Britain," *Times,* 15 August 1956, 6; Laurence Collier et al. "Dealing with Dictators," *Times,* 10 August 1956, 9. See also Neff 1981, 276–77.

44. French prime minister Guy Mollet made the comparison publicly immediately after news of nationalization broke (Neff 1981, 280).

45. *Hansard,* vol. 557, col. 1613, 2 August 1956.

46. Ibid., vol. 558, col. 15, 12 September 1956.

47. Ibid., vol. 557, col. 1602, 2 August 1956.

48. Ibid., vol. 557, col. 1614, 2 August 1956.

49. Ibid.

50. PREM 11/1098, "Record of a Meeting Held at the Foreign Office, 1 August, 12 noon."

51. PREM 11/1098, "Record of a Meeting at the Foreign Office, July 27, 5.15pm."

52. The confluence of British and French interests was immediately apparent. See "Anglo-French Unity Urged," *Times,* 28 July 1956, 6.

53. *FRUS,* 1955–57, vol. 16, doc. 24, "Telegram from UK Embassy to State, July 29, 11pm."

54. Ibid.

55. Ibid., doc. 48, "Message from the Secretary of State to the President, August 2."

56. PREM 11/1098, "Conversation between the Secretary of State (Lloyd) and French Ambassador (Jebb) on July 29."

57. PREM 11/1098, "Record of a Meeting Held in Council Chamber, July 30, Noon (Third Tripartite Meeting)."

58. PREM 11/1098, "Conversation between the Secretary of State (Lloyd) and French Ambassador (Jebb) on July 29."

59. PREM 11/1102, "Confidential Annex to Cabinet Meeting, 3 October, 10.45am." See also, e.g., "France Determined to Be Firm," *Times,* 3 September 1956, 8.

60. This is the case for the structural realism of Waltz 1979, the classical realism of Morgenthau 1993, and the historical analysis of Kennedy 1988. For a good discussion about the varied historical and more contemporary uses of the term in international theory, see Little 2007.

61. See Bull 2002.

62. Neff 1981, 25.

63. PREM 11/1100, "Letter from Paul-Henri Spaak to Selywn Lloyd, 21 August."

64. *Hansard,* vol. 557, col. 1718, 2 August 1956. See also, e.g., "Lord Kilmuir Defines 'Britain's Duty' in Suez Dispute," *Times,* 24 September 1956, 5.

65. *Hansard,* vol. 557, col. 1717, 2 August 1956.

66. Ibid., vol. 558, col. 1464, 31 October 1956.

67. PREM 11/1105, "Prime Minister's Personal Telegram T520/56, Letter from Eden to Eisenhower, November 5."

68. *FRUS,* 1955–57, vol. 16, doc. 33, "Telegram from the Embassy in the United Kingdom to the Department of State, July 29, 2am."

69. Ibid.

70. PREM 11/1100, "Prime Minister's Personal Telegram T387/56, Message from PM to Eisenhower, 6 September."

71. PREM 11/1096, "Prime Minister's Personal Telegram T497/56, Letter from Robert Menzies to Eden, 1 November."

72. Ibid.

73. *Hansard,* vol. 558, col. 1353, 30 October 1956.

74. PREM 11/1098, "Record of a Meeting Held in Secretary of State's Room in the Commons, 31 July, 9pm."

75. Murphy 1964, 381.

76. *FRUS,* 1955–57, vol. 16, doc. 7, "Telegram from UK Embassy to State Dept., 27 July, 8pm."

77. Ibid., doc. 35, "Letter from Eisenhower to Eden, 31 July."

78. Murphy informed Washington that he would be using these words, and it can be safely assumed that they were close to those actually spoken during the subsequent meeting. See *FRUS,* 1955–57, vol. 16, doc. 21, "Telegram from the Embassy in the UK to the Dept. of State, 29 July, 6pm."

79. Ibid., doc. 42, "Memorandum of Conversation between Eden and Dulles, 1 August, 12.45pm."

80. PREM 11/1098, "Telegram from Washington to the Foreign Office, 30 July."

81. *FRUS,* 1955–57, vol. 16, doc. 28, "Telegram from Dept. of State to UK Embassy, 30 July, 12.59pm."

82. Ibid.

83. PREM 11/1098, "Record of the 7th Tripartite Meeting held in the Council Chamber at the Foreign Office, 2 August, 10am."

84. Ibid.

85. Nutting 1967, 52.

86. Ibid., 53.

87. PREM 11/1098, "Record of a Meeting between Harold Caccia and Dulles, 1 August."

88. Nutting 1967, 52–53.

89. PREM 11/1102, "Prime Minister's Personal Telegram T437/56, Message for Foreign Secretary from the Prime Minister, 6 October."

90. Quoted in Richardson 1996, 59.

91. *FRUS,* 1955–57, vol. 16, doc. 33, "Telegram from UK Embassy to Dept. of State, 31 July 2am."

92. PREM 11/1102, "Letter from Harold Macmillan to the Prime Minister, 26 September."

93. Ibid.; emphasis added.

94. PREM 11/1100, "Prime Minister's Personal Telegram T391/56, Letter from Eisenhower to Eden, 9 September."

95. *FRUS,* 1955–57, vol. 16, doc. 34, "Memorandum of a Conference with the President, at the White House, July 31, 9.45am."

96. *Hansard,* vol. 558, col. 85, 12 September 1956.

97. Ibid.

98. *FRUS,* 1955–57, vol. 16, doc. 34, "Memorandum of a Conference with the President, at the White House, July 31, 9.45am."

99. Ibid.

100. Ibid., vol. 16, doc. 46, "Memorandum of a Conversation between Macmillan and Dulles, 11 Downing St., 1 August, 6.30pm."

101. PREM 11/1100, "Prime Minister's Personal Telegram T381/56, Letter from Eisenhower to Eden, 3 September."

102. See, e.g. Gaitskell's attacks on Eden in the Commons for sidestepping questions about whether Her Majesty's Government had already decided to use force, attacks that Gaitskell repeated in a letter to the *Times.* See Hugh Gaitskell, "Suez Canal Dispute," *Times,* 15 September 1956, 7.

103. PREM 11/1098, "Record of a Meeting held at 1, Carlton Gardens, 29 July, 6pm (Second Tripartite Meeting)."

104. PREM 11/1100, "Letter from Eden to Eisenhower, 27 August."

105. The French were particularly irate at the American position. See e.g. "Bitterness in France," *Times,* 24 September 1956, 8.

106. PREM 11/1098, "Makins to Foreign Office, 29 July."

107. *FRUS,* 1955–57, vol. 16, doc. 38, "Telegram from French Embassy to Dept. of State, 31 July, 8pm."

108. Ibid.

109. PREM 11/1103, "Extract from the *Times*, "Sir A. Eden in Paris for Talks," 17 October."

110. Ibid., PREM 11/1094, "Possible Attitudes Commonwealth Delegations May Adopt at Suez Conference, 9 August."

111. Ibid.

112. PREM 11/1094, "The Use of Force over Suez: Possible Commonwealth Reactions."

113. Ibid.

114. "S. African Attitude on Suez," *Times*, 2 August 1956, 7.

115. PREM 11/1105, "Prime Minister's Personal Telegram T458/56, Letter from Eden to Eisenhower, 30 October."

116. *Hansard*, vol. 557, col. 1717, 2 August 1956.

117. *FRUS*, 1955–57, vol. 16, doc. 38, "Telegram from French Embassy to State Dept., 31 July, 8pm."

118. *Hansard*, vol. 557, col. 1695, 2 August 1956.

119. Ibid.

120. Ibid., col. 1701, 2 August 1956.

121. *FRUS*, 1955–57, vol. 16, doc. 34, "Memorandum of Conversation with the President, at the White House, 31 July, 9.45am."

122. *Hansard*, vol. 557, col. 1707, 2 August 1956.

123. Ibid., vol. 558, col. 126–27, 12 September 1956.

124. Ibid.

125. Ibid., vol. 557, col. 1622, 2 August 1956.

126. Ibid., col. 1616–17, 2 August 1956.

127. Ibid.

128. Ibid., col. 1649, 2 August 1956.

129. Ibid., col. 1642, 2 August 1956.

130. Ibid., col. 1646, 2 August 1956.

131. Ibid., vol. 558, col. 1638, 1 November 1956.

132. Ibid., col. 1347, 30 October 1956.

133. Ibid., vol. 557, col. 1626, 2 August 1956.

134. Ibid., col. 1630, 2 August 1956.

135. Ibid., vol. 558, col. 1454, 31 October 1956.

136. Ibid., col. 243, 13 September 1956.

137. Ibid., col. 1454, 31 October 1956.

138. PREM 11/1105, "Dixon to Foreign Office, 2 November."

139. Ibid.

140. PREM 11/1105, "Dixon to Foreign Office, 1 November."

141. Bially Mattern 2005, 130. Bially Mattern terms her approach "postconstructivist" for a number of reasons related to its poststructuralist orientation.

142. Sanders 1990, 95.

143. Bially Mattern 2005, 130.

144. Ibid., 131.

Chapter Three

1. See, e.g. "Special Relationship on Trial," *Times,* 17 December 1962, 9.

2. See, e.g., Murray 2000, 31. For an interesting personal take, see Harlech 1971.

3. See Trachtenberg 1999, 362, which places the blame on Britain and Macmillan in particular. See also Nunnerley 1972, 148.

4. Following the usage of British policymakers, the term *Europe* here refers specifically to the EEC.

5. The standard source on Skybolt remains a report commissioned by President John F. Kennedy and written by political scientist Richard Neustadt, sections of which underpin Neustadt 1970 and which was later published in monograph form (Neustadt 1999). See also Brandon 1963. The crisis also represents a central theme of both Ian Clark 1994 and Murray 2000, both of which make extensive use of archival resources.

6. See esp. Ian Clark 1994; Trachtenberg 1999. Trachtenberg (1999, 362) thus questions the extent to which Skybolt can be considered a crisis at all.

7. Theodore Sorensen 1965, 564–65.

8. See Nunnerley 1972; Watkinson 1986.

9. The act was signed by the president on 1 January 1947. On the McMahon Act, particularly in the context of Anglo-US nuclear diplomacy, see Gormly 1984; Melissen 1992. See also Gowing 1974, 105–6; Groom 1974, 29–30.

10. On Britain's relationship with nuclear weapons, see Pierre 1972; Groom 1974; Freedman 1980.

11. On Operation Hurricane, the first test of a British nuclear bomb, see Gowing 1974, 449–50.

12. As Harold Watkinson noted, "Britain retained its subscription to the nuclear club, but was increasingly struggling to scrape together the fee." See Files of the Minister of Defence 13/617, "Watkinson to Chief of the Defence Staff, 9 January 1962." See also Mangold 2006, 187.

13. See Barbier 1995.

14. Skybolt was to be attached to the Mark II versions of the Victor Vulcan bomber and perhaps to the Handley-Paige Victor. See AIR 2/15637, "Loose Minute on Skybolt, Group Captain D. Witt, 7 May 1960." Mid-decade was the point at which it was expected that improvements to Soviet air defenses would render the V-Bombers obsolete (Ian Clark 1994, 228–34).

15. While the early 1960s was to be the dawn of the missile age, Britain's geographical situation meant that immobile forces such as the Thor and Blue Streak missiles would be a more inviting target than a viable weapon. See Clark 1994, especially chapter 5, "The Politics of the Blue Streak Programme," 157–89.

16. AIR 2/15603, "Memorandum of Understanding on Skybolt, Signed by Harold Watkinson, Minister of Defence of the United Kingdom, and Thomas S. Gates Jr., Secretary of Defense of the United States, June 1960."

17. See Murray 2000, 38–44.

18. See Brandon 1963. Skybolt was but one of a number of missile development projects begun in the later Eisenhower years and required overcoming a number of serious technical difficulties. Skybolt's launch relied on an advanced star-tracker guidance system and the correct functioning of more than 150,000 separate components: an error of only one foot per second at launch corresponded to one thousand meters at target. The powerful US Air Force lobby may thus have been fully behind the project, but others felt that the development of the submarine Polaris system, together with Minuteman land-based missiles, rendered the Skybolt program surplus to requirements, even if it could be brought swiftly to the production phase. See AIR 20/11493, "Aide Memoire by United States Secretary of Defense Robert S. McNamara, 11 December 1962."

19. For a personal recollection of the periodic rumors regarding Skybolt's progress by the chief scientific adviser to the British government, see Zuckerman 1988.

20. Murray 2000, 81.

21. UK ambassador to Washington David Ormsby-Gore used his personal channels with the White House to assure them that canceling the missile would be "political dynamite" in London. See AIR 19/1036 "Message from David Ormsby-Gore to London, 9 November 1962."

22. FRUS, 1961–63, vol. 13, doc. 113, "Memorandum for the Record, Hyannis Port, 23 November 1962."

23. Files of the Minister of Defence 19/2161, "Extract of Statement by McNamara, 11 December 1962."

24. See "Skybolt Fears Deepened by London Talks," Times, 12 December 1962, 10.

25. PREM 11/3716, "Note for the Record by Timothy Bligh, 9 December 1962."

26. See Macmillan 1973, 342, where he recalls, "The arrangement about Skybolt was not merely a verbal understanding but a formal and binding agreement. At the same time and partly in return for our making bases on the west coast of Scotland available for the American Polaris submarine, which fired nuclear rockets, President Eisenhower gave us a firm, although not legal, assurance that if by some mischance the development of Skybolt proved unsatisfactory we would be able to obtain in substitution the essential elements of Polaris to be fitted to submarines of our own construction." As Ian Clark notes, however, this account does not tally with the archival record (1994, 267–74).

27. CAB 21/4979, "Record of a Meeting at Nassau, Wednesday, 19 December 1962, 9.50 am."

28. Ibid.

29. See Winand 1993.

30. See CAB 21/4979, "Record of a Meeting at Nassau, Wednesday 19 December, 1962, 4.30pm."; "U.S. Views on Duty to Britain," Times, 12 December 1962, 10. On the plane to Nassau, Kennedy and UK ambassador to Washington Ormsby-Gore also hatched a plan by which Britain could take over the development of Skybolt with the US paying half of the costs. See Murray 2000, 82–87.

31. CAB 21/4979, "Record of a Meeting at Nassau, Wednesday 19 December, 1962, 9.50am."

32. Ibid., "Record of a Meeting at Nassau, Thursday 20 December, 1962, 12 noon."

33. Schlesinger 1965, 738.

34. See Macmillan 1973, 362.

35. *Hansard,* vol. 618, col. 861, 29 February 1960.

36. Macmillan 1973, 357.

37. Zuckerman 1988, 235–6.

38. AIR 2/15603, "Memo from Harold Watkinson to the Secretary of State for Air, Hugh Fraser, 29 April 1960."

39. AIR 2/15603, "Personal Minute from the Prime Minister to the Minister of Defence, 10 May 1960."

40. PREM 11/3761, "Note for the Record by Principal Private Secretary to the PM, Timothy Bligh, 9 December 1962."

41. See "Mr. Macmillan Confident of Skybolt Solution," *Times,* 18 December 1962, 8.

42. AIR 2/10697 "Secret Memorandum, Heathcoat-Amory to Macmillan, 1 March 1960."

43. Zuckerman 1988, 235–36.

44. Files of the Office of the Admiralty, 1/27389, "Letter from Burke to Lamb, 27 March 1960."

45. Ibid.

46. As Groom notes, "The debate on the independent deterrent was a depressing affair, for it revealed that in many quarters there had been no real reconciliation to Britain's reduced rôle on the international scene"(1974, 501).

47. AIR 19/1036, "Minute to Permanent Under Secretary at the Ministry of Aviation from Assistant Under Secretary for Air, Ronald C. Kent, 12 November 1962."

48. CAB 21/4979, "Record of Meeting at Nassau, Thursday, 20 December 1962, 10.30am."

49. See Groom 1974, 1–19. Indeed, British policymakers continued to refer to the project by its original name despite its new location. See Holland 1991, 196.

50. Gowing 1974, 3. For a good discussion, see Hymans 2009.

51. Ian Clark 1994, 298.

52. Reynolds 1991, 182.

53. CAB 21/4979, "Record of Meeting at Nassau, Thursday, 20 December 1962, 10.30am."

54. The example of Kuwait is interesting in this regard because in 1961, British reserve troops had been rushed to the country to stave off an expected Iraqi invasion in what was seen as a successful preventative intervention by British forces and therefore as evidence of its ability to continue to play a useful global military role. See Darby 1973, 216–23.

55. On the discussions on the issue of the nuclear deterrent, see Groom 1974, 421–58.

56. *Hansard,* vol. 669, col. 897, 17 December 1962.

57. Ibid., vol. 625, col. 395, 22 June 1960.

58. See chapter 4.

59. CAB 21/4979, "Record of Meeting at Nassau, Wednesday, 20 December 1962."

60. Ibid.

61. Ibid.

62. For a detailed examination of the notion of "interdependence," see Ashton 2002.

63. PREM 11/3379, "Memorandum by the Prime Minister, n.d." The document can be presumed to date from the beginning of 1961 since it opens, "The Free World cannot, on any realistic assessment, enter on 1961 with any great degree of satisfaction."

64. Ibid.

65. Reynolds 1986, 2.

66. *Hansard,* vol. 622, col. 28, 26 April 1960.

67. Britain's financial contribution was to take the form of a secure order for one hundred missiles. This arrangement suited the Americans concerned with the weapon, in particular the US Air Force, by making the Royal Air Force into a pro-Skybolt voice in Washington while playing down British requests for legal assurances that Skybolt would confirm to British specifications. See Ian Clark 1994, 258–64.

68. *Hansard,* vol. 625, col. 396, 22 June 1960.

69. PREM 11/3379, "Personal Telegram from Macmillan to President Kennedy, 19 June 1962."

70. Ibid., 11/3706, "Memorandum from the Prime Minister's Private Secretary Philip de Zulueta to the PM, 24 August 1962."

71. On a disagreement over the US decision to approve the sale of Hawk surface-to-air missiles to Israel in August 1962 despite earlier assurances to Britain that Washington did not intend to make such a sale, see Ashton 2002, 161–65.

72. PREM 11/3379, "Letter from Kennedy to Macmillan, 17 May 1962."

73. Ian Clark 1994, 278.

74. Ibid.

75. Pierre 1972, 221.

76. *Hansard,* vol. 669, col. 581, 13 December 1962.

77. Murray 2000, 89.

78. Quoted in Reynolds 1991, 161.

79. See, e.g., "Mr. Macmillan Insists on Separate Deterrent," *Times,* 20 December 1962, 8.

80. PREM 11/3079, "Letter from de Zulueta to Macmillan, 24 June 1962."

81. Ian Clark 1994, 135–40, 397–98.

82. See Zuckerman 1988, 234.

83. This is starkest in Brandon 1963.

84. Murray 2000, 1.

85. See Trachtenberg's brief review of the traditional interpretations (1999, 360).

86. See Macmillan 1973.

87. Ibid. See also Brandon 1963.

88. Trachtenberg 1999, 355–67.

89. AIR 20/11493, "Minutes of a Meeting between the Minister of Defence and the Hon. Robert S. McNamara, United States Secretary for Defense, 11 December 1962." See also Brandon 1963.

90. AIR 20/11493, "Minutes of a Meeting between the Minister of Defence and the Hon. Robert S. McNamara, United States Secretary for Defense, 11 December 1962."

91. On the Europeanists, see Winand 1993.

92. See Ball 1968, 98–108.

93. See Winand 1993, 147, and esp. chapter 7, "Kennedy's Inheritance," 161–202.

94. Ibid., chap. 7. Robert Bowie was a Harvard professor and consultant to President Kennedy.

95. Ibid.

96. On British strategy regarding the EFTA, see Milward 2002, 265–309.

97. Winand 1993, 165.

98. The standard works on which remain Schlesinger 1965; Sorensen 1965.

99. On Norstad's plan and its eventual failure, see Winand 1993, 213–21.

100. See Freedman 1980, 10–18.

101. Ibid.

102. HMSO Command Paper 124, "Defence: Outline of Future Policy, 1957."

103. On the 1957 White Paper, see Groom 1974, 205–52; Navias 1991, 134–87.

104. *FRUS,* 1961–63, vol. 13, doc. 386, "Telegram from Mission to the North Atlantic Treaty Organisation and European Regional Organisations to the Department of State, Paris, 18 December 1961."

105. Winand 1993, 218.

106. Ball 1982, 267.

107. Groom 1974, 509.

108. CAB 21/4979, "Record of a Meeting at Nassau, 19 December 1962, 9.50am." See also Trachtenberg 1999, 367.

109. Winand 1993, 224.

110. Ibid., 233.

111. Ibid., 221.

112. See Bundy's comments to Britain, reported in "U.S. Not Obliged to Provide Alternative to Skybolt," *Times,* 17 December 1962, 8.

113. Winand 1993, 157.

114. Trachtenberg 1999.

115. Ibid., 363.

116. Neustadt 1999, 27.

117. Ibid.

118. Winand 1993, 320.

119. The *Times* reported the offer to the French as representing the end of the special relationship. See "Britain to Get Polaris without Warheads," *Times,* 22 December 1962, 6.

120. See Trachtenberg 1999.

121. *FRUS,* 1961–63, vol. 13, doc. 401, "Memorandum of a Conversation, Washington, 16 December 1962."

122. Winand 1993, 229.

123. Neustadt 1999.

124. See Mendl 1970.

125. *FRUS,* 1961–63, vol. 13, doc. 402, "Memorandum of Conversation, Nassau, December 19, 9.45am." Here Lord Home makes it clear that "France is going ahead anyway."

126. On the development of the EEC, see Dinan 2004.

127. On Britain's first application, see Ludlow 1997.

128. See ibid.

129. See, e.g., Kleiman 1964.

130. Ludlow 1997, 211.

131. For the full text of the press conference, see de Gaulle 1970, 61–79.

132. Ibid.

133. See esp. Milward 2002. See also Winand 1993, 310.

134. Ludlow 1997, 208.

135. Winand 1993, 252; Trachtenberg 1999, 369.

136. See Ball 1982.

137. Although Ball's later reflections do leave the impression of genuine anti-Britishness. See Ball 1968, esp. chapter 6, "The Special Problem of the United Kingdom," 69–89, and chapter 7, "The Disadvantages of the Special Relationship," 90–117.

138. Ball 1982, 268.

139. Macmillan's (1973) reflections suggest that this was his impression at the time.

140. CAB 21/4979, "Record of Meeting at Nassau, 19 December 1962, 9.50am."

141. Ibid.

142. Pierre 1972, 237.

143. See Ball 1982, 267.

144. CAB 21/4979, "Extract from *Washington Post,* 15 December 1962."

145. Trachtenberg 1999, 359.

146. *FRUS,* 1961–63, vol. 13, doc. 64, "Summary Record of NSC Executive Committee Meeting no. 39, 31 January 1963."

147. Trachtenberg 1999, 370.

148. Ibid., 367–69.

149. The personal warmth of the relationship both highlighted the seriousness of the crisis and facilitated its solution. See, e.g., Horne 1989, 437–39. On the special relationship, see also Dimbleby and Reynolds 1988.

150. See, e.g., Kleiman 1964; Mangold 2006.

151. On the issue of the independent deterrent, see Dillon 1983; Simpson 1983; Malone 1984.

152. See Bartlett 1972; Dilks 1981; Peter Clarke and Trebilock 1997; Lieber 1999; Fry 2003.

153. Brandon 1963.

154. Neustadt 1999.

155. Ken Young 2004.

Chapter Four

1. During the 2010 general election, the Conservatives under David Cameron promised not to transfer more powers to the EU except if such a move was explicitly approved by a referendum. See http://www.conservatives.com/~/media/Files/Activist%20Centre/Press%20and%20Policy/Manifestos/Manifesto2010, accessed 23 August 2012.

2. See, e.g., CAB 148/10, "Report of the Oversea and Defence Policy (Official) Committee Long-Term Study Group, 23 October 1964."

3. Cited in Toomey 2007, 9.

4. Ibid., 8.

5. Cited in ibid.

6. PREM 13/317, "Notes for the Record: Meeting between Wilson and Krag, 29 January 1965."

7. Vickers 2011, 59.

8. Ibid.

9. See *Hansard,* vol. 735, cols. 1539–40, 10 November 1966.

10. PREM 13/910, "Personal Telegram from Johnson to Wilson, 15 November 1966."

11. FCO 13/170, "Letter from Blankenhorn to George Brown, 11 May 1967."

12. *Hansard,* vol. 735, cols. 1539–40, 10 November 1966.

13. See Toomey 2007, 82–99.

14. *Hansard,* vol. 735, cols. 1061–1184, 1281–1414, 1504–1656, 8, 9, 10 May 1967.

15. Ibid., 1516. See "For Entry to Europe 488–Against 62: Down to Business by Autumn," *Times,* 11 May 1967, 6.

16. PREM 13/1481, "Letter Addressed to the President of the Council of Ministers of the EEC, 11 May 1967." "Dear Mr. President [Mr. Renaat Van Elslande]," the letter read, "I have the honour, on behalf of Her Majesty's Government in the United Kingdom of Great Britain and Northern Ireland, to inform Your Excellency that the United Kingdom hereby applies to become a member of the European Economic Community under the terms of Article 237 establishing the European Economic Community."

17. PREM 13/1482, "Charles de Gaulle's Press Conference, 16 May 1967."

18. PREM 13/2464, "General de Gaulle's Press Conference, 27 November 1967." On the subsequent vote in the French parliament finalizing the decision, see also

"France Votes to Bar Britain's Entry to Common Market," *Times*, 20 December 1967, 1.

19. See Vickers 2011, 57–90.

20. Saki Dockrill 2002.

21. PREM 13/32, "UK Economic Situation: Minute by Sir W. Armstrong in Preparation for a Meeting between Mr Wilson, Mr Brown and Mr Callaghan, 16 October 1964." The UK's was said to have an international advantage as the only country with connections to the circles of Europe, the Atlantic, and the Commonwealth. Churchill painted this picture at the 1948 Conservative Party conference (cited in Deighton 2005).

22. See O'Hara and Parr 2006. See also Wilson 1971, 27–38; Ziegler 1993, 186–217. In the foreign policy sphere, this task fell to new minister of defence, Denis Healey. See Reed and Williams 1971; Healey 1990.

23. Cited in Pimlott 1992, 385. While the need for savings affected the British defense establishment as a whole and not simply East of Suez, the nuclear deterrent—which Healey won the battle to save at the Chequers weekend, probably noting that it accounted for less than 10 percent of the defense budget (Reed and Williams 1971, 169)—was viewed as Britain's second priority. An aide told LBJ that the deterrent had escaped for the "simple" reason that it "is the most important of the great power symbols still in British possession" (cited in Ziegler 1993, 210).

24. FCO 30/154, "O'Neill, 'The Political Case for Going into Europe,' 11 April 1967."

25. Ibid.

26. Ibid.

27. T312/1011, "O'Neill to Foreign Secretary, 23 July 1964."

28. See Milward 2002.

29. PREM 13/905, "Letter from Brown to Wilson, 'Policy towards France,' 1 February 1966."

30. Ibid. "Defeat in Rhodesia" referred to the November 1965 unilateral declaration of independence by Ian Smith's Rhodesian Front, which Britain did not seek to overturn by force.

31. See the comments by George Brown during the November debate. *Hansard,* vol. 736, col. 447, 16 November 1966.

32. Parr 2006, 20; emphasis added.

33. FO 30/154, "O'Neill, 'The Political Case for Going into Europe,' 11 April 1967."

34. FO 371/188347, "Chequers Meeting Briefs, 21 October 1966."

35. FCO 30/154, "O'Neill, 'The Political Case for Going into Europe,' 11 April 1967."

36. *Hansard,* vol. 746, col. 1101, 8 May 1967.

37. Gilbert Longden, ibid., col. 1145, 8 May 1967.

38. Ibid., vol. 736, col. 456, 16 November 1966.

39. Ibid., cols. 456–57, 16 November 1966.

40. See McCourt 2009.

41. CAB 134/1772, "Note by Official Committee on External Economic Policy, 'Defence and Foreign Policy Aspects of the United Kingdom Joining the European Economic Community,' 6 April 1965."

42. Ibid.

43. *Hansard,* vol. 746, col. 1095, 8 May 1967.

44. See esp. Saki Dockrill 2002.

45. *Hansard,* vol. 746, col. 1124, 8 May 1967.

46. Ibid., col. 1094, 8 May 1967.

47. CAB 148/69, "Cabinet Defence and Oversea Policy (Official) Committee, 'Britain and the EEC: Political and Military Commitments Involved in Membership of the EEC,' 29 July 1966."

48. *Hansard,* vol. 746, col. 1120, 8 May 1967.

49. FO 371/188346, "Foreign Office Paper, 'How to Get Into the Common Market,' Sent to Brown by Con O'Neill, 18 August 1966."

50. *Hansard,* vol. 746, col. 1174, 8 May 1967.

51. FCO 30/154, "O'Neill, 'The Political Case for Going into Europe,' 11 April 1967."

52. *Hansard,* vol. 746, col. 1174, 8 May 1967.

53. Ibid., col. 1089, 8 May 1967.

54. Ibid., col. 1152, 8 May 1967.

55. CAB 134/1772, "Official Committee on External Economic Policy, 'The Development of the European Communities, and the Implications for British Policy,' 25 March 1965."

56. FO 371/188346, "Meeting on Britain and Europe, Draft Note by the First Secretary and the Foreign Secretary, 26 September 1966."

57. Ibid.

58. Trevor Park, *Hansard,* vol. 746, col. 1168, 8 May 1967.

59. Ibid.

60. FCO 30/154, "O'Neill, 'The Political Case for Going into Europe,' 11 April 1967."

61. FO 371/188337, "Extract of Nora Beloff, 'Secret Talks on Market Entry at Expense of Sterling Bloc,' *The Observer,* 8 May 1966."

62. See, e.g., PREM 13/897, "Letter from Michael Palliser to Oliver Wright, 21 October, 1966."

63. PREM 13/1476, "Extract of 'Debate Is Meaningless,' *Daily Express,* 3 February 1967."

64. *Hansard,* vol. 746, col. 1344, 9 May 1967.

65. Ibid., col. 1097, 8 May 1967.

66. Ibid.

67. PREM 13/909, "Telegram from Washington to the Foreign Office, Sir Richard Powell's Visit to Washington, 2 November 1966."

68. PREM 13/1475, "Letter from Dean to the Secretary of State, 13 January 1967."

69. Ibid.

70. *FRUS,* 1964–68, vol. 13, doc. 173, "Memorandum by the Acheson Group: Measures to Increase the Cohesion of NATO and the North Atlantic Community, n.d."

71. PREM 13/910, "Prime Minister's Personal Telegram T 364/66, Letter from Johnson to Wilson, 15 November 1966."

72. PREM 13/910, "'United States Policy towards Europe,' Speech to Delegates at the National Conference of Editorial Writers, 12 October 1966."

73. PREM 13/907, "Extract of a Conversation between the Prime Minister, the Chancellor of the Exchequer and Mr. [Henry] Fowler, 27 July 1966."

74. Ibid.

75. *FRUS,* 1964–68, vol. 12, doc. 264, "Memorandum from the Under-Secretary of State (Ball) to President Johnson, 22 July 1966."

76. Ibid.

77. Ibid.

78. FCO 30/170, "Telegram from Dean to Foreign Office, 'Britain and the EEC,' 20 May 1967."

79. Ibid.

80. Ibid.

81. PREM 13/907, "Extract of *The Times,* 27 July 1966."

82. *Hansard,* vol. 746, col. 1152, 8 May 1967.

83. PREM 13/905, "Speech at Signing of Proclamation on the Polish Christian Millennium Anniversary, 3 May 1966."

84. Ibid.

85. PREM 13/906, "Prime Minister's Personal Telegram T 196/66, Johnson to Wilson, 23 May 1966."

86. Ibid.

87. PREM 13/1475, "Letter from Dean to Secretary of State, 13 January 1967."

88. Ibid.

89. PREM 13/904, "Extract from a Conversation between the Prime Minister and Mr. Ball on 8 September 1965."

90. *FRUS,* 1964–68, vol. 13, Doc. 251, "Summary Notes of the 569th Meeting of the National Security Council, 3 May 1967."

91. Ibid.

92. PREM 13/909, "Powell to FO, 2 November 1966."

93. FCO 30/154, "O'Neill, 'The Political Case for Going into Europe,' 11 April 1967."

94. *FRUS,* 1964–68, vol. 13, doc. 250, "Circular Telegram from the Department of State to Certain Posts in Europe, 2 May 1967."

95. Ibid.

96. *FRUS,* 1964–68, vol. 13, doc. 257, "Memorandum of a Conversation, 9 June 1967."

97. Ibid.

98. PREM 13/907, "Extract of a Conversation between the Prime Minister, Chancellor of the Exchequer and US Trade Secretary Henry Fowler, 27 July 1966."

99. PREM 13/910, "Prime Minister's Personal Telegram T360/66, Letter from Wilson to Johnson, 11 November 1966."

100. *FRUS, 1964–68*, vol. 13, doc. 278, "Memorandum of a Conversation, 6 December 1967."

101. PREM 13/1475, "Letter from Dean to Secretary of State, 13 January 1967."

102. PREM 13/1475, "Letter from Patrick Dean to the Secretary of State (via Con O'Neill), 13 January 1967."

103. PREM 13/1478, "Record of a Meeting between the Prime Minister and the Foreign Secretary and the Italian Prime Minister at Palazzo Chigi, Rome, 16 January 1967, 10am."

104. PREM 13/906, "Record of a Meeting between the Prime Minister and the Foreign Secretary and the Federal German Chancellor and Foreign Minister in the Palais Schaumburg, Bonn, 15 February 1967, 10am." For an earlier communication of the same message, see "Germany Urges Britain to Join Six," *Times,* 13 December 1966, 7.

105. PREM 13/1476, "Record of a Meeting held between the Prime Minister and Foreign Secretary and the Belgian Prime Minister and the Belgian Foreign Minister at the Ministry of Foreign Affairs, Brussels, 1 February, 1967, at 9.30am."

106. See "Five Back Britain in Face of France," *Times,* 27 June 1967, 4.

107. Wilson 1971, 335–36.

108. PREM 13/1476, "Record of a Meeting between the Prime Minister and the Foreign Secretary, and the Belgian Prime Minister and Foreign Minister at the Chateau de Val Duchesse, Brussels, Tuesday 31 January, 1967."

109. See Ludlow 2007.

110. PREM 13/1478, "Record of a Meeting between the Prime Minister and the Foreign Secretary and the Italian Prime Minister at Palazzo Chigi, Rome, on 16th January, 1967, at 10am."

111. PREM 13/1477, "Record of a Meeting between the British Prime Minister and Foreign Secretary and the Federal German Chancellor and Foreign Minister in the Palais Schaumburg, Bonn, Wednesday, 15 February, 1967."

112. See Edgerton 1996.

113. PREM 13/1477, "Record of a Meeting between the Prime Minister and Secretary of State and the Netherlands Prime Minister and Foreign Minister, at the Rolzaal, the Hague, 27 February 1967, 10am."

114. PREM 13/1477, "Record of a Meeting between the British Prime Minister and Foreign Secretary and the Federal German Chancellor and Foreign Minister in the Palais Schaumburg, Bonn, Wednesday, 15 February, 1967, 10am."

115. PREM 13/1477, "Record of a Meeting between the British Prime Minister and Foreign Secretary and the Federal German Chancellor and Foreign Minister in the Palais Schaumburg, Bonn, Wednesday, 15 February, 1967, 10.35am."

116. PREM 13/1477, "Extract from Interview with German Chancellor Kiesinger, Televised 18 February 1967."

117. PREM 13/1477, "Telegram from British Embassy in Bonn to Foreign Office, 18 February 1967."

118. For a good discussion of the significance of the crisis, see Ludlow 1999.

119. PREM 13/1477, "Record of a Meeting between the British Prime Minister and Foreign Secretary and the Federal German Chancellor and Foreign Minister in the Palais Schaumburg, Bonn, Wednesday, 15 February, 1967."

120. Ibid.

121. PREM 13/1476, "Record of a Meeting held between the Prime Minister and Foreign Secretary and the Belgian Prime Minister and the Belgian Foreign Minister at the Ministry of Foreign Affairs, Brussels, 1 February, 1967, at 9.30am."

122. Ibid.

123. PREM 13/909, "Telegram from Sir Peter Garran in the Hague to London, 2 November 1966."

124. Ibid.

125. PREM 13/1477, "Record of a Meeting between the British Prime Minister and Foreign Secretary and the Netherlands Prime Minister and Foreign Minister at the Rolzaal, the Hague, 27 February 1967, 10am."

126. PREM 13/1477, "Record of a Meeting between the British Prime Minister and Foreign Secretary and the Federal German Chancellor and Foreign Minister in the Palais Schaumburg, Bonn, Wednesday, 15 February, 1967."

127. Cited in Toomey 2007, 58.

128. PREM 13/1475, "Record of a Meeting between the Foreign Secretary and the President of the French Republic at the Palais de l'Élysée, 16 December 1966."

129. Parr 2006, 152.

130. Ibid.

131. Ibid., 152–53.

132. PREM 13/897, "Letter from Michael Palliser to Oliver Wright, 21 October 1966."

133. *FRUS,* 1964–68, vol. 13, doc. 188, "Memorandum from the Assistant Secretary of State for Economic Affairs (Solomon) and the Deputy Assistant Secretary of State for European Affairs (Stoessel) to the Under Secretary of State (Ball), 19 July 1966."

134. PREM 13/1479, "Observations on EEC Entry after Visits of the Prime Minister and Foreign Secretary to the Capitals of the Six, 31 March 1967."

135. PREM 13/1475, "Telegram from Patrick Reilly (Paris) to Foreign Office, 9 January 1967."

136. Ibid.

137. CAB 148/69, "Cabinet Defence and Oversea Policy (Official) Committee, 'The International Consequences of de Gaulle,' 18 March 1966."

138. See Cerny 1980.

139. CAB 134/2705, "Cabinet Ministerial Committee on Europe, 'Politico-Military Implications of United Kingdom Entry into the European Communities,' 23 August 1960." The paper notes that these objectives could be found in de Gaulle's memoirs (3).

140. See Milward 1992.

141. PREM 13/1477, "Record of a Meeting between the British Prime Minister and Foreign Secretary and the Federal German Chancellor and Foreign Minister, at the Palais Schaumburg, Bonn, 16 February, 1967."

142. PREM 13/1475, "The Foreign Secretary's Conversations in Paris with President de Gaulle and Monsieur Couve de Murville, 30 December 1966."

143. CAB 134/2705, "Cabinet Ministerial Committee on Europe, 'Politico-Military Implications of United Kingdom Entry into the European Communities,' 23 August 1960."

144. *Hansard,* vol. 746, col. 1121, 8 May 1967.

145. PREM 13/906, "Note by Michael Palliser, 11 May 1966."

146. Ibid.

147. PREM 13/907, "Record of a Conversation during the French Prime Minister's Luncheon for the Prime Minister, at the French Embassy, 8 July 1966."

148. PREM 13/1483, "Extract from a Record of a Conversation between the Prime Minister and the President of France at the Grand Trianon, Versailles, 19 June 1967."

149. PREM 13/1479, "Observations on EEC Entry after Visits of the Prime Minister and the Foreign Secretary to the Capitals of the Six, 31 March 1967."

150. PREM 13/1475, "Record of a Meeting between the Foreign Secretary and the President of the French Republic at the Palais de l'Élysée, 16 December 1966."

151. PREM 13/1483, "Extract from a Record of a Conversation between the Prime Minister and the President of France at the Grand Trianon, Versailles, 19 June 1967."

152. Ibid.

153. Ibid.

154. PREM 13/1482, "General de Gaulle's Press Conference, 16 May 1967."

155. Ibid.

156. FCO 30/170, "Reilly to the Foreign Office, 5 October 1967."

157. FCO 30/83, "Letter from Brown to Wilson, 9 April 1967."

158. FCO 30/170, "Reilly to the Foreign Office, 6 October 1967."

159. PREM 13/1483, "Extract from a Record of a Conversation between the Prime Minister and the President of France at the Grand Trianon, Versailles, 19 June 1967."

160. PREM 13/1481, "Personal Telegram from Wilson to De Gaulle, 1 May 1967."

161. *Hansard,* vol. 746, col. 1283, 9 May 1967.

162. See Catterall 2003. On the post-veto progress of the bid, see Pine 2007.

163. *Hansard,* vol. 746, col. 1506, 10 May 1967.

164. Ibid.

165. Milward 2002.

166. PREM 13/907, "Extract from a Record of a Meeting between the Prime Minister and His Advisers and President Johnson and His Advisers at the White House, 29 July 1966."

167. Parr 2006, 20.

Chapter Five

1. The British Nationality Act of 1981 renamed the "Crown Colonies" "British Dependent Territories." In addition to the Falkland Islands, Britain in 1982 retained control over Belize and Gibraltar, where sovereignty was also at issue, and a number of other territories. For an overview, see Central Office of Information 1992. For British force deployments outside of the NATO area, see also Michael Dockrill 1988, 108.

2. Ibid., 115. For Minister of Defence John Nott's reflections, see Nott 2003.

3. Michael Dockrill 1988, 99–110. Britain retained sea-based aerial capacity through the deftly titled "through-deck cruisers"—effectively small aircraft carriers.

4. The Falkland Islands are Las Islas Malvinas in Spanish. Throughout this chapter, *the Falklands* will be used in reference to British discourse regarding the islands, whereas *Las Malvinas* will be used in reference to Argentine discourse.

5. This famous remark was made by Enoch Powell at the beginning of the conflict. See *Hansard* (6th ser.), vol. 21, col. 644, 3 April 1982.

6. See Metford 1968; Freedman 2005a.

7. The previous settlers were removed in 1833. On the islands' complex and contested legal status, see Goebel 1927; Bologna 1983; Myhre 1983; Bluth 1987.

8. See Bologna 1983.

9. On the issue of Las Malvinas in Argentine domestic politics, see esp. Calvert 1992; more generally, Bicheno 2006.

10. See Freedman 2005a, 20–21.

11. On Argentine preparations for war, see esp. Gamba 1987; Freedman and Stonehouse-Gamba 1990.

12. See Ellerby 1992.

13. See "Saga of Misjudgment in the Talks That Failed," *Times*, 6 April 1982, 3. On the contested nature of sovereignty in international politics, including a discussion of the Falklands dispute, see Kratochwil, Rohrlich, and Mahajan 1985. A related body of literature has emerged, specifically within constructivism, on the question of how territory is constructed as divisible or indivisible. See esp. Goddard 2006; Hassner 2009.

14. See, e.g., Bicheno 2006. See also Reagan's (1990) assessment of the conflict in his autobiography.

15. Kinney 1989, 76.

16. Freedman 2005b, 16.

17. "Task Force Ordered 'Full Speed Ahead,'" *Times*, 5 April 1982, 1. The total exclusion zone replaced the maritime exclusion zone around the islands that Nott had announced in the Commons on 7 April. See Central Office of Information 1982, 43.

18. "Cruiser Torpedoed by Royal Navy Sinks," *Times*, 4 May 1982, 1. On the attacks on the *Belgrano* and *Sheffield*, see Freedman 2005b, 284–93, 294–311. On the *Belgrano*, see also Freedman and Stonehouse-Gamba 1990, 247–71.

19. There are a growing number of studies on the military aspects of the Falklands conflict. See esp. Sunday Times Insight Team 1982; Hastings and Jenkins 1983; Middlebrook 1985; Freedman 2005b; Bicheno 2006. For a personal perspective, see Woodward 1992.

20. Charlton 1989, 158.

21. For his personal recollections, see Haig 1984.

22. See Toase 2005.

23. For a good discussion of the Haig mission, see Freedman and Stonehouse-Gamba 1990, 238–43. See also Freedman 2005b, 127–78.

24. See Freedman 2005b, 341–75. For a personal account, see Pérez de Cuellar 1997.

25. "Third Division Takes on Britain," *Times,* 3 April 1982, 3.

26. On the military aspects of the war, see Middlebrook 1985; Freedman 2005b.

27. See Freedman 2005b, 39–47.

28. Freedman and Stonehouse-Gamba 1990, 78.

29. See the reply of Eduardo Roca, Argentina's ambassador to the UN, to Anthony Parsons during the early debate in the UN Security Council, in Freedman 2005b, 44.

30. See "Galtieri Pledges 'No Disruption,'" *Times,* 3 April 1982, 1.

31. Cited in Freedman 2005b, 42.

32. Freedman and Stonehouse-Gamba 1990, 205.

33. "World Blows Hot and Cold," *Times,* 5 April 1982, 4.

34. Pérez de Cuellar 1997, 381.

35. Cited in Freedman 2005b, 47.

36. *Hansard,* vol. 24, col. 511, 20 May 1982.

37. Ibid.

38. Dillon 1989, 55.

39. Ibid., 89.

40. *Hansard,* vol. 21, col. 633, 3 April 1982.

41. Ibid.

42. Central Office of Information 1982, 24.

43. See ibid., 134–37.

44. *Hansard,* vol. 21, col. 633, 3 April 1982.

45. Femenia 1996, 134.

46. Sharp 1997, 67.

47. *Hansard,* vol. 23, cols. 25–26, 4 May 1982.

48. As Pym told the Commons on 4 May, for example, "The truth is—and cannot be said too often—that the Argentines started this trouble. They invaded the islands, which they had no right to do" (*Hansard,* vol. 23, col. 26, 4 May 1982).

49. Ibid., vol. 21, col. 659, 3 April 1982.

50. See Simpson and Bennett 1985.

51. *Hansard,* vol. 23, col. 990, 13 May 1982.

52. Ibid., vol. 21, col. 639, 3 April 1982.

53. Freedman and Stonehouse-Gamba 1990, 138.

54. See "Argentines Fail to Rally Support," *Times,* 8 April 1982, 4.

55. Bicheno 2006, 67.

56. *Hansard Digest,* vol. 21, col. 1148, 14 April 1982.

57. Freedman and Stonehouse-Gamba 1990, 151.

58. Ibid., 140.

59. Freedman 2005b, 41.

60. See Adams 1986.

61. *Hansard,* vol. 21, col. 638, 3 April 1982.

62. On the conflict's European dimension, see Lisa L. Martin 1992; Stavridis and Hill 1996; Bicheno 2006, 81–82.

63. Edwards 1996, 41. See also "Falklands Crisis," *Times,* 14 April 1982, 4, which notes that the "EEC supported Britain with dramatic speed."

64. Edwards 1996, 42.

65. *Hansard,* vol. 21, col. 1206, 14 April 1982.

66. Ibid., vol. 23, cols. 970–71, 13 May 1982.

67. Ibid., vol. 21, col. 1148, 14 April 1982.

68. On French opinions, see Stavridis and Regelsberger 1996. During the conflict, French prime minister Pierre Mauroy visited similar French possession off the coast of Canada in what was explained as a mere coincidence but which seemed anything but. See "Mauroy Visits France's Other Islands," *Times,* 22 April 1982, 8.

69. Freedman and Stonehouse-Gamba 1990, 154.

70. Ibid.

71. Nott 2002, 305.

72. *Hansard,* vol. 21, col. 639, 3 April 1982.

73. Ibid., 9 June 1982.

74. Ibid.

75. E.g., Andrew Mayer, in ibid., col. 193.

76. Ibid., vol. 24, col. 468, 20 May 1982.

77. Ibid., vol. 22, col. 418, 22 April 1982.

78. Ibid., vol. 23, col. 953, 13 May 1982.

79. See Sharp 1997, 74–78.

80. *Hansard,* vol. 21, col. 1024, 7 April 1982.

81. Ibid., col. 863, 7 April 1982.

82. Ibid., col. 1051, 14 April 1982.

83. Ibid., vol. 23, col. 28, 4 May 1982.

84. Ibid., vol. 21, col. 961, 7 April 1982.

85. Freedman and Stonehouse-Gamba 1990, 6.

86. Ibid., 152.

87. Although few observers now believe that oil was an important factor in British decision making with regard to the Falklands. See Freedman 2005a, 22–23. Oil has, however, recently become an important issue. See "Argentina Threatens Legal Action over Falklands Oil," http://www.bbc.co.uk/news/world-latin-america-17390911, accessed 6 September 2012. On the place of shame and

jingoism in the conflict, see Bicheno 2006, 84–97. For a discussion of the argument concerning Thatcher's position, see Sharp 1997, 65–66.

88. The main spokesman for this line was Denis Healey, now on the opposition benches. See, e.g., his intervention in the Commons on 7 May (*Hansard,* vol. 23, cols. 396–97, 7 May 1982).

89. Central Office of Information 1982, 34.

90. See Freedman and Stonehouse-Gamba 1990, 151.

91. Central Office of Information 1982, 34.

92. *Hansard,* vol. 22, col. 992, 29 April 1982.

93. Ibid., vol. 24, col. 190, 18 May 1982.

94. Ibid., col. 477, 20 May 1982.

95. Ibid., vol. 21, col. 571, 2 April 1982.

96. Ibid.

97. Ibid., col. 1147, 14 April 1982.

98. Ibid., vol. 22, col. 720, 27 April 1982.

99. Ibid., col. 1054, 29 April 1982.

100. Ibid., col. 1003, 29 April 1982.

101. Ibid., vol. 21, col. 1155, 14 April 1982.

102. Ibid., col. 1170, 14 April 1982.

103. Ibid., vol. 22, col. 610, 26 April 1982.

104. Ibid., col. 986, 29 April 1982.

105. See, e.g., "The Death of the Belgrano," in the special section of the *Sunday Times,* 9 May 1982, 15–19.

106. "Sympathy for Britain Wanes," *Times,* 5 May 1982, 2.

107. See Freedman and Stonehouse-Gamba 1990, 272–91.

108. Member of Parliament Tam Dalyell in particular was convinced this was the case. See Henderson 1994, 455. For a discussion of this suggestion, see Freedman 2005b. See also Dalyell 1983; Ponting 1985; Rossiter 2007.

109. See Freedman 2005b, 687–702.

110. "Victory Yes, but Don't Rub It In," *Times,* 7 June 1982, 14.

111. Hastings and Jenkins 1983, 169. See Freedman and Stonehouse-Gamba 1990, 323.

112. Thatcher 1993, 173.

113. Cited in Sharp 1997, 68.

114. *Hansard,* vol. 21, col. 645, 3 April 1982.

115. Ibid., col. 336, 3 April 1982.

116. Alan Clark 2001, 310.

117. *Hansard,* vol. 21, col. 332, 3 April 1982.

118. Bicheno 2006, 87.

119. Hastings and Jenkins 1983, 84.

120. *Hansard,* vol. 21, col. 1032, 7 April 1982.

121. Quoted in Bicheno 2006, 95.

122. *Hansard,* vol. 21, col. 1021, 7 April 1982.

123. Peter Hennessy 2000, 416.

124. *Hansard,* vol. 21, col. 965, 7 April 1982.

125. Ibid., col. 960, 7 April 1982

126. Ibid., col. 1084, 8 April 1982.

127. Thatcher 1993, 181.

128. *Hansard,* vol. 21, col. 990, 7 April 1982.

129. Ibid., col. 1038, 7 April 1982.

130. For an explanation of Thatcher's response to the conflict based on the notion of painful choices in international politics, see Welch 2005.

131. Haig 1984, 296.

132. Alan Clark 2001, 318.

133. Dumbrell 2001.

134. See Windsor 1983, 92. On US-Argentine relations prior to the war, see Freedman and Stonehouse-Gamba 1990, 32–33.

135. Henderson 1987, 86.

136. "Reagan Dispatches Haig on Peace Mission to London," *Times,* 8 April 1982, 1. See also Freedman and Stonehouse-Gamba 1990, 238–39.

137. Freedman and Stonehouse-Gamba 1990, 187.

138. Ibid., 239–40.

139. Haig 1984, 271.

140. Ibid., 151.

141. Kinney 1989, 76.

142. Nott 2002, 291.

143. See Freedman 2005b, 124–25; "Kirkpatrick Explains Embassy Dinner," *Times,* 12 April 1982, 4.

144. See esp. Freedman and Stonehouse-Gamba 1990, 354–56.

145. Haig 1984, 294.

146. Ibid., 282.

147. Henderson 1994, 452.

148. Ibid.

149. Weinberger 1990, 144.

150. Ibid.

151. See esp. Nott 2002, 288.

152. Freedman 2005b, 71.

153. See, e.g., "An Ally Not an Umpire," *Times,* 12 April 1982, 7.

154. Haig 1984, 266.

155. Ibid., 273.

156. Freedman 2005b, 179. See also Thatcher 1993, 188.

157. "US Imposes Economic and Military Curbs on Argentina," *Times,* 1 May 1982, 1.

158. Haig 1984, 293.

159. *Hansard,* vol. 23, col. 281, 9 May 1982.

160. See "By Jingo, We're All Rooting for You," *Times,* 7 April 1982, 10. See also Freedman and Stonehouse-Gamba 1990, 237–38; "Pro-British Mood Grows on Capitol Hill," *Times,* 23 April 1982, 8.

161. See Haig 1984. See also Freedman 2005b, 178.

162. See Richardson 1996.

163. *Hansard,* vol. 25, col. 724, 15 June 1982.

164. Bicheno 2006, 24.

165. Dodds 2002, 6.

166. Cited in Boyce 2005, 221.

167. Thatcher 1993, 8–9.

168. Calvocoressi (1979, 199) nevertheless argues that there is no such thing as a world power grade two.

169. "Retaking the Falklands," *Sunday Times,* 4 April 1982, 17.

170. Sharp 1997, 70.

171. Ibid., 71.

172. "Argentina Calls on Cameron to Reopen Falklands Talks," *BBC News Online,* 18 May 2010, http://news.bbc.co.uk/2/hi/uk_news/8689991.stm, accessed 14 September 2012.

173. As indicated by the strong reaction to recent tensions, including the sending of one of the Royal Navy's newest destroyers. See, e.g., "HMS Dauntless Sails for the Falklands," *BBC News Online,* 4 April 2012, www.bbc.co.uk/news/uk-17606130, accessed 14 September 2012.

Conclusion

1. See McNay 2001.

2. Ibid., 197.

3. The desire to ensure top-quality military hardware through "interdependence" with the US, even if doing so meant buying off the shelf remains a prominent aspect of British defense policy. During the Falklands conflict, this tendency was manifest in the combination of American Sidewinder 9-L missiles and Sea Harrier jets—British-built but used by the US Navy. This American connection was also meant to augment rather than replace Britain's own armaments industry. As Edgerton (2006) has suggested, postwar Britain was in every way as much a "warfare state" as a "welfare state." At the time of this writing, Britain remains on course to purchase from the US the successor to the Polaris-Trident nuclear missile system. See "Brown Backs Trident Replacement," 21 June 2006, news.bbc.co.uk/2/hi/5103764.stm, accessed 28 August 2012.

4. As was made clear during the discussions over the withdrawal from East of Suez. The option of stationing Polaris east of Suez as part of a thinned-down military capability in the area was briefly entertained before being swiftly shelved. See Jones and Young 2010.

5. Simms (2001, 6) refers to the Major government's foreign policy doctrine as "profoundly conservative philosophical realism."

6. Michael Clarke 2007, 593.

7. Blair 2010.

8. Barnett 1997.

9. Curtis 2003; Williams 2005; McCourt 2013.

10. David Miliband, "Strong Britain in a Strong Europe," Speech at the International Institute for Strategic Studies, London, 26 October 2009, www.iiss.org/EasySiteWeb/getresource.axd?AssetID=32217, accessed 22 February 22, 2013.

11. Ibid.

12. Blair 2003.

13. Wendt 1999, 227-28.

14. Waltz 1979, 121.

15. Ibid., 126. Waltz attributes the term to Stephen Van Evera.

16. Alker 1996, 356.

17. Ibid.

18. See, e.g., Lake 2011.

19. Onuf 1989, 163.

20. Indeed, a number of scholars have recently converged on the notion of hierarchy as a more fruitful starting point for analysis in IR. See Cooley 2005; Bially Mattern 2005; Nexon 2009b; Towns 2010; Zarakol 2013.

21. See Jackson 2007; Nexon 2009b; Neumann and Sending 2010; Pouliot 2011; Zarakol 2011.

22. Goffman 1990. Jervis 1970 places these issues more centrally and might therefore have points of significant correlation with my research.

23. Along these lines, see Cynthia Weber 1998.

24. Jackson 2007 is strongly Weberian; Nexon 2009b draws on the insights of Charles Tilly; Neumann and Sending 2010 focuses on the insights of Foucault; and Zarakol 2010 uses Goffman, to refer to just the examples cited here.

25. Bell 2001. Although the relationship between Morgenthau's thought and the work of Max Weber and the way in which Morgenthau's intellectual lineage was shaped by his critique of liberal democracy suggest that realists, too, need to consider the implications of the resocialization of IR theory. See Barkawi 1998.

26. Kratochwil 1989; Onuf 1989. As noted, Wendt (1999) also drew heavily on Mead and Parsons.

Epilogue

1. "Blair Wins War Backing amid Revolt," *BBC News Online* http://news.bbc.co.uk/1/hi/uk_politics/2862325.stm, accessed 11 April 2013; "'Million' March against Iraq War," http://news.bbc.co.uk/1/hi/2765041.stm, accessed 11 April 2013.

2. See Jackson 2007.

3. "David Cameron Promises in/out Referendum on EU," http://www.bbc.co.uk/news/uk-politics-21148282, accessed 22 February 2013.

4. See, e.g., in terms entirely in line with the findings of chapter 5, "UK Risks 'Turning Inwards over EU Referendum—US Official," http://www.bbc.co.uk/news/uk-politics-20961651, accessed 22 February 2013.

5. See the warnings by senior Conservative Ken Clarke and Liberal Demo-

cratic deputy prime minister Nick Clegg in "EU Exit Would Be a 'Fatal Mistake'
says Ken Clarke," http://www.bbc.co.uk/news/uk-politics-21269658, accessed 22
February 2013; "Nick Clegg Warning to PM over EU Referendum," http://www.
bbc.co.uk/news/uk-politics-21024123, accessed 22 February 2013.

   6. "Germans Want EU Budget Commissioner for Greece," http://www.bbc.
co.uk/news/world-europe-16773974, accessed 11 April 2013; "Cyprus Bailout:
Deal   Reached   in   Eurogroup   Talks,"   http://www.bbc.co.uk/news/world
-europe-21916102, accessed 11 April 2013.

   7. "Scottish Independence: Cameron and Salmond Strike Referendum Deal,"
http://www.bbc.co.uk/news/uk-scotland-scotland-politics-19942638,   accessed
19 April 2013.

   8. "Scottish Independence: How Do You Defend a Small Country?" http://
www.bbc.co.uk/news/uk-scotland-scotland-politics-21628443, accessed 19 April
2013.

References

Primary Sources

Manuscript Collections at The National Archives of the UK

Files of the Cabinet Office
Files of the Foreign and Commonwealth Office
Files of the Foreign Office
Files of the Minister of Defence
Files of the Minister of State for Air
Files of the Office of the Admiralty
Files of the Prime Minister's Office

Published Primary Sources

Acheson, Dean. "Our Atlantic Alliance: The Political and Economic Strands." *Vital Speeches* 29, no. 6 (1963): 163–64.
Britain's Associated States and Dependencies. London: HMSO, 1981.
Central Office of Information. *Britain and the Falklands Crisis: A Documentary Record*. London, 1982.
De Gaulle, Charles. *Discours et Messages*. Vol. 4, *Août 1962–Décembre 1965*. Paris: Plon, 1970.
Foreign Relations of the United States. http://history.state.gov/historicaldocuments. Accessed 16 August 2012.

Secondary Sources

Abbott, Andrew. "What Do Cases Do? Some Notes on Activity in Sociological Analysis." In *What Is a Case? Exploring the Foundations of Social Inquiry,* ed. Charles C. Ragin and Howard S. Becker. Cambridge: Cambridge University Press, 1992.
Abbott, Andrew. *Time Matters: On Theory and Method*. Chicago: University of Chicago Press, 2001.

Acuff, Jonathan. "Spectacle and Space in the Creation of Premodern and Modern Polities: Toward a Mixed Ontology of Collective Identity." *International Political Sociology* 6, no. 2 (2012): 132–48.

Adams, Valerie. *The Media and the Falklands Campaign.* Basingstoke: Macmillan, 1986.

Adamthwaite, Anthony. "Britain and the World, 1945–9: The View from the Foreign Office." *International Affairs* 61, no. 2 (1985): 223–35.

Adler, Emanuel. "Seizing the Middle Ground: Constructivism in World Politics." *European Journal of International Relations* 3, no. 3 (1997): 319–63.

Adler, Emanuel, and Michael N. Barnett. *Security Communities.* Cambridge: Cambridge University Press, 1998.

Adler, Emanuel, and Vincent Pouliot. *International Practices.* Cambridge: Cambridge University Press, 2011.

Aggestam, Lisbeth. *Role Conceptions and the Politics of Identity in Foreign Policy.* Oslo: ARENA, 1999.

Aggestam, Lisbeth, and Adrian Hyde-Price, eds. *Security and Identity in Europe: Exploring the New Agenda.* New York: St. Martin's, 2000.

Alker, Hayward. *Rediscoveries and Reformulations: Humanistic Methodologies for International Studies.* Cambridge: Cambridge University Press, 1996.

Allingham, Michael, ed. *Rational Choice Theory: Critical Concepts in the Social Sciences.* London: Routledge, 2006.

Anderson, Benedict. *Imagined Communities.* London: Verso, 1983.

Aristotle. *The Physics.* Oxford: Oxford University Press, 1979.

Ashley, Richard. "The Poverty of Neorealism." *International Organization* 38, no. 2 (1984): 225–86.

Ashton, Nigel J. *Kennedy, Macmillan, and the Cold War: The Irony of Interdependence.* Basingstoke: Palgrave Macmillan, 2002.

Athens, Lonnie. "Mead's Lost Conception of Society." *Symbolic Interactionism* 28, no. 3 (2005): 305–25.

Baldwin, John. *George Herbert Mead.* London: Sage, 1986.

Ball, George W. *The Discipline of Power: Essentials of a Modern World Structure.* London: Bodley Head, 1968.

Ball, George W. *The Past Has Another Pattern.* London: Norton, 1982.

Banton, Michael. *Roles: An Introduction to the Study of Social Relations.* London: Tavistock, 1965.

Barbier, Collette. "The French Decision to Develop a Military Nuclear Programme in the 1950s." *Diplomacy and Statecraft* 4, no. 1 (1993): 103–13.

Barder, Alexander J., and Daniel D. Levine. "'The World Is Too Much with Us': Reification and the Depoliticising of *Via Media* Constructivist IR." *Millennium: Journal of International Studies* 40, no. 3 (2012): 585–604.

Barder, Brian. "Britain: Still Looking for That Role?" *Political Quarterly* 72, no. 3 (2001): 366–74.

Barkawi, Tarak. "Strategy as Vocation: Weber, Morgenthau, and Modern Strategic Studies." *Review of International Studies* 24, no. 2 (1998): 159–84.

Barker, Elisabeth. *The British between the Superpowers, 1945–50.* London: Macmillan, 1983.

Barnes, Jonathan, ed. *The Cambridge Companion to Aristotle.* Cambridge: Cambridge University Press, 1995.

Barnett, Corelli. *The Collapse of British Power.* London: Methuen, 1972.

Barnett, Corelli. *Audit of War: The Illusion and Reality of Britain as a Great Nation.* London: Macmillan, 1986.

Barnett, Corelli. *The Lost Victory: British Dreams, British Realities, 1945–1990.* London: Macmillan, 1995.

Barnett, Corelli. "Britain Is Still Far Too Big for Its Army Boots." *Sunday Times,* 26 October 1997.

Bartelson, Jens. "Second Natures: Is the State Identical with Itself?" *European Journal of International Relations* 4, no. 3 (1998): 295–326.

Bartlett, C. J. *The Long Retreat: A Short History of British Defence Policy, 1945–70.* London: Macmillan, 1972.

Bartlett, C. J. *"The Special Relationship": A Political History of Anglo-American Relations since 1945.* London: Longman, 1992.

Baylis, John. *Anglo-American Defence Relations, 1939–1980.* London: Macmillan, 1981.

Beaufre, André. *The Suez Expedition 1956.* New York: Praeger, 1969.

Bell, Duncan. "International Relations: The Dawn of a Historiographical Turn?" *British Journal of Politics and International Relations* 3, no. 1 (2001): 115–26.

Berger, Peter L., and Thomas Luckmann. *The Social Construction of Reality: A Treatise in the Sociology of Knowledge.* London: Penguin, 1967.

Bevir, Mark. "Meta-Methodology: Clearing the Underbrush." In *The Oxford Handbook of Political Methodology,* ed. J. Box-Steffensmeier, H. Brady, and D. Collier. Oxford: Oxford University Press, 2008.

Bevir, Mark, and R. A. W. Rhodes. "Interpretive Theory." In *Theory and Methods in Political Science,* ed. Gerry Stoker and David Marsh. Basingstoke: Palgrave Macmillan, 2003.

Bially Mattern, Janice. *Ordering International Politics: Identity, Crisis, and Representational Force.* New York: Routledge, 2005.

Bicheno, Hugh. *Razor's Edge: The Unofficial History of the Falklands War.* London: Weidenfeld and Nicolson, 2006.

Biddle, Bruce J., and Edwin J. Thomas, eds. *Role Theory: Concepts and Research.* New York: Wiley, 1966.

Biersteker, Thomas J., and Cynthia Weber., eds. *State Sovereignty as Social Construct.* Cambridge: Cambridge University Press, 1996.

Blair, Tony. Speech at the Lord Mayor's Banquet, 10 November 2003.

Blair, Tony. *A Journey: My Political Life.* New York: Knopf, 2010.

Bloom, William. *Personal Identity, National Identity, and International Relations.* Cambridge: Cambridge University Press, 1990.

Blumer, Herbert. "Sociological Implications of the Thought of George Herbert Mead." *American Journal of Sociology* 71, no. 5 (1966): 535–44.

Blumer, Herbert. *Symbolic Interactionism: Perspective and Method.* Berkeley: University of California Press, 1986.

Blumer, Herbert. *George Herbert Mead and Human Conduct.* Walnut Creek, CA: Altamira, 2004.

Bluth, Christopher. "The British Resort to Force in the Falklands/Malvinas Conflict of 1982: International Law and Just War Theory." *Journal of Peace Research* 24, no. 1 (1987): 5–20.

Blyth, Mark. *Great Transformations: Economic Ideas and Institutional Change in the Twentieth Century.* Cambridge: Cambridge University Press, 2002.

Boetcher, Williams A., III. "The Prospects for Prospect Theory: An Empirical Evaluation of International Relations Applications of Framing and Loss Aversion." *Political Psychology* 25, no. 3 (2004): 331–62.

Bologna, Alfredo Bruno. "Argentine Claims to the Malvinas under International Law." *Millennium: Journal of International Studies* 12, no. 1 (1983): 39–48.

Borges, Jorge Luis. "On Exactitude in Science." In *Collected Fictions,* trans. Andrew Hurley. New York: Viking, 1998.

Boyce, D. George. *The Falklands War.* Basingstoke: Palgrave Macmillan, 2005.

Brandon, Henry. "Skybolt: The Full inside Story of How a Missile Nearly Split the West." *Sunday Times,* 8 December 1963.

Brinkley, Douglas. "Dean Acheson and the 'Special Relationship': The West Point Speech of December 1962." *Historical Journal* 33, no. 3 (1990): 599–608.

Brown, Chris. "'Turtles All the Way Down': Anti-Foundationalism, Critical Theory, and International Relations." *Millennium: Journal of International Studies* 23, no. 2 (1994): 213–36.

Brubaker, Rogers, and Frederick Cooper. "Beyond Identity." *Theory and Society* 29, no. 1 (2000): 1–47.

Bueger, Christian, and Frank Gadinger. "Reassembling and Dissecting: International Relations Practice from a Science Studies Perspective." *International Studies Perspectives* 8, no. 1 (2007): 90–110.

Bukovansky, Mlada. "American Identity and Neutral Rights from Independence to the War of 1812." *International Organization* 51, no. 2 (1997): 209–43.

Bukovansky, Mlada. *Legitimacy and Power Politics: The American and French Revolutions in International Political Culture.* Princeton: Princeton University Press, 2002.

Bull, Hedley. *The Anarchical Society: A Study of Order in World Politics.* 1977; Basingstoke: Palgrave Macmillan, 2002.

Bullock, Alan. *Ernest Bevin: A Biography.* London: Politico's, 2002.

Buzan, Barry, and Richard Little. *International Systems in World History: Remaking the Study of International Relations.* Oxford: Oxford University Press, 2000.

Callero, Peter. "Role-Identity Salience." *Social Psychology Quarterly* 48, no. 3 (1985): 203–15.

Callero, Peter L. "Toward a Meadian Conceptualization of Role." *Sociological Quarterly* 27, no. 3 (1986): 343–58.

Calvert, Peter. "The Malvinas as a Factor in Argentine Politics." In *International*

Perspectives on the Falklands Conflict, ed. Alex Danchev. Basingstoke: St. Martin's, 1992.

Calvocoressi, Peter. *The British Experience, 1945–75.* London: Pelican, 1979.

Carr, E. H. *The Twenty Years' Crisis, 1919–1939: An Introduction to the Study of International Relations.* London: Macmillan, 1946.

Catterall, Peter. "The Ironies of "Successful Failure." In *Harold Wilson and European Integration: Britain's Second Application to Join the EEC,* ed. Oliver J. Daddow. London: Cass, 2003.

Cerny, Philip G. *The Politics of Grandeur: Ideological Aspects of de Gaulle's Foreign Policy.* Cambridge: Cambridge University Press, 1980.

Chang, Johannes Han-Ying, "Mead's Theory of Emergence as a Framework for Multilevel Sociological Inquiry." *Symbolic Interaction* 27, no. 3 (2004): 405–27.

Charlton, Michael. *The Little Platoon: Diplomacy and the Falklands Dispute.* Oxford: Blackwell, 1989.

Charon, Joel M. *Symbolic Interactionism: An Introduction, an Interpretation, an Integration.* 6th ed. Upper Saddle River, NJ: Prentice Hall, 1998.

Checkel, Jeffrey T. "The Constructivist Turn in International Relations Theory." *World Politics* 50, no. 2 (1998): 324–48.

Choi, Wooseon. "Structural Realism and Dulles' China Policy." *Review of International Studies* 38, no.1 (2012): 119–40.

Clark, Alan. *Diaries: Into Politics, 1972–1982.* London: Phoenix, 2001.

Clark, Ian. *Nuclear Diplomacy and the Special Relationship: Britain's Deterrent and America, 1957–1962.* Oxford: Oxford University Press, 1994.

Clarke, Michael. "Foreign Policy." In *Blair's Britain, 1997–2007,* ed. Anthony Seldon. Cambridge: Cambridge University Press, 2007.

Clarke, Peter, and Clive Trebilock, eds. *Understanding Decline: Perceptions and Realities of British Economic Performance.* Cambridge: Cambridge University Press, 1997.

Coates, David, and Joel M. Krieger. *Blair's War.* Cambridge: Polity, 2004.

Coles, John. *Making Foreign Policy: A Certain Idea of Britain.* London: Murray, 2000.

Collins, Randall. "On the Microfoundations of Macrosociology." *American Journal of Sociology* 86, no. 5 (1981): 984–1014.

Collins, Randall. *Four Sociological Traditions.* New York: Oxford University Press, 1985.

Cooley, Alexander. *Logics of Hierarchy: The Organization of Empires, States, and Military Occupations.* Ithaca: Cornell University Press, 2005.

Cooper, Chester L. *The Lion's Last Roar: Suez, 1956.* New York: Harper and Row, 1978.

Coutu, Walter. "Role-Playing vs. Role-Taking: An Appeal for Clarification." *American Sociological Review* 16, no. 2 (1951): 180–87.

Crawford, Neta. "*Homo Politicus* and Argument (Nearly) All the Way Down." *Perspectives on Politics* 7, no. 1 (2009): 103–24.

Croft, Stuart. *The End of Superpower: British Foreign Office Conceptions of a Changing World.* Aldershot: Dartmouth, 1994.

Curtis, Mark. *Web of Deceit: Britain's Real Role in the World*. London: Vintage, 2003.

Curtis, Mark. *Unpeople: Britain's Secret Human Rights Abuses*. London: Vintage, 2004.

Daddow, Oliver J., ed. *Harold Wilson and European Integration: Britain's Second Application to Join the EEC*. London: Frank Cass, 2003.

Dalyell, Tam. *Thatcher's Torpedo: The Sinking of the "Belgrano."* London: Cecil Woolf, 1983.

Danchev, Alex. "Tony Blair's Vietnam: Iraq and the 'Special Relationship' in Historical Perspective." *Review of International Studies* 33, no. 2 (2007): 189–203.

Darby, Phillip. *British Defence Policy East of Suez, 1947–1968*. London: Oxford University Press, 1973.

Deighton, Anne. *The Foreign Policy of British Prime Minister Tony Blair: Radical or Retrograde?* Berlin: Humboldt University of Berlin, Centre for British Studies, 2005.

Dessler, David. "What's at Stake in the Agent-Structure Debate?" *International Organization* 43, no. 3 (1989): 441–73.

Dilks, David. *Retreat from Power: Studies in Britain's Foreign Policy of the Twentieth Century*. London: Macmillan, 1981.

Dillon, G. M. *Dependence and Deterrence: Success and Civility in the Anglo-American Special Nuclear Relationship, 1962–1982*. Aldershot: Gower, 1983.

Dillon, G. M. *The Falklands, Politics, and War*. New York: St. Martin's, 1989.

Dimbleby, David, and David Reynolds. *An Ocean Apart: The Relationship between Britain and America in the Twentieth Century*. New York: Random House, 1988.

Dinan, Desmond. *Europe Recast: A History of European Union*. Basingstoke: Palgrave Macmillan, 2004.

Dockrill, Michael. *British Defence since 1945*. Oxford: Basil Blackwell, 1988.

Dockrill, Michael, and John W. Young. *British Foreign Policy, 1945–56*. Basingstoke: Macmillan, 1989.

Dockrill, Saki. *Britain's Retreat from East of Suez: The Choice between Europe and the World?* Basingstoke: Palgrave Macmillan, 2002.

Dodds, Klaus. *Pink Ice: Britain and the South Atlantic Empire*. New York: I. B. Tauris, 2002.

Doty, Roxanne Lynn. "Desire All the Way Down." *Review of International Studies* 26, no. 1 (2000): 137–40.

Dreyfus, Hubert. *Being-in-the-World: A Commentary on Heidegger's* Being and Time, *Division I*. Cambridge: MIT Press, 1991.

Dumbrell, John. "The Johnson Administration and the British Labour Government: Vietnam, the Pound, and East of Suez." *Journal of American Studies* 30, no. 2 (1996): 211–31.

Dumbrell, John. *A Special Relationship: Anglo-American Relations in the Cold War and After*. Basingstoke: Macmillan, 2001.

Durkheim, Emile. *The Rules of Sociological Method*. 1895; New York: Free Press, 1982.

Eden, Anthony. *The Suez Crisis of 1956*. Boston: Beacon, 1960.

Edgerton, David. "The 'White Heat' Revisited: The British Government and Technology in the 1960s." *Twentieth Century British History* 7, no. 1 (1996): 53–82.

Edgerton, David. *Warfare State: Britain, 1920–1970*. Cambridge: Cambridge University Press, 2006.

Edkins, Jenny. "Legality with a Vengeance: Famines and Humanitarian Relief in 'Complex Emergencies.'" *Millennium: Journal of International Studies* 25, no. 3 (1996): 547–75.

Edwards, Geoffrey. "Europe and the Falkland Islands Conflict." In *Domestic Sources of Foreign Policy: Western European Reactions to the Falklands Conflict,* ed. Stelios Stavridis and Christopher Hill. Oxford: Berg, 1996.

Ellerby, Clive. "The Role of the Falkland Lobby, 1968–1990." In *International Perspectives on the Falklands Conflict,* ed. Alex Danchev. Basingstoke: St. Martin's, 1992.

Ellison, James. *The United States, Britain, and the Transatlantic Crisis: Rising to the Gaullist Challenge, 1963–68*. Basingstoke: Palgrave Macmillan, 2007.

Emirbayer, Mustafa. "Manifesto for Relational Sociology." *American Journal of Sociology* 103, no. 2 (1997): 281–317.

Fawzi, Mohammad. *Suez 1956: An Egyptian Perspective*. London: Farouk, 1956.

Fearon, James D. "Domestic Political Audiences and the Escalation of International Disputes." *American Political Science Review* 88, no. 3 (1994): 577–92.

Fearon, James D. "What Is Identity (As We Now Use the Word)?" Unpublished manuscript, Stanford University, 1999.

Fearon, James D., and Alexander Wendt. "Rationalism vs. Constructivism." In *Handbook of International Relations,* ed. Walter Carlsnaes, Beth A. Simmons, and Thomas Risse. London: Sage, 2000.

Femenia, Nora. *National Identity in Time of Crises: The Scripts of the Falklands-Malvinas War*. Commack, NY: Nova Science, 1996.

Fierke, Karin. "Constructivism." In *International Relations Theories: Discipline and Diversity,* ed. Tim Dunne, Milja Kurki and Steve Smith. 2nd ed. Oxford: Oxford University Press, 2010.

Fine, Gary Alan. "The Sad Demise, Mysterious Disappearance, and Glorious Triumph of Symbolic Interactionism." *Annual Review of Sociology* 19 (1993): 61–87.

Finnemore, Martha. *National Interests in International Society*. Ithaca: Cornell University Press, 1996.

Finnemore, Martha, and Kathryn Sikkink. "Taking Stock: The Constructivist Research Program in International Relations and Comparative Politics." *Annual Review of Political Science* 4 (2001): 391–416.

Fisher, Nigel. *Harold Macmillan*. London: Weidenfeld and Nicolson, 1982.

Fox, William T. R. *The Superpowers: The United States, Britain, and the Soviet Union—Their Responsibility for Peace*. New York: Harcourt, Brace, 1944.

Frankel, Joseph. *British Foreign Policy, 1945–1973*. Oxford: Oxford University Press, 1975.

Freedman, Lawrence. *Britain and Nuclear Weapons*. London: Macmillan, 1980.

Freedman, Lawrence. "The War of the Falkland Islands." *Foreign Affairs* 61, no. 1 (1982): 196–210.

Freedman, Lawrence. *The Official History of the Falklands Campaign.* Vol. 1, *The Origins of the Falklands War.* London: Routledge, 2005a.

Freedman, Lawrence. *The Official History of the Falklands Campaign.* Vol. 2, *War and Diplomacy.* London: Routledge, 2005b.

Freedman, Lawrence. "The Special Relationship, Then and Now." *Foreign Affairs* 85, no. 3 (2006): 61–73.

Freedman, Lawrence. "Defence." In *Blair's Britain, 1997–2007,* ed. Anthony Seldon. Cambridge: Cambridge University Press, 2007.

Freedman, Lawrence, and Virginia Stonehouse-Gamba. *Signals of War: The Falklands Conflict of 1982.* London: Faber and Faber, 1990.

Freiberger, Steven Z. *Dawn over Suez: The Rise of American Power in the Middle East, 1953–1957.* Chicago: Van R. Dee, 2007.

Friedrichs, Joerg, and Friedrich V. Kratochwil. "On Acting and Knowing: How Pragmatism Can Advance International Relations Research and Methodology." *International Organization* 63, no. 4 (2009): 701–31.

Fry, Geoffrey K. *The Politics of Decline: An Interpretation of British Politics from the 1940s to the 1970s.* New York: Palgrave Macmillan, 2003.

Gamba, Virginia. *The Falklands/Malvinas War: A Model for North-South Crisis Prevention.* London: Allen and Unwin, 1987.

Garfinkel, Harold. *Studies in Ethnomethodology.* Cambridge: Polity Press, 1967.

Garfinkel, Harold. *Ethnomethodology's Program: Working Out Durkheim's Aphorism.* Lanham, MD: Rowman and Littlefield, 2002.

Garfinkel, Harold. *Seeing Sociologically: The Routine Grounds of Social Action.* Edited with Introduction by Anne Rawls Warfield. Boulder: Paradigm, 2006.

Geertz, Clifford. *The Interpretation of Cultures.* New York: Basic Books, 1973.

George, Stephen. *An Awkward Partner: Britain in the European Community.* Oxford: Oxford University Press, 1998.

Gheciu, Alexandra. *NATO in the "New Europe": The Politics of International Socialization after the Cold War.* Stanford: Stanford University Press, 2005.

Giddens, Anthony. *The Constitution of Society: Outline of a Theory of Structuration.* Cambridge: Polity Press, 1984.

Giddens, Anthony. *Modernity and Self-Identity: Self and Society in the Late Modern Age.* Stanford: Stanford University Press, 1991.

Gilpin, Robert. *War and Change in World Politics.* Cambridge: Cambridge University Press, 1981.

Glaser, Charles. *Rational Theory of International Politics.* Princeton: Princeton University Press, 2010.

Goddard, Stacie. "Uncommon Ground: Indivisible Territory and the Politics of Legitimacy." *International Organization* 60, no. 1 (2006): 35–68.

Goddard, Stacie, and Daniel H. Nexon. "Paradigm Lost? Reassessing *Theory of International Politics.*" *European Journal of International Relations* 11, no. 1 (2005): 9–61.

Goebel, Julius. *The Struggle for the Falkland Islands.* New Haven: Yale University Press, 1927.

Goffman, Erving. *Frame Analysis: An Essay on the Organization of Experience*. London: Harper and Row, 1974.

Goffman, Erving. *The Presentation of Self in Everyday Life*. 1959; London: Penguin, 1990.

Goldstein, Judith, and Robert O. Keohane, eds. *Ideas and Foreign Policy: Beliefs, Institutions, and Political Change*. Ithaca: Cornell University Press, 1993.

Gordon, Michael R. *Conflict and Consensus in Labour's Foreign Policy, 1914–1965*. Stanford: Stanford University Press, 1969.

Gormly, James L. "The Washington Declaration and the 'Poor Relation': Anglo-American Atomic Diplomacy, 1945–46." *Diplomatic History* 8, no. 2 (1984): 125–43.

Gouldner, Alvin. *The Coming Crisis of Western Sociology*. New York: Basic Books, 1971.

Gowing, Margaret. *Independence and Deterrence: Britain and Atomic Energy, 1945–1952*. Vol. 1, *Policy Making*. London: Macmillan, 1974.

Groom, A. J. R. *British Thinking about Nuclear Weapons*. London: Pinter, 1974.

Gurowitz, Amy. "The Diffusion of International Norms: Why Identity Matters." *International Politics* 43, no. 3 (2006): 305–41.

Guzzini, Stefano, and Anna Leander, eds. *Constructivism and International Relations: Alexander Wendt and His Critics*. London: Routledge, 2006.

Haig, Alexander M. *Caveat: Realism, Reagan, and Foreign Policy*. New York: Macmillan, 1984.

Hall, Peter A., ed. *The Political Power of Economic Ideas: Keynesianism Across Nations*. Princeton: Princeton University Press, 1989.

Hall, Rodney Bruce. *National Collective Identity: Social Constructs and International Systems*. New York: Columbia University Press, 1999.

Hamilton, Peter. *Talcott Parsons: Critical Assessments*. 4 vols. London: Routledge, 1992.

Hankinson, R. J. "Philosophy of Science." In *The Cambridge Companion to Aristotle,* ed. Jonathan Barnes. Cambridge: Cambridge University Press, 1995.

Hastings, Max, and Simon Jenkins. *The Battle for the Falklands*. London: Book Club, 1983.

Harlech, Lord (David Ormsby-Gore). "Opinion: Suez Snafu, Skybolt Sabu." *Foreign Policy* 2 (Spring 1971): 38–50.

Harnisch, Sebastian. "'Dialogue and Emergence': George Herbert Mead's Contribution to Role Theory and His Reconstruction of International Politics." In *Role Theory in International Relations: Approaches and Analyses,* ed. Sebastian Harnisch, Cornelia Franck and Hans Maull. London: Routledge, 2011.

Harnisch, Sebastian, Cornelia Franck, and Hans Maull, eds. *Role Theory in International Relations: Approaches and Analyses*. London: Routledge, 2011.

Hassner, Ron. *War on Sacred Grounds*. Ithaca: Cornell University Press, 2009.

Healey, Denis. *The Time of My Life*. London: Penguin, 1990.

Heidegger, Martin. *Being and Time*. 1927; Oxford: Blackwell, 1962.

Heikal, Mohamed. *Cutting the Lion's Tail: Suez through Egyptian Eyes*. London: Arbor House, 1987.

Heiss, Jerold. *Social Roles*. New York: Basic Books, 1981.

Hempel, Carl G. "The Function of General Laws in History." *Journal of Philosophy* 39, no. 2 (1942): 35–48.

Henderson, Nicholas. *Channels and Tunnels: Reflections on Britain and Abroad*. London: Weidenfeld and Nicolson, 1987.

Henderson, Nicholas. *Mandarin*. London: Weidenfeld and Nicolson, 1994.

Hennessy, Peter. *The Prime Minister: The Office and Its Holders since 1945*. London: Penguin, 2000.

Hewitt, John P. *Self and Society: A Symbolic Interactionist Social Psychology*. 7th ed. Boston: Allyn and Bacon, 1997.

Hobbes, Thomas. *Leviathan*. 1651; London: Penguin, 1985.

Hobson, John M. *The State and International Relations*. Cambridge: Cambridge University Press, 2000.

Holland, Robert F. *The Pursuit of Greatness: Britain and the World Role, 1900–1970*. London: Fontana Press, 1991.

Hollis, Martin, and Steve Smith. *Explaining and Understanding International Relations*. Oxford: Clarendon, 1991.

Holsti, K. J. "National Role Conceptions in the Study of Foreign Policy." *International Studies Quarterly* 14, no. 3 (1970): 233–309.

Homans, George C. "Bringing Men Back In." *American Sociological Review* 29, no. 6 (1964): 809–18.

Hopf, Ted. "The Promise of Constructivism in International Relations Theory." *International Security* 23, no. 1 (1998): 171–200.

Hopf, Ted. "Constructivism All the Way Down." *International Politics* 37, no. 3 (2000): 369–78.

Hopf, Ted. *Social Construction of International Politics: Identities and Foreign Policies, Moscow, 1955 and 1999*. Ithaca: Cornell University Press, 2002.

Hopf, Ted. "The Logic of Habit in International Relations." *European Journal of International Relations* 16, no. 4 (2010): 539–61.

Hopf, Ted. *Reconstructing the Cold War: The Early Years, 1945–1958*. Oxford: Oxford University Press, 2012.

Horne, Alistair. *Macmillan*. Vol. 2, 1957–86. London: Macmillan, 1989.

Hurd, Douglas. *Memoirs*. London: Abacus, 2003.

Husserl, Edmund. *Ideas*. 1913; The Hague: Nijhoff, 1982.

Husserl, Edmund. *Cartesian Meditations*. 1931; Dordrecht: Kluwer, 1988.

Hymans, Jacques C. *The Psychology of Nuclear Proliferation: Identity, Emotions, and Foreign Policy*. Cambridge: Cambridge University Press, 2006.

Hymans, Jacques C. "Britain and Hiroshima." *Journal of Strategic Studies* 32, no. 5 (2009): 769–97.

Hynek, Nick, and Andrea Teti. "Saving Identity from Postmodernism? The Normalization of Constructivism in International Relations." *Contemporary Political Theory* 9, no. 2 (2010): 171–99.

Ikenberry, G. John. *Liberal Leviathan: The Origins, Crisis, and Transformation of the American World Order*. Princeton: Princeton University Press, 2011.

Isacoff, Jonathan B. "On the Historical Imagination of International Relations: The Case for a 'Deweyan' Reconstruction." *Millennium: Journal of International Studies* 31, no. 3 (2002): 603–26.

Jackson, Patrick Thaddeus. "Hegel's House; or, 'People Are States Too.'" *Review of International Studies* 30, no. 2 (2004): 281–87.

Jackson, Patrick Thaddeus. *Civilizing the Enemy: German Reconstruction and the Invention of the West*. Ann Arbor: University of Michigan Press, 2007.

Jackson, Patrick Thaddeus. *The Conduct of Inquiry in International Relations*. London: Routledge, 2011.

Jackson, Patrick Thaddeus, and Daniel H. Nexon. "Relations before States: Substance, Process, and the Study of World Politics." *European Journal of International Relations* 5, no. 3 (1999): 291–332.

Jackson, Patrick Thaddeus, and Daniel H. Nexon. "Paradigmatic Faults in International-Relations Theory." *International Studies Quarterly* 53, no. 4 (2009): 907–30.

Jervis, Robert. *The Logic of Images in International Relations*. Princeton: Princeton University Press, 1970.

Joas, Hans. *Pragmatism and Social Theory*. Chicago: University of Chicago Press, 1993.

Jones, Matthew, and John W. Young. "Polaris, East of Suez: British Plans for a Nuclear Force in the Indo-Pacific." *Strategic Studies* 33, no. 6 (2010): 847–70.

Kaiser, Wolfram. *Using Europe, Abusing the Europeans: Britain and European Integration, 1945–63*. Basingstoke: Macmillan, 1999.

Kampfner, John. *Blair's Wars*. London: Simon and Schuster, 2003.

Katzenstein, Peter J., ed. *The Culture of National Security: Norms and Identity in World Politics*. New York: Columbia University Press, 1996.

Kedar, Asaf. "Ideal Types as Hermeneutic Concepts." *Journal of the Philosophy of History* 1, no. 3 (2007): 318–45.

Kennedy, Paul. *The Realities behind Diplomacy: Background Influences on British External Policy, 1865–1980*. London: Fontana, 1981.

Kennedy, Paul. *The Rise and Fall of the Great Powers*. London: Fontana, 1988.

Kent, John W. *British Imperial Strategy and the Origins of the Cold War*. Leicester: Leicester University Press, 1993.

Keohane, Robert O. *After Hegemony: Cooperation and Discord in the World Political Economy*. Princeton: Princeton University Press, 1984.

Keohane, Robert O., ed. *Neorealism and Its Critics*. New York: Columbia University Press, 1986.

Keohane, Robert O. "International Institutions: Two Approaches." *International Studies Quarterly* 32, no. 4 (1988): 753–75.

Keohane, Robert O. "Ideas Part-Way Down." *Review of International Studies* 26, no. 1 (2000): 125–30.

Kindleberger, Charles. *The World in Depression, 1929–1939*. London: Allen Lane, 1973.

King, Gary, Robert O. Keohane, and Sidney Verba. *Designing Social Inquiry: Scientific Inference in Qualitative Research*. Princeton: Princeton University Press, 1994.

Kinney, Douglas. *National Interest/National Honor: The Diplomacy of the Falklands Crisis*. New York: Praeger, 1989.

Kleiman, Robert. *Atlantic Crisis: American Diplomacy Confronts a Resurgent Europe*. New York: W.W. Norton, 1964.

Klotz, Audie. *Norms in International Relations: The Struggle against Apartheid*. Ithaca: Cornell University Press, 1995.

Klotz, Audie, and Cecilia Lynch. *Strategies for Research in Constructivist International Relations*. Armonk, NY: Sharpe, 2007.

Knorr Cetina, Karin. *Epistemic Cultures: How the Sciences Make Knowledge*. Cambridge: Harvard University Press, 1999.

Kratochwil, Friedrich V. *International Order and Foreign Policy: A Theoretical Sketch of Post-War International Relations*. Boulder: Westview, 1978.

Kratochwil, Friedrich V. "On the Notion of 'Interest' in International Relations." *International Organization* 36, no. 1 (1982): 1–30.

Kratochwil, Friedrich V. *Rules, Norms, and Decisions: On the Conditions of Practical and Legal Reasoning in International Relations and Domestic Affairs*. Cambridge: Cambridge University Press, 1989.

Kratochwil, Friedrich V. "The Embarrassment of Changes: Neo-Realism as the Science of Realpolitik without Politics." *Review of International Studies* 19, no. 1 (1993): 63–80.

Kratochwil, Friedrich V. "Constructing a New Orthodoxy? Wendt's 'Social Theory of International Politics' and the Constructivist Challenge." *Millennium: Journal of International Studies* 29, no. 1 (2000): 73–101.

Kratochwil, Friedrich V. "Constructing a New Orthodoxy? Wendt's *Social Theory of International Politics* and the Constructivist Challenge." In *Constructivism and International Relations: Alexander Wendt and His Critics,* ed. Stefano Guzzini and Anna Leander. London: Routledge, 2006a.

Kratochwil, Friedrich V. "History, Action, and Identity: Revisiting the 'Second' Great Debate and Assessing Its Importance for Social Theory." *European Journal of International Relations* 12, no. 1 (2006b): 5–29.

Kratochwil, Friedrich V. "Constructivism: What It Is (Not) and Why It Matters." In *Approaches and Methodologies in the Social Sciences: A Pluralist Perspective,* ed. Donatella Della Porta and Michael Keating, 80–98. Cambridge: Cambridge University Press, 2008.

Kratochwil, Friedrich V., Paul Rohrlich, and Harpeet Mahajan. *Peace and Disputed Sovereignty: Reflections on Conflict over Territory*. Lanham, MD: University Press of America, 1985.

Kratochwil, Friedrich V., and John Gerard Ruggie. "International Organization: A State of the Art on an Art of the State." *International Organization* 40, no. 4 (1986): 753–75.

Krebs, Ron, and Patrick Thaddeus Jackson. "Twisting Tongues and Twisting Arms: The Power of Political Rhetoric." *European Journal of International Relations* 13, no. 1 (2007): 35–66.

Krotz, Ulrich. *National Role Conceptions and Foreign Policies: France and Germany*

Compared. Cambridge: Harvard University/Minda de Gunzburg Center for European Studies, 2002.

Kunz, Diane. *The Economic Diplomacy of the Suez Crisis.* Chapel Hill: University of North Carolina Press, 1991.

Kupchan, Charles. *No One's World: The West, the Rising Rest, and the Coming Global Turn.* Oxford: Oxford University Press, 2012.

Kurki, Milja. "Causes of a Divided Discipline: Rethinking the Concept of Cause in International Relations Theory." *Review of International Studies* 32, no. 2 (2006): 189–216.

Kurki, Milja. *Causation in International Relations.* Cambridge: Cambridge University Press, 2008.

Kyle, Keith. *Suez.* London: Weidenfeld and Nicolson, 1991.

Lake, David. *Hierarchy in International Relations.* Ithaca: Cornell University Press, 2011.

Lapid, Yosef, and Friedrich V. Kratochwil, eds.. *The Return of Culture and Identity in IR Theory.* Boulder: Lynne Rienner, 1996.

Layne, Christopher. "The Unipolar Illusion: Why New Great Powers Will Rise." *International Security* 17, no. 4 (1993): 5–51.

Layne, Christopher. *The Peace of Illusions: American Grand Strategy from 1940 to the Present.* Ithaca: Cornell University Press, 2006.

Layne, Christopher. "This Time It's Real: The End of Unipolarity and the *Pax Americana.*" *International Studies Quarterly* 56, no. 1 (2012): 203–13.

Leeds, Brett Ashley. "Domestic Political Institutions, Credible Commitments, and International Cooperation." *American Political Science Review* 43, no. 4 (1999): 979–1002.

Legro, Jeffrey W. "Culture and Preferences in the International Cooperation Two-Step." *American Political Science Review* 90, no. 1 (1996): 118–37.

Legro, Jeffrey. Rethinking the World: Great Power Strategies and International Order. Ithaca: Cornell University Press, 2005.

Legro, Jeffrey W. "The Plasticity of Identity under Anarchy." *European Journal of International Relations* 15, no. 1 (2009): 37–65.

Leites, Nathan. *The Operational Code of the Politburo.* New York: McGraw-Hill, 1956.

Le Prestre, Philippe G., ed. *Role Quests in the Post–Cold War Era.* Montreal: McGill-Queen's University Press, 1997.

Lieber, Robert J. "Great Britain: Decline and Recovery." In *A Century's Journey: How the Great Powers Shape the World,* ed. Robert A. Pastor. New York: Basic Books, 1999.

Little, Richard. *The Balance of Power in International Relations: Myths, Metaphors, and Models.* Cambridge: Cambridge University Press, 2007.

Little, Richard, and Steve Smith. *Belief Systems and International Relations.* Oxford: Blackwell, 1988.

Lloyd, Selwyn. *Suez 1956: A Personal Account.* New York: Mayflower, 1978.

Louis, W. R., and Hedley Bull, eds. *The "Special Relationship": Anglo-American Relations since 1945.* Oxford: Clarendon, 1986.

Love, Kennett. *Suez: The Twice-Fought War.* New York: McGraw-Hill, 1969.

Lucas, W. Scott. *Divided We Stand: Britain, the US, and the Suez Crisis.* London: Hodder and Stoughton, 1991.

Lucas, W. Scott. *Britain and Suez: The Lion's Last Roar.* Manchester: Manchester University Press, 1996.

Luce, Edward. *Time to Start Thinking: America in the Age of Descent.* New York: Atlantic Monthly Press, 2012.

Ludlow, N. Piers. *Dealing with Britain: The Six and the First UK Application to the EEC.* Cambridge: Cambridge University Press, 1997.

Ludlow, N. Piers. "Challenging French Leadership in Europe: Germany, Italy, the Netherlands, and the Outbreak of the Empty Chair Crisis, 1965–1966." *Contemporary European History* 8, no. 2 (1999): 231–48.

Ludlow, N. Piers, ed. *European Integration and the Cold War: Ostpolitik-Westpolitik, 1965–1973.* London: Routledge, 2007.

Lukes, Steven. Introduction to Emile Durkheim, *The Rules of Sociological Method.* New York: Free Press, 1982.

Lynch, Cecilia. *Beyond Appeasement: Interpreting Interwar Peace Movements.* Ithaca: Cornell University Press, 1999.

Macmillan, Harold. *At the End of the Day, 1961–1963.* London: Macmillan, 1973.

Magid, Alvin. "'Role Theory,' Political Science, and African Studies." *World Politics* 32, no. 2 (1980): 311–30.

Mahan, Erin R. *Kennedy, De Gaulle, and Western Europe.* Basingstoke: Palgrave Macmillan, 2002.

Maliniak, Daniel, Amy Oakes, Susan Peterson, and Michael J. Tierney. "International Relations in the US Academy." *International Studies Quarterly* 55, no. 1 (2011): 1–28.

Malone, Peter. *The British Nuclear Deterrent.* London: Croom Helm, 1984.

Mangold, Peter. *The Almost Impossible Ally: Harold Macmillan and Charles de Gaulle.* London: I. B. Tauris, 2006.

Maoz, Zeev. "Framing the National Interest: The Manipulation of Foreign Policy Decisions in Group Settings." *World Politics* 43, no. 1 (1990): 77–110.

March, James G. *The Logic of Appropriateness.* Oslo: ARENA, 2004.

March, James G., and Johan P. Olsen. *Rediscovering Institutions: The Organizational Basis of Politics.* New York: Free Press, 1989.

Martin, Jon Levi. *The Explanation of Social Action.* Oxford: Oxford University Press, 2011.

Martin, Lisa L. "Institutions and Cooperation: Sanctions during the Falkland Islands Conflict." *International Security* 16, no. 4 (1992): 143–78.

McCourt, David M. "What Was Britain's 'East of Suez Role'? Reassessing the Withdrawal, 1964–1968." *Diplomacy and Statecraft* 20, no 3 (2009): 453–72.

McCourt, David M. "Rethinking Britain's *Role in the World* for a New Decade: The Limits of Discursive Therapy and the Promise of Field Theory." *British Journal of Politics and International Relations* 13, no. 2 (2011): 145–64.

McCourt, David M. "Embracing Humanitarian Intervention: Atlanticism and the UK Interventions in Bosnia and Kosovo." *British Journal of Politics and International Relations* 15, no. 2 (2013): 246–62.

McNay, John T. *Acheson and Empire: The British Accent in American Foreign Policy.* Columbia: University of Missouri Press, 2001.

McPhail, Clark, and Cynthia Rexroat. "Mead vs. Blumer: The Divergent Methodological Perspectives of Social Behaviorism and Symbolic Interactionism." *American Sociological Review* 44, no. 3 (1979): 449–67.

Mead, George Herbert. *Mind, Self, and Society: From the Standpoint of a Social Behaviorist.* Chicago: University of Chicago Press, 1934.

Mead, Walter Russell. *God and Gold: Britain, America, and the Making of the Modern World.* New York: Knopf, 2007.

Mead, Walter Russell. "The Myth of America's Decline." *Wall Street Journal,* 9 April 2012.

Mearsheimer, John J. "The False Promise of International Institutions." *International Security* 19, no. 3 (1994–95): 5–49.

Mearsheimer, John J. *The Tragedy of Great Power Politics.* New York: Norton, 2001.

Melissen, Jan. "The Restoration of the Nuclear Alliance: Great Britain and Atomic Negotiations with the United States, 1957–58." *Contemporary Record* 6, no. 1 (1992): 72–106.

Mendl, Wolf. *Deterrence and Persuasion: French Nuclear Armament in the Context of National Policy, 1945–1969.* London: Faber, 1970.

Metford, J. C. J. "Falklands or Malvinas? The Background to the Dispute." *International Affairs* 44, no. 3 (1968): 463–81.

Middlebrook, Martin. *Operation Corporate: The Story of the Falklands War, 1982.* London: Viking, 1985.

Milner, Helen. "The Assumption of Anarchy in International Relations Theory: A Critique." *Review of International Studies* 17, no. 1 (1991): 67–85.

Milner, Helen V. *Interests, Institutions, and Information: Domestic Politics and International Relations.* Princeton: Princeton University Press, 1997.

Milward, Alan S. *The European Rescue of the Nation-State.* Berkeley: University of California Press, 1992.

Milward, Alan. S. *The UK and the European Community.* Vol. 1, *The Rise and Fall of a National Strategy, 1945–1963.* London: Frank Cass, 2002.

Mitzen, Jennifer. "Ontological Security in World Politics: State Identity and the Security Dilemma." *European Journal of International Relations* 12, no. 3 (2004): 341–70.

Moravcsik, Andrew. "Taking Preferences Seriously: A Liberal Theory of International Politics." *International Organization* 51, no. 4 (1997): 513–55.

Morgenthau, Hans J. *Politics among Nations: The Struggle for Power and Peace.* Brief ed. New York: McGraw-Hill, 1993.

Morris, Justin. "How Great Is Britain? Power, Responsibility, and Britain's Future Global Role." *British Journal of Politics and International Relations* 13, no. 3 (2011): 326–47.

Morrow, James D. *Game Theory for Political Scientists.* Princeton: Princeton University Press, 1994.

Mullins, Nicholas C. *Theories and Theory Groups in American Sociology*. New York: Harper and Row, 1973.

Murphy, Robert. *Diplomat among Warriors: The Unique World of a Foreign Service Expert*. New York: Doubleday, 1964.

Murray, Donette. *Kennedy, Macmillan, and Nuclear Weapons*. Basingstoke: Macmillan, 2000.

Nagel, Thomas. *The View from Nowhere*. New York: Oxford University Press, 1986.

Narizny, Kevin. *The Political Economy of Grand Strategy*. Ithaca: Cornell University Press, 2007.

Navias, Martin S. *Nuclear Weapons and British Strategic Planning, 1955-1958*. Oxford: Clarendon, 1991.

Neff, Donald. *Warriors at Suez: Eisenhower Takes America into the Middle East*. New York: Linden/Simon and Schuster, 1981.

Neumann, Iver. *Uses of the Other: "The East" in European Identity Formation*. Minneapolis: University of Minnesota Press, 1999.

Neumann, Iver. "Returning Practice to the Linguistic Turn: The Case of Diplomacy." *Millennium: Journal of International Studies* 31, no. 3 (2002): 627–51.

Neumann, Iver, and Ole Jacob Sending. *Governing the Global Polity: Practice, Mentality, Rationality*. Ann Arbor: University of Michigan Press, 2010.

Neustadt, Richard N. *Alliance Politics*. New York: Columbia University Press, 1970.

Neustadt, Richard N. *Report to JFK: The Skybolt Crisis in Perspective*. Ithaca: Cornell University Press, 1999.

Nexon, Daniel H. "The Balance of Power in the Balance." *World Politics* 61, no. 2 (2009a): 330–59.

Nexon, Daniel H. *The Struggle for Power in Early Modern Europe: Religious Conflict, Dynastic Empires, and International Change*. Princeton: Princeton University Press, 2009b.

Nichols, David A. *Eisenhower 1956: The President's Year of Crisis: Suez and the Brink of War*. New York: Simon and Schuster, 2011.

Northedge, F. S. *Descent from Power: British Foreign Policy, 1945-1973*. London: Allen and Unwin, 1974.

Nott, John. *Here Today, Gone Tomorrow: Memoirs of an Errant Politician*. London: Politico's, 2003.

Nott, John. "A View from the Centre." In *The Falklands Conflict Twenty Years On: Lessons for the Future,* ed. Stephen Badsey, Rob Havers, Mark Grove. London: Frank Cass, 2005.

Nunnerley, David. *President Kennedy and Britain*. New York: St. Martin's, 1972.

Nutting, Anthony. *No End of a Lesson: The Inside Story of the Suez Crisis*. New York: Potter, 1967.

Nye, Joseph. "The Twenty-First Century Will Not Be a 'Post-American' World." *International Studies Quarterly* 56, no. 1 (2012): 215–17.

O'Hara, Glen, and Helen Parr. *The Wilson Governments 1964-1970 Reconsidered*. London: Routledge, 2006.

Onuf, Nicholas Greenwood. *World of Our Making: Rules and Rule in Social Theory and International Relations*. Columbia: University of South Carolina Press, 1989.

Oros, Andrew. *Normalizing Japan: Politics, Identity, and the Origins of Security Practice*. Stanford: Stanford University Press, 2008.

Ovendale, Ritchie. *The Foreign Policy of the British Labour Governments, 1945–1951*. Leicester: Leicester University Press, 1984.

Parmar, Inderjeet. *Think Tanks and Power in Foreign Policy: A Comparative Study of the Role and Influence of the Council on Foreign Relations and Royal Institute of International Affairs, 1939–1945*. Basingstoke: Palgrave Macmillan, 2004.

Parr, Helen. *Britain's Policy towards the European Community: Harold Wilson and Britain's World Role, 1964–1967*. London: Routledge, 2006.

Parsons, Craig. "Showing Ideas as Causes: The Origins of the European Union." *International Organization* 56, no. 1 (2002): 47–84.

Parsons, Talcott. *The Social System*. Glencoe, IL: Free Press, 1951.

Pastor, Robert A., ed. *A Century's Journey: How the Great Powers Shape the World*. New York: Basic Books, 1999.

Patomäki, Heikki, and Colin Wight. "After Postpositivism? The Promises of Critical Realism." *International Studies Quarterly* 44, no. 2 (2000): 213–37.

Pelling, Henry. *The Labour Governments, 1945–51*. London: Macmillan, 1984.

Pérez de Cuellar, Javier. *Pilgrimage for Peace: A Secretary General's Memoir*. Basingstoke: Macmillan, 1997.

Pickering, Jeffrey. *Britain's Withdrawal from East of Suez: The Politics of Retrenchment*. Basingstoke: Macmillan, 1998.

Pierre, Andrew J. *Nuclear Politics: The British Experience with an Independent Strategic Force, 1939–1970*. London: Oxford University Press, 1972.

Pierson, Paul. *Politics in Time: History, Institutions, and Social Analysis*. Princeton: Princeton University Press, 2004.

Pimlott, Ben. *Wilson*. London: Harper Collins, 1992.

Pine, Melissa. *Harold Wilson and Europe: Pursuing Britain's Membership of the European Community*. London: I.B. Tauris, 2007.

Plummer, Ken. "Symbolic Interactionism in the Twentieth Century: The Rise of Empirical Social Theory." In *The Blackwell Companion to Social Theory*, ed. Bryan S. Turner. Oxford: Blackwell, 1996.

Ponting, Clive. *The Right to Know: The Inside Story of the Belgrano Affair*. London: Sphere, 1985.

Pouliot, Vincent. "'Sobjectivism': Towards a Constructivist Methodology." *International Studies Quarterly* 51, no. 2 (2007): 359–84.

Pouliot, Vincent. "The Logic of Practicality: A Theory of Practice of Security Communities." *International Organization* 62, no. 2 (2008): 257–88.

Pouliot, Vincent. *International Security in Practice: The Politics of NATO-Russia Diplomacy*. Cambridge: Cambridge University Press, 2011.

Prestowitz, Clyde V. *The Betrayal of American Prosperity: Free Market Delusions, America's Decline, and How We Must Compete in the Post-Dollar Era*. New York: Free Press, 2010.

Price, Richard. "A Genealogy of the Chemical Weapons Taboo." *International Organization* 49, no. 1 (1995): 73–103.

Puchala, Donald J. *Theory and History in International Relations.* London: Routledge, 2003.

Rathbun, Brian. *Partisan Interventions: European Party Politics and Peace Enforcement in the Balkans.* Ithaca: Cornell University Press, 2004.

Rawls, John. "Two Concepts of Rules." *Philosophical Review* 64, no. 1 (1955): 3–32.

Reagan, Ronald. *An American Life.* New York: Simon and Schuster, 1990.

Reus-Smit, Christian. *The Moral Purpose of the State: Culture, Social Identity, and Institutional Rationality in International Relations.* Princeton: Princeton University Press, 1999.

Reynolds, David. "A 'Special Relationship'? America, Britain, and the International Order since the Second World War." *International Affairs* 62, no. 1 (1986): 1–20.

Reynolds, David. *Britannia Overruled: British Policy and World Power in the Twentieth Century.* London: Longman, 1991.

Richardson, Louise. *When Allies Differ: Anglo-American Relations during the Suez and Falklands Crises.* New York: St. Martin's, 1996.

Ringmar, Erik. *Identity, Interest, and Action: A Cultural Explanation of Sweden's Intervention in the Thirty Years War.* Cambridge: Cambridge University Press, 1996.

Robertson, Terence. *Crisis: The Inside Story of the Suez Conspiracy.* London: Hutchison, 1965.

Rosenau, James N. *Turbulence in World Politics: A Theory of Change and Continuity.* Princeton: Princeton University Press, 1990.

Rossiter, Mike. *Sink the Belgrano.* London: Bantam, 2007.

Rousseau, David. *Identifying Threats and Threatening Identities: The Social Construction of Realism and Liberalism.* Stanford: Stanford University Press, 2006.

Ruggie, John Gerard. *Constructing the World Polity: Essays on International Institutionalization.* London: Routledge, 1998a.

Ruggie, John Gerard. "What Makes the World Hang Together? Neo-Utilitarianism and the Social Constructivist Challenge." *International Organization* 52, no. 4 (1998b): 855–85.

Ryle, Gilbert. "The Thinker of Thoughts: What Is 'Le Penseur' Doing?" *University Lectures* 18 (1968).

Sanders, David. *Losing an Empire, Finding a Role: British Foreign Policy since 1945.* Basingstoke: Macmillan, 1990.

Sartori, Giovanni. "Concept Misformation in Comparative Politics." *American Political Science Review* 64, no. 4 (1970): 1033–53.

Schlesinger, Arthur M. *A Thousand Days: John F. Kennedy in the White House.* London: Deutsch, 1965.

Schutz, Alfred. *The Phenomenology of the Social World.* 1932; Chicago: Northwestern University Press, 1967.

Schutz, Alfred, and Thomas Luckmann. *The Structures of the Life-World.* Vol. 1. Chicago: Northwestern University Press, 1973.

Schutz, Alfred, and Thomas Luckmann. *The Structures of the Life-World*. Vol. 2. Chicago: Northwestern University Press, 1989.

Searle, John. *Speech Acts: An Essay in the Philosophy of Language*. London: Cambridge University Press, 1969.

Sen, Amartya. *Identity and Violence: The Illusion of Destiny*. New York: W.W. Norton, 2006.

Shannon, Vaughn P., and Paul A. Kowert. *Psychology and Constructivism in International Relations: An Ideational Alliance*. Ann Arbor: University of Michigan Press, 2011.

Sharp, Paul. *Thatcher's Diplomacy: The Revival of British Foreign Policy*. Basingstoke: Macmillan, 1997.

Shaw, Tony. *Eden, Suez, and the Mass Media: Propaganda and Persuasion during the Suez Crisis*. London: I.B.Tauris, 1996.

Shih, Chih-yu. "National Role Conceptions as Foreign Policy Motivation: The Psychocultural Bases of Chinese Diplomacy." *Political Psychology* 9, no. 4 (1988): 599–631.

Shlaim, Avi. "Britain's Quest for a World Role." *International Relations* 5, no. 1 (1975): 835–65.

Shotter, John. *Cultural Politics of Everyday Life: Social Constructionism, Rhetoric, and Knowing of the Third Kind*. Toronto: University of Toronto Press, 1993.

Simms, Brendan. *Unfinest Hour: Britain and the Destruction of Bosnia*. London: Penguin, 2001.

Simpson, John. *The Independent Nuclear State: The United States, Britain, and the Military Atom*. London: Macmillan, 1983.

Simpson, John, and Jana Bennett. *The Disappeared: Voices from a Secret War*. London: Robson, 1985.

Slonim, Shlomo. "Origins of the 1950 Tripartite Declaration on the Middle East." *Middle Eastern Studies* 23, no. 2 (1987): 135–49.

Smith, Thomas W. *History and International Relations*. London: Routledge, 1999.

Sørensen, Georg. "The Case for Combining Material Forces and Ideas in the Study of IR." *European Journal of International Relations* 14, no. 1 (2008): 5–32.

Sorensen, Theodore. *Kennedy*. London: Hodder and Stoughton, 1965.

Stavridis, Stelios, and Christopher Hill, eds. *Domestic Sources of Foreign Policy: Western European Reactions to the Falklands Conflict*. Oxford: Berg, 1996.

Stavridis, Stelios, and Elfriede Regelsberger. "The Converging National Reactions (I): The Big States—France and Germany." In *Domestic Sources of Foreign Policy: Western European Reactions to the Falklands Conflict,* ed. Stelios Stavridis and Christopher Hill. Oxford: Berg, 1996.

Steele, Brent. "Liberal-Idealism: A Constructivist Critique." *International Studies Review* 9, no. 1 (2007): 23–52.

Steele, Brent. *Ontological Security in International Relations: Self-Identity and the IR State*. London: Routledge, 2008.

Stryker, Sheldon, and Anne Statham. "Symbolic Interaction and Role Theory." In

Handbook of Social Psychology, ed. G. Lindzey and E. Aronson. New York: Random House, 1985.

Sunday Times Insight Team. *The Falklands War: The Full Story.* London: Deutsch, 1982.

Swidler, Ann. "Culture in Action: Symbols and Strategies." *American Sociological Review* 51, no, 2 (1986): 273–86.

Tannenwald, Nina. *The Nuclear Taboo: The United States and the Non-Use of Nuclear Weapons since 1945.* Cambridge: Cambridge University Press, 2005.

Taylor, Charles. "Interpretation and the Sciences of Man." In *Readings in the Philosophy of Social Science,* ed. Michael Martin and Lee C. McIntyre. Cambridge: MIT Press, 1994.

Taylor, Peter J. *Britain and the Cold War: 1945 as Geopolitical Transition.* London: Pinter, 1991.

Thatcher, Margaret. *The Downing Street Years.* London: Harper Collins, 1993.

Thies, Cameron. "Explaining Zones of Negative Peace in Interstate Relations: West Africa's Regional Culture of Interstate Rivalry." *European Journal of International Relations* 16, no. 3 (2010a): 391–415.

Thies, Cameron. "Role Theory and Foreign Policy." In *The International Studies Encyclopedia,* ed. Robert A. Denemark. Malden, MA: Wiley-Blackwell, 2010b.

Thies, Cameron. "State Socialization and Structural Realism." *Security Studies* 19, no. 4 (2010c): 689–717.

Thomas, Hugh. *The Suez Affair.* London: Pelican, 1970.

Thorne, Christopher. "International Relations and the Prompting of History." *Review of International Studies* 9, no. 2 (1983): 123–36.

Toase, Francis. "The United Nations Security Resolution 502." In *The Falklands Conflict Twenty Years On: Lessons for the Future,* ed. Stephen Badsey, Rob Havers and Mark Grove. London: Frank Cass, 2005.

Toomey, Jane. *Harold Wilson's EEC Application: Inside the Foreign Office.* Dublin: University College Dublin Press, 2007.

Towns, Ann. *Women and States: Norms and Hierarchies in International Studies.* Cambridge: Cambridge University Press, 2010.

Trachtenberg, Marc. *A Constructed Peace: The Making of the European Settlement, 1945-1963.* Princeton: Princeton University Press, 1999.

Tucker, Robert C. *The Marx-Engels Reader.* New York: W.W. Norton, 1978.

Tugendhat, Ernst. *Self-Consciousness and Self-Determination.* Cambridge: MIT Press, 1986.

Turner, Jonathan H. *A Theory of Social Interaction.* Cambridge: Polity, 1988.

Turner, Ralph H. "Role-Taking, Role Standpoint, and Reference-Group Behavior." *American Journal of Sociology* 61, no. 4 (1956): 316–28.

Turner, Ralph H. "The Role and the Person." *American Journal of Sociology* 84, no. 1 (1978): 1–23.

Vaughan-Williams, Nick. "International Relations and the 'Problem of History.'" *Millennium: Journal of International Studies* 34, no. 1 (2005): 115–36.

Vickers, Rhiannon. *The Labour Party and the World.* Vol. 2, *Labour's Foreign Policy since 1951.* Manchester: Manchester University Press, 2011.

Waever, Ole. "The Sociology of a Not So International Discipline: American and

European Developments in International Relations." *International Organization* 52, no. 4 (1998): 687–727.

Waever, Ole. "Waltz's Theory of Theory." *International Relations* 23, no. 2 (2009): 201–22.

Walker, Stephen G., ed. *Role Theory and Foreign Policy Analysis*. Durham: Duke University Press, 1987.

Walker, Stephen G. *Role Theory and the Cognitive Architecture of British Appeasement Decisions: Symbolic and Strategic Interaction in World Politics*. London: Routledge, 2013.

Wall, Stephen. *A Stranger in Europe: Britain and the EU from Thatcher to Blair*. Oxford: Oxford University Press, 2008.

Wall, Stephen. *The Official History of Britain and the European Community*. Vol. 2, *From Rejection to Referendum, 1963–1975*. London: Routledge, 2012.

Wallace, William. "Foreign Policy and National Identity in the United Kingdom." *International Affairs* 67, no. 1 (1991): 65–80.

Wallace, William, and Christopher Philips. "Reassessing the Special Relationship." *International Affairs* 85, no. 2 (2009): 263–84.

Walsh, James I. "Do States Play Signaling Games?" *Cooperation and Conflict* 42, no. 4 (2007): 441–59.

Walt, Stephen. *The Origins of Alliances*. Ithaca: Cornell University Press, 1987.

Waltz, Kenneth N. *Theory of International Politics*. New York: Random House, 1979.

Waltz, Kenneth N. "Evaluating Theories." *American Political Science Review* 91, no. 4 (1986): 913–17.

Waltz, Kenneth N. "International Politics Is Not Foreign Policy." *Security Studies* 6, no. 1 (1996): 54–57.

Waltz, Kenneth N. *Realism and International Politics*. New York: London, 2008.

Ward, Hugh. "Rational Choice." In *Theory and Methods in Political Science*, ed. David Marsh and Gerry Stoker. Basingstoke: Palgrave Macmillan, 2002.

Watkinson, Harold. *Turning Points: A Record of Our Times*. Salisbury: Michael Russell, 1986.

Watt, Donald Cameron. *Succeeding John Bull: America in Britain's Place, 1900–1975*. Cambridge: Cambridge University Press, 1984.

Weber, Cynthia. "Performative States." *Millennium: Journal of International Studies* 27, no. 1 (1998): 77–95.

Weber, Max. *The Methodology of the Social Sciences*. New York: Free Press, 1949.

Weinberger, Caspar. *Fighting for Peace: Seven Critical Years at the Pentagon*. London: Michael Joseph, 1990.

Weinstein, Eugene A., and Paul Deutschberger, "Some Dimensions of Alter-Casting." *Sociometry* 26, no. 4 (1963): 454–66.

Welch, David A. *Painful Choices: A Theory of Foreign Policy Change*. Princeton: Princeton University Press, 2005.

Weldes, Jutta. *Constructing National Interests: The United States and the Cuban Missile Crisis*. Minneapolis: University of Minnesota Press, 1999.

Weldes, Jutta, Mark Laffey, Hugh Gusterson, and Raymond Duvall, eds. *Cultures* of Insecurity: States, Communities, and the Production of Danger. Minneapolis: University of Minnesota Press, 1997.

Wendt, Alexander. "Anarchy Is What States Make of It: The Social Construction of Power Politics." *International Organization* 46, no. 2 (1992): 391–425.

Wendt, Alexander. "On Constitution and Causation in International Relations." *Review of International Studies* 24, no. 5 (1998): 101–17.

Wendt, Alexander. *Social Theory of International Politics*. New York: Cambridge University Press, 1999.

Wendt, Alexander. "On the Via Media: A Response to the Critics." *Review of International Studies* 26, no. 1 (2000): 165–80.

Wendt, Alexander. "Why a World State Is Inevitable." *European Journal of International Relations* 9, no. 4 (2003): 491–542.

Wendt, Alexander. "The State as Person in International Theory." *Review of International Studies* 30, no. 2 (2004): 289–316.

Wight, Colin. "They Shoot Dead Horses Don't They? Locating Agency in the Agent-Structure Problematique." *European Journal of International Relations* 5, no. 1 (1999): 109–42.

Wight, Colin. *Agents, Structures and International Relations: Politics as Ontology*. Cambridge: Cambridge University Press, 2006.

Williams, Michael C. "Why Ideas Matter in International Politics: Hans Morgenthau, Classical Realism, and the Moral Construction of Power Politics." *International Organization* 58, no. 4 (2004): 633–65.

Williams, Paul. *British Foreign Policy under New Labour, 1997–2005*. Basingstoke: Palgrave Macmillan, 2005.

Wilson, Harold. *The Labour Government, 1964–1970: A Personal Record*. London: Weidenfeld and Nicolson, 1971.

Winand, Pascaline. *Eisenhower, Kennedy, and the United States of Europe*. New York: St. Martin's, 1993.

Windsor, Philip. "Diplomatic Dimensions of the Falklands Crisis." *Millennium: Journal of International Studies* 12, no. 1 (1983): 88–96.

Wish, Naomi Bailin. "Foreign Policy Makers and Their National Role Conceptions." *International Studies Quarterly* 24, no. 4 (1980): 532–54.

Wittgenstein, Ludwig. *Philosophical Investigations*. Oxford: Blackwell, 1953.

Wohlforth, William. "How Not to Evaluate Theories." *International Studies Quarterly* 56, no. 1 (2012): 219–22.

Woodward, Admiral Sandy, with Patrick Robinson. *One Hundred Days: The Memoirs of the Falklands Battle Group Commander*. London: Book Club, 1992.

Wrong, Dennis H. "The Oversocialized Conception of Man in Modern Sociology." *American Sociological Review* 26, no. 2 (1961): 183–93.

Youde, Jeremy. "Is Universal Access to Antiretroviral Drugs an Emerging International Norm?" *Journal of International Relations and Development* 11, no. 4 (2008): 415–40.

Young, Hugo. *This Blessed Plot: Britain and Europe from Churchill to Blair*. London: Macmillan, 1998.

Young, Ken. "The Skybolt Crisis of 1962: Muddle or Mischief?" *Journal of Strategic Studies* 27, no. 4 (2004): 614–35.

Zakaria, Fareed. *From Wealth to Power: The Unusual Origins of America's World Role.* Princeton: Princeton University Press, 1998.

Zakaria, Fareed. *The Post-American World.* New York: W.W. Norton, 2008.

Zametica, John. *British Officials and British Foreign Policy.* Leicester: Leicester University Press, 1990.

Zarakol, Ayşe. *After Defeat: How the East Learned to Live with the West.* Cambridge: Cambridge University Press, 2010.

Zarakol, Ayşe. "Revisiting Second Image Reversed: Lessons from Turkey and Thailand." *International Studies Quarterly* 57, no. 1 (2013): 150–62.

Ziegler, Philip. *Wilson.* London: Weidenfeld and Nicolson, 1993.

Zuckerman, Solly. *Monkeys, Men, and Missiles: An Autobiography, 1946–88.* London: Collins, 1988.

Index

Abbott, Andrew, 54
abstraction, 47
Acheson, Dean, report of 1961, 99; West Point speech, ix, x, xi, 3, 86, 113, 164, 166
Acheson Group, 119
action, 12, 25–26, 29–30, 38, 44–45, 48, 50, 56–57; habitual, 44; state, 20, 23, 37, 43
Adler, Emanuel, 8, 44
Afghanistan (War, 2001-), 3
agency, x, 6, 22, 30; constraint on, 47; corporate, 34–37; role-conceptions, 171; state, 7
agency-structure debate, 7, 15, 25, 31
Ahmed, Rafeeudin, 143
Algeria, French War in, 59, 67
alliance leader, 1; United States as, 59, 71, 73–74, 76, 78, 85–86, 103, 108
Alker, Hayward, 173
alter, 29
alter-casting, 15, 171, 178; of Argentina, 142, 146–47; and conceptual framework, 20, 32, 33, 35, 41, 52, 56–57; of Friendly Five, 128, 131; and Skybolt affair, 102, 108; Suez Crisis (1956), 66, 71, 74–77
Amery, Julian, 79, 156
analyticism, 52
anarchy, 12, 22; culture(s) of, 14, 40; problematic, 173; what states make of it, 10, 23
Anderson, Benedict, 36
Ascension Island, 148
Australia, 78; embargo on Argentina, 149
apperception, 51
Argentina, 16, 18, 141, 144, 150; Beagle Channel Islands dispute, 151; Dirty War, 145; expected US support, 162; interpre-

tation of Resolution 502, 152; invasion of Falklands/Malvinas, 138–39, 141; ruling junta, 144, 160; and Soviet Union, 146
Aristotle, 47–48
Atkins, Humphrey, 153
Attlee, Clement, 15

Baghdad Pact, 59
Bahamas. *See* Nassau
balancing, 12, 172–73
Baldwin, John, 27
Ball, George, 98, 102, 105, 107; second EEC application, 120–21, 124; victim of the Nassau decision, 103
bargaining, 20, 41–42; and Suez Crisis, 60
Barnett, Corelli, 169
Bartelson, Jens, 35–36
Belgium, 111, 116, 127, 164
Belgrano, 140, 144, 155
beliefs, 17; and interpretivism, 55; and motivations, 50; systems of foreign policy-makers, 24
Bevin, Ernest, 4, 96
Bevinite consensus, 4, 9, 15–16, 164–65
Bevir, Mark, 55
Bially Mattern, Janice, 84–85
Bicheno, Hugh, 145, 163
Blair, Tony, x, 169, 176–77; foreign policy style, 170
Blankenhorn, Herbert, 111
Blue Steel Mark II (missile), 94
Blue Streak (missile), 88, 93–94
Blumer, Herbert, 24–25, 38, 55
Boothroyd, Betty, 154
Bourdieu, Pierre, 174